BlackBerry®

FOR

DUMMIES®

5TH EDITION

BlackBerry® FOR DUMMIES® 5TH EDITION

by Robert Kao and Dante Sarigumba

WILEY

John Wiley & Sons, Inc.

BlackBerry® For Dummies®, 5th Edition

Published by
John Wiley & Sons, Inc.
111 River Street
Hoboken, NJ 07030-5774

www.wiley.com

WILEY

About the Authors

Robert Kao is one well-rounded professional. His ability to translate his technical knowledge and communicate with users of all types led him to cowrite *BlackBerry For Dummies, BlackBerry Pearl For Dummies, BlackBerry Storm For Dummies, BlackBerry Bold For Dummies,* and *BlackBerry Curve For Dummies*. He started out as a BlackBerry developer for various financial firms in New York City, that truly global city. Kao is currently the Founder and CEO of a mobile software start-up. A graduate of Columbia University, with a Computer Engineering degree, he currently lives in South Brunswick, New Jersey.

Dante Sarigumba is a long-time user of BlackBerry and a gizmo enthusiast. He, along with Robert, has been developing BlackBerry and mobile applications since early millennium. He currently works as a "development wizard" and lives in South Brunswick, New Jersey, with his wife, Rosemarie, and two sons, Dean and Drew.

Dedication

I would like to thank my father (MHK), my mother (SYT), and the rest of the Kao family for everything they've done for me. I wouldn't be here without their kindness and understanding. I would also like to thank my lovely wife Marie-Claude, my daughter Jade, and my newborn son for all their support. In addition, thanks to Manon Lalancette and the rest of Gamelin family for all your cheers!

— Robert Kao

To Yosma, Dean, and Drew: My greatest treasures. Thank you for your thoughts, understanding, and support.

— Dante Sarigumba

Authors' Acknowledgments

Collectively, we want to give a big thanks to everyone at Wiley.

In addition, we'd like to thank the following people:

- Katie Mohr, our acquisitions editor, for making sure we hit our targets.
- Laura Miller, for crossing our T's and dotting our I's.
- Carol McClendon, our agent, for presenting our proposal to the right people.
- Victoria Berry of Research In Motion, for getting us access to proper channels at the right time.

— Rob & Dante

Publisher's Acknowledgments

We're proud of this book; please send us your comments at http://dummies.custhelp.com. For other comments, please contact our Customer Care Department within the U.S. at 877-762-2974, outside the U.S. at 317-572-3993, or fax 317-572-4002.

Some of the people who helped bring this book to market include the following:

Acquisitions, Editorial, and Media Development

Project Editor: Laura K. Miller

Acquisitions Editor: Katie Mohr

Copy Editor: Laura K. Miller

Technical Editor: Richard Evers

Editorial Manager: Jodi Jensen

Media Development Project Manager: Laura Moss-Hollister

Media Development Assistant Project Manager: Jenny Swisher

Media Development Associate Producers: Josh Frank, Marilyn Hummel, Douglas Kuhn, and Shawn Patrick

Editorial Assistant: Amanda Graham

Sr. Editorial Assistant: Cherie Case

Cover Photos: © istockphoto.com/ centauria; Images of phones courtesy of Research in Motion; © istockphoto.com/ Lee Pettet; © istockphoto.com/Rosemarie Gearhart; © istockphoto.com/Ken Canning

Cartoons: Rich Tennant (www.the5thwave.com)

Composition Services

Project Coordinator: Sheree Montgomery

Layout and Graphics: Kim Tabor, Laura Westhuis

Proofreaders: Rebecca Denoncour, Cynthia Fields

Indexer: BIM Indexing & Proofreading Services

Publishing and Editorial for Technology Dummies

Richard Swadley, Vice President and Executive Group Publisher

Andy Cummings, Vice President and Publisher

Mary Bednarek, Executive Acquisitions Director

Mary C. Corder, Editorial Director

Publishing for Consumer Dummies

Kathy Nebenhaus, Vice President and Executive Publisher

Composition Services

Debbie Stailey, Director of Composition Services

Contents at a Glance

Table of Contents

Introduction

*I*f you already have a BlackBerry, *BlackBerry For Dummies,* 5th Edition can help you discover new features, or you can slap it open and use it as a quick reference. If you don't have a BlackBerry yet and have some basic questions (such as "What's a BlackBerry?" or "How can a BlackBerry help me be more productive?"), you can benefit by reading this book cover to cover. No matter what your current BlackBerry user status — BUS, for short — this book can help you get the most out of your BlackBerry.

Right off the bat, we can tell you that a BlackBerry isn't a fruit you find at the supermarket, nor is it related to nasty weather patterns. It's an always-connected smartphone that has e-mail capabilities, a built-in Internet browser, advanced media features, and a camera.

On top of that, a BlackBerry has all the features you expect from a personal organizer, including a calendar, to-do lists, and memos. Oh, and did we mention that a BlackBerry also has a built-in mobile phone? Talk about multitasking! Imagine being stuck on a commuter train: With your BlackBerry by your side, you can compose an e-mail while conducting a conference call — all from the comfort of your seat.

In this book, we show you all the basics, and then go the extra mile by highlighting some of the lesser-known (but still handy) features of the BlackBerry. Your BlackBerry can work hard for you when you need it to — and it can play hard when you want it to.

About This Book

BlackBerry For Dummies, 5th Edition is a comprehensive user guide, as well as a quick user reference. We designed this book so that you can read it cover to cover if you want, but you don't need to read one chapter after the other. Feel free to jump around while you explore the different functionalities of your BlackBerry.

We cover basic and advanced topics, but we stick to those topics that we consider the most practical and frequently used. If you use or want to use a certain function of your BlackBerry, we likely cover it here.

Who Are You?

In this book, we try to be considerate of your needs, but because we've never met you, we make some assumptions about who you might be:

- ✔ You have a BlackBerry and want to find out how to get the most from it.
- ✔ You don't have a BlackBerry yet, but you're wondering what one could do for you.
- ✔ You're looking for a book that doesn't assume you know all the jargon and tech terms used in the smartphone industry.
- ✔ You want a reference that shows you, step by step, how to do useful and cool things with a BlackBerry — but that doesn't bog you down by giving you unnecessary background or theory.
- ✔ You're tired of hauling your 10-pound laptop with you on trips, and you're wondering how to turn your BlackBerry into a miniature traveling office.
- ✔ You no longer want to be tied to your computer system for the critical activities in your life, such as sending and receiving e-mail, checking your calendar for appointments, and surfing the web.
- ✔ You like to have some fun, play games, and be entertained by a device but don't want to carry an extra game gadget around with you.

What's in This Book

BlackBerry For Dummies, 5th Edition consists of six parts, and each part contains different chapters related to that part's theme.

Part 1: Getting Started with BlackBerry

Part I starts with the basics of your BlackBerry. You know: What it is, what you can do with it, and what the parts are. We also show you how to personalize and express yourself through your BlackBerry. This part wraps up with must-knows about security and where to go for help when you get into trouble with your BlackBerry.

Part II: Organizing with BlackBerry

Part II deals with the fact that your BlackBerry is also a full-fledged organizer. We show you how to get your BlackBerry to keep your contacts in Contacts, as well as how to manage your appointments and meetings in Calendar. You also can find out how to set an alarm by using the Clock application, use it as a timer, and set your device to Bedside mode. We explore the Password Keeper application, which can centralize your passwords. And finally, we show you how most BlackBerry applications interconnect, working hard for you.

Part III: Getting Online with Your BlackBerry

Part III shows you what made BlackBerry what it is today: always-connected e-mail. We also get into the other strengths of the BlackBerry — web-surfing functionality — but we don't stop there. We point out how you can use other forms of messages, such as text messaging and Instant Messaging. You can find out about unique forms of messages on the BlackBerry: PIN-to-PIN messages and BlackBerry Messenger. And best of all, you get the lowdown on social networking.

Part IV: Applications and Media on Your BlackBerry

You can find the fun stuff in Part IV. Use the BlackBerry GPS to navigate your way around, and rock your world by using your BlackBerry to play music, watch videos, and take pictures. You also get the scoop on how to record videos and sample ringtones. Plus, we give you timesaving shortcuts that you can use on the Media applications and offer ways to manage your media files.

Part V: Working with BlackBerry Desktop Software

In Part V, we detail BlackBerry Desktop Software and show you some of the hoops you can put it through with your BlackBerry, including making backups and installing BlackBerry applications from your PC to your smartphone. You can find out how to transfer data from your older devices — BlackBerry or not — to your new BlackBerry. And we didn't forget to cover important stuff, such as data syncing your appointments and contacts with desktop applications, such as Outlook. And finally, you can find all the possible ways you can install third-party applications.

Part VI: The Part of Tens

All *For Dummies* books include The Part of Tens, and this book is no different. In Part VI, we show you where to get cool BlackBerry accessories and (of course) great applications for your BlackBerry.

Icons in This Book

 This icon highlights an important point that you don't want to forget because it just might come up again. We'd never be so cruel as to spring a pop quiz on you, but paying attention to these details can definitely help you.

 This book rarely delves into the geeky, technical details, but when it does, this icon warns you. Read the text that this icon points to if you want to get under the hood a little, or just skip ahead if you aren't interested in the gory details.

 Here's where you can find not-so-obvious tricks that can make you a BlackBerry power-user in no time. Pay special attention to the paragraphs that feature this icon so that you can get the most out of your smartphone.

 Look out! This icon tells you how to avoid trouble before it starts. Be sure to read and follow the accompanying directions.

Where to Go from Here

Now, you can dive in! Give Chapter 1 a quick look if you want to get a sense of where this book takes you — or feel free to head straight to your chapter of choice.

If you want to find out more about the book, or have a question or comment for the authors, please visit us at www.blackberryfordummies.com.

Part I
Getting Started with BlackBerry

The 5th Wave   By Rich Tennant

"This model comes with a particularly useful function – a simulated static button for breaking out of long-winded conversations."

In this part . . .

The road to a happy and collaborative relationship with your BlackBerry starts here. We cover all the nuts and bolts — how things work, the BlackBerry's look and feel, and connectivity. We also discuss how you can navigate with ease to the world of BlackBerry, offering timesaving shortcuts. Finally, you can figure out how to customize BlackBerry and make it your own.

Chapter 1

Your BlackBerry Isn't an Edible Fruit

*Y*our BlackBerry can help you do more things than you could ever think of. For example, your BlackBerry is a whiz at making phone calls, but it's also a computer that you can use to check your e-mail, as well as surf the web. We're talking *World Wide* Web here, so the sky's the limit. Help is always at your fingertips, not sitting on some desk at home or at the office. Need to check out the reviews of that restaurant on the corner? Need to see (right now) what's showing in your local movie theaters, or what the weather will be like later tonight, or the best place to shop? Need to get directions to that cozy bed and breakfast, or see the latest news headlines, or look over stock quotes? Want to do some online chatting, or view some pictures online and download them? You can do all these things (and more) by using your BlackBerry.

BlackBerry is also a full-fledged personal digital assistant (PDA). Out of the box, it provides you with the organizational tools you need to set up to-do lists, manage your appointments, take care of your address books, and more.

By arming yourself with a device that's a sleek phone, a camera, a portal flash drive, an Internet connection, and a PDA all built into one, you become a power person. With your BlackBerry (along with this resourceful book), you really can improve your productivity, better organize yourself, and increase your cool factor. Watch out, world! Person bearing a BlackBerry smartphone coming through!

Knowing Your BlackBerry History

Your BlackBerry smartphone is truly a wondrous device, boasting many features beyond your ordinary mobile phone. But its sudden popularity actually didn't happen overnight. Like any other good product out there, BlackBerry has come a long way from its (relatively humble) beginnings.

In the days when the Palm Pilot ruled the PDA world, Research in Motion (RIM, the maker of the BlackBerry) was busy in its lab, ignoring the then-popular graffiti input method to design its own device with the QWERTY keyboard — the kind of keyboard people already knew from working on their computers. RIM didn't stop there, however. It also added an always-connected e-mail capability, making this device a must-have among government officials, as well as professionals in the finance and health industries.

To meet the needs of government officials and industry professionals, RIM made reliability, security, and durability the priorities when manufacturing its devices. Today, the BlackBerry smartphone comes from the same line of RIM family products, inheriting all the good genes, and also boosting usability and especially multimedia capabilities.

How It Works: The Schematic Approach

For those of you who always ask, "How do they do that?" you don't have to go far; the following sections answer just that question.

The role of the network service provider

Along with wondering how your BlackBerry actually works, you might also be wondering why you didn't get your BlackBerry from RIM, rather than a network service provider such as AT&T or Verizon Wireless. Why did you need to go through a middle-person? After all, RIM makes BlackBerry.

Those are excellent questions — and here's a quick-and-dirty answer. RIM needs a delivery system — a communication medium — for its technology to work. Not in a position to come up with such a delivery system all by its lonesome, RIM partnered and built alliances across the globe with what developed into its network service providers — the usual suspects, meaning the big cellphone companies.

These middle-providers support the wireless network for your BlackBerry so that you have signals to connect to the BlackBerry Internet Service — which means you can get all those wonderful e-mails (and waste so much valuable time surfing the Internet). See Figure 1-1 for a schematic overview of this process.

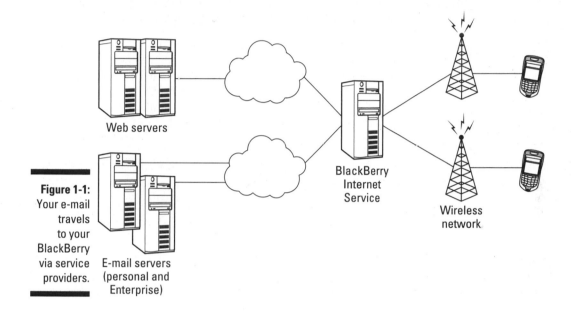

Figure 1-1: Your e-mail travels to your BlackBerry via service providers.

Web servers

E-mail servers (personal and Enterprise)

BlackBerry Internet Service

Wireless network

Network service providers don't build alliances for nothing, right? In return, RIM gave those providers the right to brand their names on the BlackBerry they offer for sale. For example, a Verizon BlackBerry may look different from a similar model that you can get from Vodafone. This point leads to another question: Do BlackBerry functionalities differ from phone model to phone model? Quick answer: In the core BlackBerry applications (such as Tasks and Address Book), you find no major differences. However, the network service provider might or might not support some BlackBerry features, such as Instant Messaging. (See Chapter 10 for more details on Instant Messaging.)

Connecting to your personal computer

Nowadays, personal computers are household necessities because we spend so much time on them and so much information is stored in them. It should come as no surprise that BlackBerry works hand-in-hand with your computer. The USB cable that comes with your BlackBerry does more than just charge your device. All the chapters in Part V in this book are dedicated to guiding you in making use of this important connection with the help of BlackBerry Desktop Software and all the utilities that come with it. For example, Chapter 19 guides you through how to back up almost anything in your BlackBerry, down to your desktop. Also, Chapter 16 shows you how to use the BlackBerry and its microSD slot as storage that goes where you go.

Doing the BlackBerry world-traveler thing

If you purchased your BlackBerry from Verizon or AT&T, chances are that your BlackBerry will continue to work when you travel to, say, London or Beijing. You need to worry about only turning on your BlackBerry (and maybe the extra roaming charges). Because your BlackBerry is quad band, it can work in more than 90 different countries.

What's quad band? Basically, different cellphone networks in different countries operate in different frequencies. For example, the United States and Canada operate in two frequencies: 850 and 1900 MHz; Europe and the Asia Pacific, 900 and 1800 MHz. Your BlackBerry is designed to work in these four frequencies — 850/900/1800/1900 MHz — so you're covered no matter where you go. Well, almost. Check with your network service provider before you hop on a plane, just to be sure.

Two dominant technologies compete in the worldwide cellphone industry today:

- ✔ **Code Division Multiple Access (CDMA):** Available in the United States through Verizon Wireless.
- ✔ **Global System for Mobile Communications (GSM):** A tad older than its CDMA rival, GSM is available in the United States through Cingular and T-Mobile.

Back in the day, if you purchased a BlackBerry from a GSM-based carrier (for example, AT&T or T-Mobile), you could travel with your BlackBerry without worrying about losing service because most carriers outside of North America are GSM based. If you purchased a BlackBerry from a CDMA-based carrier (including Verizon and Sprint), then you definitely couldn't use your BlackBerry to check your e-mail while traveling. That was then; this is now.

If you have a CDMA BlackBerry, quad-band technology allows you to run it on a GSM-based carrier as well, making your BlackBerry a phone that can travel the world. So, regardless of whether you have a CDMA- or GSM-based carrier, the only thing you need to do before traveling is call your carrier to make sure you have your international plan activated.

Oh, the Things You Can Do!

Your BlackBerry is a work of art when it comes to smartphones. But besides its looks, the always-connected e-mail is likely first in the long list of reasons why you got your BlackBerry in the first place. And if you need to go global, you can use your BlackBerry in more than 90 countries. Just hop off your flight, turn on your BlackBerry, and *voilà!* — e-mails on your BlackBerry while you're 6,000 miles away from home. (See the preceding section for more info about traveling with your BlackBerry.) Generally speaking, you can receive and send e-mails from your BlackBerry just like you can from your computer at home.

Although e-mail is BlackBerry's strength, that's not the only thing it can do. The following sections go beyond e-mail to point out some of the other major benefits you can get from your device.

All-in-one multimedia center

In the early days of the BlackBerry, many consumers were hesitant about purchasing a BlackBerry because it didn't offer multimedia functions such as a camera and audio playback. But RIM changed all that, adding more features to the BlackBerry than a typical consumer might expect. Not only does the BlackBerry have a high-resolution, multi-mega-pixel camera (see Chapter 14), but it also has a memory slot for a microSD chip (see Chapter 16). So, your BlackBerry can function as an MP3 player, a portal video player, a portable flash drive, and your personal photo collection (see Chapter 14).

Internet at your fingertips

Yup, you can browse the web by using your BlackBerry, which has full HTML5 and CSS3 support (this just means that a site you access on your BlackBerry appears like it would on a computer). Even better, you can continue chatting with your friends through Instant Messenger, just as though you never left your computer (see Chapter 10). You can also get up-to-the-minute information when you want it — or when you need it. Imagine getting an alert when your stock is tanking. True, you don't want that to happen, but you absolutely need this information if you want to act in a timely manner.

If you're not into stocks, how about getting sports and weather information? Or maybe traffic alerts? Say that you want to know the best restaurants in town for that special evening — birthday, anniversary, first date. Many services that you can access on the Internet from a computer, you also can access on your BlackBerry.

Download? Absolutely! BlackBerry supports the downloading of applications and games from the BlackBerry App World's vast selection. For example, you can download more productivity tools than what come standard on your BlackBerry, such as PDF readers, or an exciting game of Texas Hold 'Em.

Me and my great personal assistant

You might be saying, "But I'm really a busy person, and I don't have time to browse the web. What I *do* need is an assistant to help me better organize my day-to-day tasks." If you can afford one, by all means, go ahead and hire a personal assistant. If not, the next best thing is a personal *digital* assistant (PDA). You can find many PDAs on the market today; the most popular ones are marketed by Palm and WinCE. Getting a PDA can really help you get organized — and for much less than hiring a secretary.

So, are we telling you to go out and buy a PDA? No way! Put away that credit card because you don't need to go that route.

Whip out your BlackBerry and take a closer look. That's right, your BlackBerry is also a full-fledged PDA, able to help you remember all your acquaintances (see Chapter 4), manage your appointments (Chapter 5), and much more.

Me and my chatty self

Besides all the features that we describe in the preceding sections, your BlackBerry is also a full-featured phone. By offering voice dialing and the ability to carry out conference calls with you as the moderator, your BlackBerry isn't like standard cellphones. To find out more about your BlackBerry Phone, see Chapter 7.

Look, Dad, no hands!

Your BlackBerry comes equipped with an earphone that doubles as a mike for hands-free talking. This accessory is your doctor's prescription for preventing the stiff neck that comes from wedging your BlackBerry with your shoulder against your ear. At the very minimum, it helps free your hands so that you can eat Chinese take-out. And, if you happen to be residing in the United States, in most states, you're required by law to use a hands-free accessory while driving when you use a cellphone. (Not that we recommend using your cellphone while driving, but if you really need to make that call, going hands-free is safer than trying to divide your attention between the phone and the steering wheel.)

But RIM didn't stop with just your standard (wired) earphones. BlackBerry also supports cool wireless earphones/mikes — the ones based on Bluetooth technology. "But how could a bizarrely colored tooth help me here?" you might ask. Fooled you! *Bluetooth* is a codename for a (very) short-distance wireless technology first used to connect simple devices (such as computer accessories) that's now commonly used on cellphones, specifically on wireless earphones/mikes.

Chewing on Hardware

The main concerns most of us have when buying a product are quality and reliability. Will the product last? Does it perform the way that the flier says? Will I regret having bought this item six months down the road? The following sections look at some of the hardware features that make buying the BlackBerry a wise purchase.

Power efficiency

Now, anyone who's had an ear to the ground regarding BlackBerry knows its reputation as a highly efficient little machine when it comes to power consumption. Even with the colored, high-resolution screen, the power consumption of the BlackBerry still has a 15-day standby time and close to four hours talk time. So, when the salesperson offers you a special deal on a second battery, simply tell him or her that you'll think about it. With the BlackBerry's standard battery, you'll have more than enough power.

Memory management

When you first receive your BlackBerry, the device definitely has ample free memory. However, that memory — which your BlackBerry uses for pre-installed applications and other applications that you download — doesn't grow while you use BlackBerry. You're stuck with a fixed amount of memory, which can prove limiting over time. While you install more and more applications, this free memory gets used up. In fact, you could eventually run out of memory altogether.

Don't confuse this fixed amount of memory with the memory available through the microSD slot. A microSD chip can store MP3s, portable videos, and pictures that you download or load from your PC.

Does your device die when you run out of memory? No, thank goodness. Your BlackBerry is capable of monitoring the free memory on your device. If you're ever in danger of reaching your upper limits, the BlackBerry has a memory management tool that cleans house to free this limited resource.

Right out of the box, BlackBerry applications are capable of figuring out what data it doesn't really need. For example, the BlackBerry Browser caches data to enhance your experience when you browse the web. *Caches* use local copies of web pages to speed up the reloading of previously visited websites, so generally, the pages load faster, and you can view pages you've previously visited, even if you don't have good coverage. However, this cache also takes up memory space. When the operating system (OS) tells the Browser that the device is reaching its upper memory limit and it needs to do some house cleaning, the Browser deletes this cache. Similarly, BlackBerry Messages deletes e-mails that you've already read, starting from the oldest and working its way forward in time.

Curious about how much available space your device has? Follow these steps to find out:

1. **From the Home screen, press the Menu key.**

2. **In the menu that appears, scroll to highlight Options in the list of applications, and then press the trackpad.**

   The Options screen opens.

3. **Select the Device option, and then select Device and Status Information from the Device screen that appears.**

   In the Device and Status Information screen that appears, the File Free field tells you how much available space is left.

A sentry is always on duty

If you look at the history of human existence, you can see some nasty things that human beings are capable of doing. Unfortunately, the virtual world isn't exempt; in fact, every day a battle is fought between those who are trying to attack a system and those who are trying to protect it. Included among the people attacking the system are those who are trying to steal corporate data for their advantage, as well as individuals trying to steal personal data to carry out identity theft.

A computer connected to the Internet faces an extra risk of being hacked or becoming infected by a computer virus intent on simply annoying the heck out of you or (even worse) wreaking havoc on your computer. Fortunately, security is one of the strong points of the BlackBerry.

RIM has built features into its software that allow companies to curtail activities for their BlackBerry users that they deem risky, such as installing or running a third-party application. Data transmitted on and from the device are encrypted to prevent possible snooping. RIM also has a Signature process for application developers, which forces developers to identify themselves and their programs if they're developing any applications that run on the BlackBerry platform and need to integrate with either BlackBerry core applications or the OS.

The security measures that RIM implemented on the BlackBerry platform have gained the trust of the U.S. government, as well as many of the Forbes Top 500 enterprises in the financial and health industries.

Remember the *I love you* and *Anna Kournikova* viruses? These virtual evils were transmitted through e-mail, a script, or sets of instructions in the e-mail body or attachment that either the host e-mail program or, in the case of an attachment, the program associated with the attached file could execute. Fortunately, BlackBerry Messages doesn't support scripting languages. As for attachments, out of the box, BlackBerry supports few file types, mostly images and text documents. BlackBerry's viewer for such files doesn't support scripting either, so you don't have to worry about threats from e-mails that contain these attachments.

Chapter 2

Navigating the BlackBerry

In This Chapter

▶ Taking a course in BlackBerry Anatomy

▶ Understanding general navigating guidelines

▶ Using common shortcut keys

*R*egardless of whether you've previously owned a BlackBerry, you might have heard that the new BlackBerry is different. You might be wondering how you spot a new BlackBerry. Looks aren't deceiving in this case. From the outside, the new BlackBerry is a lot slimmer than the older BlackBerry handhelds. The new design has a brighter and higher-resolution screen. However, what makes it fundamentally different is that it has a touch screen, along with a QWERTY keyboard.

Don't worry; new BlackBerries still have the trackpad that you can use to navigate and input data, too. Bear with us, and you can become master of your BlackBerry in no time.

Anatomy 101: The Body and Features of Your BlackBerry

In this and the following sections, we show you all the keys and features on your BlackBerry Bold Touch 9900 series and BlackBerry Pearl 3G. The two models are shown in Figures 2-1 and 2-2.

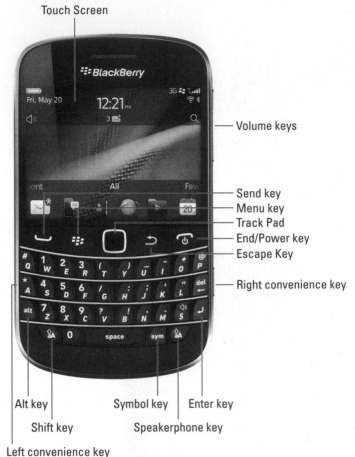

Touch Screen

Volume keys

Send key
Menu key
Track Pad
End/Power key
Escape Key

Right convenience key

Figure 2-1:
Main
features
on a
BlackBerry
Bold 9900
series.

Alt key

Shift key

Left convenience key

Symbol key

Speakerphone key

Enter key

First, the major features:

- ✔ **Display screen:** The graphical user interface (GUI) on your BlackBerry. BlackBerry models such as the BlackBerry Torch or BlackBerry Bold Touch have touch screens, in addition to the QWERTY keyboard.

- ✔ **QWERTY keyboard:** The input for your BlackBerry — very straightforward.

- ✔ **SureType keyboard:** The input for your BlackBerry Pearl 3G.

- ✔ **Escape key:** Cancels a selection or returns you to a previous page within an application. If you hold it down, it returns you to the Home screen from any program.

- ✔ **Menu key:** Displays the full menu of the application you're using.

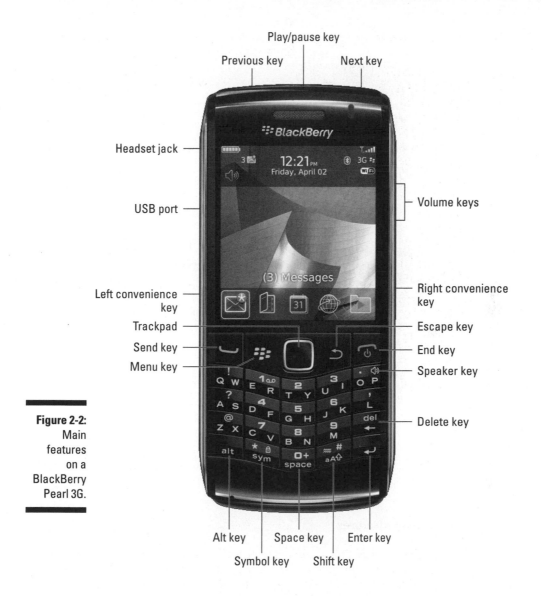

Figure 2-2:
Main
features
on a
BlackBerry
Pearl 3G.

✔ **Trackpad:** You navigate the display screen of your BlackBerry with the trackpad. It allows you four directional movements (up, down, left, and right). When you press the trackpad, the short menu of the application you're using appears.

✔ **Convenience keys:** Depending on which BlackBerry model you have, it includes one or two convenience keys. By default, the convenience keys are preprogrammed to open an application. In Chapter 3, we show you how to reprogram the convenience keys so that they display the programs you use the most.

✔ **MicroSD slot:** The microSD slot is a crucial element to your BlackBerry media experience. You can store music, video, and pictures on to the microSD card.

✔ **Send key:** Because your BlackBerry can also function as a cellular phone, this key allows you to go straight to the Phone application, regardless of which application you're currently using. If you're already in the Phone application, the Send key starts dialing the number you last entered — a redial function.

✔ **End key/Power key:** While on a phone call, use this key to end your call. If not on a phone call, press this key to jump to the Home screen from wherever you are. Press and hold this key to put your BlackBerry on stand-by mode, which saves power usage.

✔ **Mute key:** Mutes your end of a conversation when you're on a call.

Two types of context menus can appear on your BlackBerry:

✔ **Full menu:** Lists all the options and features that you can perform. You access the full menu by pressing the Menu key.

✔ **Short menu:** An abbreviated list of the full menu (as shown in Figure 2-3). You access the short menu by pressing the trackpad anytime a pop-up screen isn't open. (If a pop-up screen is displayed, pressing the trackpad selects the highlighted item or dismisses the pop-up screen if it doesn't offer any choices.)

Figure 2-3: Examples of a short menu in the Memo application.

Display screen

When you first turn on your BlackBerry, you see the *Home screen,* which is your introduction to the graphical user interface (GUI) of your BlackBerry. The folks at RIM knows that, while you use your BlackBerry, your Home screen gets cluttered with various application icons. Your BlackBerry has different panels in which you can organize your BlackBerry icons. Think of the panels as different pages on which you can organize similar BlackBerry icons.

Your BlackBerry has the following panels:

- **All:** By default, all the icons that you have appear on this panel.
- **Favorite:** You can move icons that you like the most to this panel.
- **Media:** By default, this panel contains all the media-related applications.
- **Download:** Anything you download appears on this panel.
- **Frequent:** This panel keeps track of your frequently used applications.

You can specify which panels to display on your Home screen and which to hide. Follow these steps:

1. **From the Home screen, press the Menu key, and then select Manage Panel from the menu that appears.**

   The Manage Panel screen appears, listing each panel choice with its own check box.

2. **Select the check boxes for the panels you want to display on your Home screen.**

3. **Press the Menu key, and then select Save from the menu that appears to save your settings.**

The icons that appear in each panel represent the different applications in your BlackBerry. See Figure 2-4 for an example of what your Home screen might look like.

Throughout this book, we ask you to select applications from the All panel. For example, to open the Calendar application, from the All panel on the Home screen, press the Menu key twice, and then select Calendar Application. Alternatively, to maximize the panel, from the All panel on the Home screen, press the Menu key, and then select the Maximize Panel menu option.

Custom Dictionary

BlackBerry comes with a default spell check that keeps all the words you add in a safe place — a Custom Dictionary, to be precise. You can manually add custom words or proper names to the list:

1. **From the Home screen, press the Menu key twice, and then select the Options icon (which looks like a wrench).**

   The Options screen appears.

2. **Select Typing and Input, and then select Custom Dictionary from the screen.**

   Custom Dictionary, where you can see all the words that BlackBerry has picked up over the time you've used it, opens.

3. **From within Custom Dictionary, press the Menu key, and then select New from the menu that appears.**

   A pop-up message appears, prompting you to type a new word, as shown in Figure 2-5.

4. **Enter the word you want to add to the Custom Dictionary.**

   If you want to enter more words, repeat Steps 3 and 4.

5. **To save your changes, press the Menu key, and then select Save from the menu that appears.**

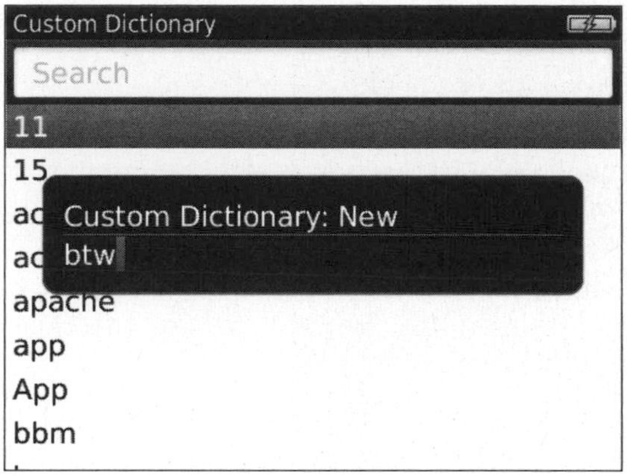

Custom Dictionary

Figure 2-5:
Adding our
favorite,
btw, to
Custom
Dictionary.

QWERTY keyboard

For those non–BlackBerry Pearl owners, this section is for you.

Unlike some PDA manufacturers — they know who they are — Research in Motion (RIM) chose as the input method for the BlackBerry the same QWERTY keyboard you know and love from your personal computer. We think that was a great decision because it means that you don't have to master some new way of writing — graffiti or whatever — to get data into your BlackBerry. You just have to type on a familiar keyboard — and you already know how to do that.

Whether you use your pinky or your index finger, how you type on your BlackBerry is up to you. However, most people find that typing with two thumbs is the most efficient method.

SureType keyboard

If you have the BlackBerry Pearl, this section is for you. The Pearl doesn't have a full QWERTY keyboard; rather, it works with a QWERTY-based keyboard known as the SureType keyboard. The idea of the SureType keyboard is that many keys share letters (refer to Figure 2-2 to see how this setup looks), and the SureType technology is smart enough to figure out what key combinations produce the words you want. With SureType, you can now type with only one thumb, and your BlackBerry Pearl adds the words that you frequently use to its Custom Dictionary.

Here are tips to speed the learning curve when you use SureType technology:

- ✔ **Always finish typing a word before correcting it.** This way, SureType can remember what you want to type next time.

- ✔ **If SureType gets the word you're typing right on the first try, keep on typing.** Simply use the Space key to move on, instead of pressing the trackpad or Enter.

- ✔ **Take advantage of Custom Wordlist, which is a list of words that you define.** We talk more about this list in the "Custom Dictionary" section, earlier in this chapter.

- ✔ **Type! Type! Type!** Because SureType figures out how you type by observing how you type, the more you use it, the smarter it becomes in adapting to your style.

Trackpad

You can perform two functions with the trackpad: scrolling and pressing. When you scroll with your trackpad, you can navigate the display screen in four directions (up, down, left, and right). In a text-filled screen, such as the body of an e-mail, you can usually navigate through the text in all four directions.

Depending on where you are on the BlackBerry's screen, different situations determine what happens when you press the trackpad, also called the *trackpad click:*

- ✔ **Display a pop-up menu.** When you're in a choice field, pressing the trackpad displays a pop-up menu of choices for that field.

- ✔ **Confirm a choice.** The trackpad can also function as a confirmation key. For example, when you need to select a choice in a pop-up menu, you can press the trackpad to confirm the highlighted choice.

- ✔ **Display a short menu.** When you're in a text-filled screen (for example, an e-mail body or web page), pressing the trackpad displays a short menu (refer to Figure 2-3), which is just an abbreviated version of the full menu. You can access the full menu by pressing the Menu key.

Escape and Menu keys

The Escape and Menu keys both help you navigate through your BlackBerry:

✔ **Escape:** Simple yet useful, the Escape key allows you to return to a previous screen or cancel a selection. The Escape key is the arrow key to the right of the trackpad.

✔ **Menu:** Brings up the full menu for the application you're using. When you're on the Home screen, pressing the Menu key displays a list of applications installed on your BlackBerry. If you want to change the order of the applications in the list, see Chapter 3.

When you're on the Home screen, the behavior of the Menu key depends on the BlackBerry theme. The behavior we describe in this section is based on the default theme. See Chapter 3 for more on changing themes.

The microSD slot

Your BlackBerry comes with some internal memory — 1GB if you have the BlackBerry Bold 9700 series or 8GB if you have the BlackBerry Bold Touch 9900 series. If you are a music or video fan, you know that 8GB (let alone 1GB) is not going to keep you entertained for a long commute. No need to worry. The folks at Research in Motion (RIM) have incorporated a microSD slot into your BlackBerry so that you can add extended memory and store all the media files you want in your BlackBerry.

You can purchase a microSD card separately for a relatively low price these days. A 16GB microSD card costs about $20, and a 32GB microSD costs about $40. Get the latest prices from an online commerce site, such as Amazon.com.

General Navigation Guidelines

In the Cheat Sheet (which you can find at `www.dummies.com/cheatsheet/ blackberry`), as well as throughout this book, we show you shortcuts that are application-specific. In this section, however, we go over general short-cuts and navigation guidelines. On a web page or an e-mail full of text, you can perform the following tasks:

✔ **Move to the top of the page.** Press the T key.

✔ **Move to the bottom of the page.** Press the B key.

✔ **Move to the top of the next page.** Press the Space key.

- ✔ **Select a line.** Press and hold the Shift key and scroll the trackpad horizontally.

- ✔ **Select multiple lines.** Press and hold the Shift key and scroll the trackpad vertically.

- ✔ **Copy selected text.** Press and hold the Shift key and press the trackpad.

- ✔ **Cut selected text.** Press and hold the Shift key and press the Delete key.

- ✔ **Paste text.** Press and hold the Shift key and press the trackpad.

- ✔ **Insert an accented character.** Hold down a letter key and scroll the trackpad.

- ✔ **Insert a symbol.** Press the Sym key and press the letter below the symbol.

- ✔ **Use Caps Lock.** Press the Alt key and the right Shift key at the same time.

- ✔ **Use Num Lock.** Press the Alt key and the left Shift key at the same time.

You can perform these functions by pressing the keys listed for the BlackBerry Pearl 3G:

- ✔ **Use Num Lock.** Press Shift+Alt.

- ✔ **Move to the top of the page.** Press the ER key.

- ✔ **Move to the bottom of the page.** Press the CV key.

- ✔ **Move to the next page.** Press the M or Space key.

- ✔ **Move to the previous page.** Press the UI key.

- ✔ **Move to the next line.** Press the BN key.

- ✔ **Move to the previous line.** Press the TY key.

- ✔ **Switch between multitap and SureType mode.** When you're typing in a text field, press and hold the * (asterisk) key.

Switching applications

When you're navigating in an application, you can press the Menu key to see an option called Switch Application. *Switch Application,* which is similar to Alt+Tab in Windows, lets you multitask between applications (see Figure 2-6).

You can most quickly get to Switch Application by pressing and holding the Menu key for two seconds.

Figure 2-6:
The Switch
Application
menu.

If you always use a particular application, such as the Tasks application, you can program the convenience key (which we explain in Chapter 3) so that you can get to that application even more quickly than by using the Switch Application function.

Changing options

Throughout this book, we give examples of changing an option field's value. You can most easily change the value in a field by using the trackpad to scroll to the field, pressing the trackpad to display a pop-up menu of choices (see Figure 2-7), scrolling until you highlight the option you want, and then pressing the trackpad again on your choice.

Figure 2-7:
An example
of an option
field's
pop-up
menu.

General Keyboard Shortcuts

The rest of this chapter covers shortcuts for QWERTY-based BlackBerry models.

In many instances in this book, when we ask you to go to a BlackBerry application (Profile, for example), you have to first scroll to it from the Home screen and then press the trackpad. You might be thinking, "Hey, there must be a shortcut for this," and you're right. This section and the following sections cover such general keyboard shortcuts, all in the name of making your life easier. (We talk about shortcuts that are more application-specific in the chapter that deals with the particular application.)

Before you get all excited about shortcuts, you need to take care of one bit of housekeeping. To use some of these general keyboard shortcuts, you have to change a Home Screen Preference option. Follow these steps to set the Launch by Typing option to the proper setting:

1. **From the BlackBerry Home screen, press the Menu key, and then select Option from the menu that appears.**

   The Home Screen Preference screen opens.

2. **Highlight Launch by Typing, and then press the trackpad.**

   A pop-up menu opens, offering two choices:

   - **Universal Search:** Pressing any key on the Home screen makes a Search text box appear.
   - **Application Shortcuts:** Pressing a key in the Home screen opens the associated application.

3. **Select Application Shortcuts.**

   This step shuts down the Dial from Home Screen option, enabling you to use Home screen shortcuts.

4. **Press the Menu key, and then select Save from the menu that appears.**

Using Home screen shortcuts

After you disable the Dial from Home Screen feature, you're free to use any Home screen shortcut. (The name for these shortcuts is actually a pretty good fit because you can use these shortcuts only while you're on the Home screen.)

Okay, here goes. To call up the application listed in the first column of Table 2-1, press the key listed in the second column.

Table 2-1	Home Screen Shortcuts
Application	*Shortcut Key*
Messages	M
Saved Messages	V
Compose	C
Search	S
Contacts	A
Tasks	T
Profile	F
Browser	B
Calendar	L
Calculator	U
MemoPad	D
Keyboard Lock	Hold A
Phone	P
Vibrate Mode	Hold Q

Other (non–Home screen) shortcuts

You can use the following shortcuts at any time, regardless of which screen you're currently on — or whether you have Dial from Home Screen enabled, for that matter:

✔ **Soft Device Reset (also known as the 3-Button Salute):** Pressing Alt+right Cap+Del forces a manual soft reset, which is just what you need when your BlackBerry has crashed or you install an application that needs a manual reset. You can do a hard reset by pulling out the battery from the back of the BlackBerry. What's the difference between a soft reset and a hard reset? Without getting into the technical jargon, from a BlackBerry user's perspective, a hard reset takes longer and is usually the last resort to try to solve any issues before you have to contact the help desk.

✔ **HelpMe:** In the BlackBerry world, SOS is spelled Alt+Cap+H. Use it when you're on the phone with technical support. (It gives support personnel info such as your BlackBerry PIN, memory space, and version number so that they have information about your BlackBerry when they try to troubleshoot your problems.)

Note: Your BlackBerry PIN isn't a security password; rather, it's a unique number that identifies your BlackBerry, sort of like a serial number. Unlike a serial number, you can message another BlackBerry by using PIN-to-PIN messages. For more on PIN-to-PIN messages, see Chapter 9.

Chapter 3

Tweaking Your BlackBerry

Regardless of how long you've had your BlackBerry — one week, one month, one year, or more — you probably want to have it around for as long as you possibly can. (At least until you have the bucks for that way-cool new model that's surely coming down the pike.) For the duration that you *do* have your device, you can trick it out so that it doesn't feel and sound exactly like the millions of other BlackBerry devices out there. (C'mon, admit it — your BlackBerry is definitely a fashion statement, so you'd better feel comfortable with what that statement is saying.)

In addition to customizing your BlackBerry so that it expresses the inner you, you can make sure that you keep your BlackBerry in tip-top shape by watching out for such things as its battery life and information security. Luckily for you, this chapter puts all such worries to rest by filling you in on all you need to know to keep your BlackBerry a finely tuned (and yet quirkily personal) little smartphone.

Making Your BlackBerry Yours

BlackBerry smartphones are increasingly popular, so much so that more than 50 million BlackBerries are serving the needs of people like you. So, we feel confident that finding ways to distinguish your BlackBerry from your colleagues' is high on your list of priorities.

Branding your BlackBerry

Like any number of other electronic gadgets, your BlackBerry comes to you automatically fitted with a collection of factory settings. This section helps you put your name on your BlackBerry, figuratively and literally. You can start by branding your name on your BlackBerry. Follow these steps:

1. **From the Home screen, press the Menu key twice, and then select Options (the icon looks like a wrench).**

   The Options screen opens.

2. **Select the Display setting, and then select Message on Lock Screen from the Display screen.**

   The screen displays fields in which you can enter your owner information.

3. **Enter your name in the Display Owner Name field and your contact information in the Display Information field.**

   Phrase a message (like the one shown in Figure 3-1) that would make sense to any possible Good Samaritan who might find your lost BlackBerry and want to get it back to you.

   If you lock or don't use your BlackBerry for a while, the standby screen comes on, displaying the owner information that you entered. You can find out how to lock your BlackBerry, either manually or by using an auto setting, in the section "Keeping Your BlackBerry Safe," later in this chapter.

4. **Press the Menu key, and then select Save from the menu that appears.**

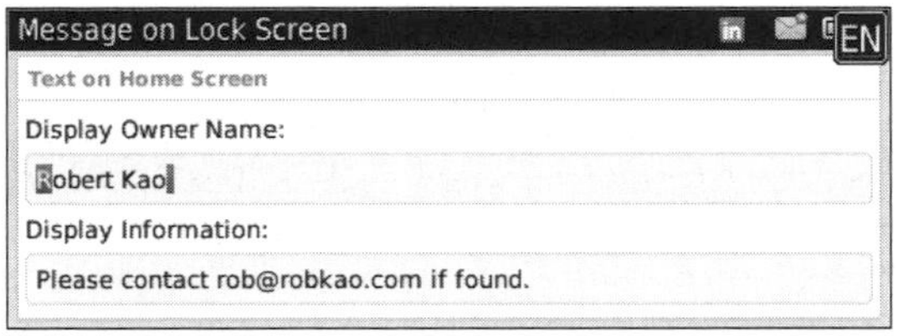

Figure 3-1:
List your owner info in the Message on Lock Screen fields.

Message on Lock Screen			in	✉	EN

Text on Home Screen

Display Owner Name:

Robert Kao

Display Information:

Please contact rob@robkao.com if found.

Choosing a language, any language

Setting your BlackBerry's language to your native tongue so that you don't need to hire a translator to use your BlackBerry is important — and easy. You can also set your input method of choice in this option, which can not only change the way you type, but also affect whether Word Substitution shows up. Don't worry: We explain Word Substitution in the following section.

Follow these steps to choose a language:

1. **From the Home screen, press the Menu key twice, and then select Options.**

    The Options screen opens.

2. **Select the Typing and Input option, and then select Language and Method from the screen that appears.**

    In the Language and Method screen that appears, you can choose the language and input method of your choice.

3. **Select your native tongue from the Display Language pop-up menu.**

    Depending on your network provider, as well as your region (North America, Europe, and so on), the language choices you have can vary. Most smartphones sold in North America default to English (UK) or English (U.S.).

    If your network provider supports it, you can install more languages in your BlackBerry by using Application Loader in BlackBerry Desktop Software. For more information on Application Loader, see Chapter 20.

4. **Press the Menu key, and then select Save from the menu that appears.**

Isn't it great when you can actually read what's onscreen?

Typing with ease using Word Substitution

Even the most devoted BlackBerry user has to admit that you can more easily type on a full keyboard than you can thumb-type on a BlackBerry. In an attempt to even the score a bit, your BlackBerry comes equipped with a Word Substitution feature (formerly known as AutoText), which is a kind of shorthand that can cut down on how much you have to type.

Word Substitution works with a pool of abbreviations that you set up. You then just type an abbreviation to get the word you associated with that abbreviation. For example, after setting up *b/c* as an AutoText word for *because,* any time you type **b/c**, you automatically get *because* onscreen.

Your BlackBerry comes with a few default Word Substitution entries. Here are some useful ones:

> ✔ **mypin:** Displays your BlackBerry PIN
>
> ✔ **mynumber:** Displays your BlackBerry phone number
>
> ✔ **myver:** Displays your BlackBerry model number and operating system (OS) version

The whole Word Substitution thing works best if you set up your own personal code, mapping your abbreviations to their meanings, which is why we discuss Word Substitution as part of personalization.

To set up your own code, follow these steps:

1. **From the Home screen, press the Menu key twice, and then select Options.**

   The Options screen opens.

2. **Select the Typing and Input option, and then select Word Substitution from the screen that appears.**

   In the Word Substitution screen that appears, you can choose to see (or search for) existing items in Word Substitution or create new ones.

3. **Press the Menu key, and then select New.**

   The Word Substitution: New screen appears, as shown in Figure 3-2.

Figure 3-2:
Create
a Word
Substitution.

4. **In the Replace field, enter the characters that you want to replace.**

   For example, we enter **b/c**.

5. **In the With field, type what replaces your characters.**

   We enter **because.**

6. **In the Using field, choose between the SmartCase and Specified Case options.**

   Here's what each option does:

   • *SmartCase:* Capitalizes the first letter when the context calls for that, such as the first word in a sentence.

   • *Specified Case:* Replaces your AutoText with the exact text found in the With field.

For example, say you entered the Word Substitution **sgms** for the term *SmrtGuard Mobile Security,* and you want it to appear as-is, in terms of letter case (keeping the *g* in the middle of SmrtGuard capitalized). If you use Specified Case, your Word Substitution always appears as exactly *SmrtGuard Mobile Security.* If you instead choose SmartCase for this particular Word Substitution, the *g* in SmrtGuard isn't capitalized because it doesn't begin a word.

7. **Select All Locales from the Language pop-up menu.**

   Whenever you create AutoText, we recommend you use the All Locales setting. Regardless of the Language input method (for example, English UK, English U.S., or French), when you select All Locales, any self-created Word Substitution is available for you to use. Therefore, in the case of the Word Substitution **sgms** (which gets replaced with *SmrtGuard Mobile Security*), whether you're typing in French or Chinese, you can use this Word Substitution. On the other hand, if you select only the French input method from the Language field, you can use this Word Substitution only if you've selected French as your Language input method.

8. **Press the Menu key, and then select Save from the menu that appears.**

If you specify a language input method other than All Locales, your Language input method must match the Language field in Word Substitution if you want to use your newly created Word Substitution. Follow these steps to make sure your word substitution works in all languages:

1. **From the Home screen, press the Menu key twice, and then select Options.**

   The Options screen opens.

2. **Select the Typing and Input option, and then select Language from the screen that appears.**

   In the Language screen that appears, you can choose the language and input method.

3. **Select the input method you need from the Input Language pop-up menu.**

   For your new Word Substitution setting to work (assuming that you didn't choose All Locales as the language for your Word Substitution), this option needs to match the input method set in your Language option.

4. **Press the Menu key, and then choose Save from the menu that appears.**

Getting your dates and times lined up

Having the correct date, time, and time zone is important when it comes to your BlackBerry for, we hope, obvious reasons. Many of the fine features that make up the BlackBerry core experience depend on accurate time, date, and time zone information.

Need an example? How about your BlackBerry calendar events? Imagine that you have a make-or-break meeting set for 9 a.m. (in your time zone) with a client in Paris, who's in who-knows-what time zone. You definitely want to be on time for that appointment, but you probably won't be if you're planning to have your BlackBerry remind you — at least, if you haven't set up the appropriate date, time, and time zone. Follow these steps to tell your BlackBerry the time and date:

1. **From the Home screen, press the Menu key twice, and then select Options.**

   The Options screen opens.

2. **Select the Display option, and then select Date and Time from the screen that appears.**

   The Date/Time screen appears.

3. **Select a time zone from the Time Zone pop-up menu.**

   The Date/Time screen confirms the time zone that you chose.

   If you travel to a different time zone, you probably don't need to adjust this field because it adjusts automatically based on information your BlackBerry receives from the network.

4. **In the Auto Update Time Zone pop-up menu, select Prompt.**

   When you travel across different time zones, your BlackBerry can detect which time zone you're currently in.

5. **In the Update Time pop-up menu, select Automatic.**

   By selecting Automatic, your date and time source is set to your service provider's server time (see Figure 3-3). By having this option set to Automatic, the time is always accurate for your current location.

   If you always set the time a few minutes earlier than the actual time (so that you can be on time for those important meetings), set this field to Manual. If you set Update Time to Manual, Time and Date pop-up menus appear. Select the proper date, hour, and minutes.

6. **Press the Menu key, and then select Save from the menu that appears.**

   Your BlackBerry saves your date and time settings in perpetuity — or until you change them.

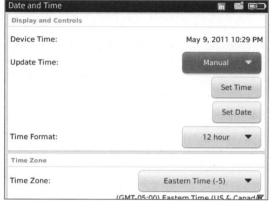

Figure 3-3:
Set the
date and
time of your
BlackBerry.

Customizing your screen's look and feel

You can set your BlackBerry's display font, font size, and screen contrast to your liking. We know that some of you don't give a hoot whether your fonts are Batang or Bookman, as long as you can read the text, but we also know that other folks won't stop configuring the fonts until they feel those fonts are absolutely right. For all you tweakers out there, follow these steps to play around with your BlackBerry's fonts:

1. **From the Home screen, press the Menu key twice, and then select Options.**

   The Options screen opens.

2. **Select the Display option, and then select Screen Display from the screen that appears.**

   The Screen Display screen appears, featuring various customizable fields, as shown in Figure 3-4.

3. **In the Font Family pop-up menu, select a font.**

   You can choose from between three to ten fonts, depending on your provider.

4. **Select a font size from the Font Size pop-up menu.**

   Keep in mind that the smaller the font size, the more you can see onscreen; however, a smallish font is harder on the eyes.

   Note: While you scroll up and down the list of fonts and font sizes, the text The quick brown fox jumps over the lazy dog below the Font Style setting takes on the look of the selected font and size so that you can preview what the particular text looks like. (In case you were wondering, that sentence uses every letter in the alphabet.)

Figure 3-4:
The Screen
Display
screen,
waiting
for person-
alization.

5. **Select an option in the Font Style pop-up menu.**

   You can set your text to Bold, Italic, or Plain (the default).

6. **From the Backlight Brightness pop-up menu, select the desired brightness.**

   You can choose 0 to 100, where 0 is the darkest and 100 is the brightest. A lower brightness level reduces your BlackBerry's battery consumption.

7. **From the Backlight Timeout pop-up menu, select how long your BlackBerry's screen uses backlighting.**

   You can choose from 10 seconds up to 2 minutes. The lower this setting, the less time your BlackBerry displays backlighting after you press a key. However, a low setting helps you conserve battery life.

8. **Deselect the Automatically Dim Backlight check box, if necessary.**

   When you're outdoors, with the bright sun shining on your BlackBerry, you probably have difficulty reading the screen. When the Automatically Dim Backlight feature is on (the default), the BlackBerry's light sensor auto-adjusts the backlight so that, for example, it's bright enough for you to read your BlackBerry while you're outdoors.

9. **To confirm your changes, press the Menu key, and then select Save from the menu that appears.**

   You can download other themes from BlackBerry App World, which we talk about in Chapter 20.

Wallpapering your BlackBerry

Like your PC, you can personalize the BlackBerry Home screen by adding wallpaper. You set an image to be your BlackBerry Home screen background by using the BlackBerry Media application. Follow these steps:

1. **From the Home screen, press the Menu key twice, and then select the Media folder.**

   The Media panel opens, displaying the following icons: Music, Video, Ring Tones, Pictures, and Voice Notes.

2. **Select the Pictures icon, and then select one of the choices on the screen that appears.**

   Four choices appear onscreen:

   - *Camera Pictures:* Turns on the BlackBerry camera
   - *All Pictures:* Displays all the pictures stored on your BlackBerry
   - *Picture Library:* Displays the pictures stored on your BlackBerry, organized by folders
   - *Wallpaper:* Displays the wallpaper that came with your BlackBerry

3. **Select the picture that you want to use for your Home screen background.**

   The selected picture appears in full-screen view.

4. **Press the Menu key, and then select Set as Home Screen Image from the menu that appears.**

   The picture is now your new Home screen wallpaper.

5. **Press and hold the Escape key to return to the Home screen and see the result.**

You can download free wallpapers from the following websites (as long as you use your BlackBerry, not your PC, to access the URLs):

- ✔ mobile.blackberry.com
- ✔ BlackBerry Wallpapers (www.blackberrywallpapers.com)
- ✔ CrackBerry.com Free Wallpapers (www.crackberry.com/free-wallpapers)

Letting freedom ring

The whole appeal of the BlackBerry phenomenon is the idea that this little electronic device can make your life easier. One of the ways it accomplishes this feat is by acting as your personal reminder service — letting you know when an appointment is coming up, a phone call is coming in, an e-mail has arrived, and so on. Your BlackBerry is set to bark at you if it knows something it thinks you should know, too.

Whether you create your own profile or customize a predefined profile, each profile is divided into several categories that represent the application for which you can define alerts.

You can find Sound and Alert Profiles as a speaker icon in the Home screen. Within the Sound and Alert Profile application, each Profile is organized into the following categories (as shown in Figure 3-5):

Figure 3-5:
Set
attention-
needy
applications
in this Edit
Profile
screen.

- ✔ **Phone:** Alerts you if you have an incoming call or new voice mail message.

- ✔ **Messages:** Alerts you if you have an incoming e-mail, SMS, MMS, or BlackBerry PIN message. Additionally, you can set different alerts for each individual e-mail account.

- ✔ **Instant Messages:** Alerts you if you have any BlackBerry Messenger Alerts; if you have third-party Instant Messaging apps installed (such as Google Talk), you can set the alerts for those apps, as well.

- ✔ **Events:** Alerts you if you've set up calendar reminders, tasks reminders, or e-mail follow-up flags (see Chapter 8).

- ✔ **Other Applications:** This category is a notification setting for third-party applications, such as Facebook, as well as the Browser application.

You can personalize all the listed applications according to how you want to be alerted. Because how you customize them is similar, we use one application, Messages, as an example in the following section.

Different people react differently to different sounds. Certain segments of the population might greatly appreciate some BlackBerry barks, whereas other segments might react to the same sound by pitching their BlackBerries under the nearest bus. The folks at Research in Motion (RIM) are well aware of these different reactions and have devised a great way for you to customize how you want your BlackBerry to bark at you — they call it your *Sound and Alert Profile*.

You can jump right into things by using a predefined profile (which we describe in the following section), or you can create your own profile (outlined in the section "Creating your own profile," later in this chapter). You may wonder why you need to create a profile if you can personalize the predefined ones. If your needs are different from the predefined settings, create a profile to get it just the way you want it.

Using factory settings

If you're okay with customizing a predefined, factory-loaded profile, just follow these steps:

1. **From the BlackBerry Home screen, press the Menu key twice, and then select the Sound and Alert Profiles application.**

   A pop-up screen appears, listing different profiles (Silent, Vibrate, Normal, Loud, Medium, Phone Calls Only, All Alerts Off).

2. **Select Change Sounds and Alerts, which appears at the end of the list.**

   The Change Sounds and Alerts screen appears.

3. **Select Sound for Selected Profile.**

   The Edit Profile screen appears, listing the applications that have alert capabilities, mentioned in the preceding section (refer to Figure 3-5).

4. **Expand the Messages heading by pressing the trackpad, and then in the list that appears, select any of your e-mail accounts for which you want to configure custom alerts.**

   A screen appears, displaying options to set the ringtone, LED, and vibration.

5. **Change the appropriate Sound Alerts options.**

   You can set the following options:

- *Notifier Tone:* The ringtone you want.

- *Volume:* How loud you want the ringtone to sound, from Silent to 10 (the loudest).

- *Count:* The number of times the ringtone repeats, from 1 to 3.

- *Play Sound:* Whether the ringtone will play while your BlackBerry is in or out of the holster, or whether it will always play.

6. **Select On from the LED pop-up menu.**

   If you enable the LED option for when messages arrive, the LED blinks when you receive a message.

7. **Select an option from the Vibration pop-up menu.**

   You can set it to On, Off, or Custom.

   If you choose Custom, the following options appear onscreen:

   - *Length:* How long each vibration lasts — Short, Medium, or Long.

   - *Count:* The number of times the vibration occurs; you can choose 1, 2, 3, 5, or 10.

   - *Vibrate:* Whether the vibration will occur while your BlackBerry is in or out of the holster, or whether it will always vibrate.

8. **Press the Menu key, and then select Save from the menu that appears.**

Creating your own profile

You need to know which applications on your BlackBerry have alert capabilities because then you can personalize each "Hey, you!" to your liking. You can have your BlackBerry so personalized that you can tell whether you have a phone call or an incoming message just by how your BlackBerry sounds.

If you're already familiar with the different applications and know how you want each one to alert you, go on and create your own profile. You can achieve the same result by personalizing the predefined profiles that come with your BlackBerry, but if you want to keep the predefined profiles the way they are, create a new profile by following these steps:

1. **From the BlackBerry Home screen, press the Menu key twice, and then select the Sound and Alert Profiles application.**

   A pop-up screen appears, listing different profiles (Silent, Vibrate, Normal, Loud, Medium, Phone Calls Only, All Alerts Off).

2. **Select Change Sounds and Alerts, which appears at the end of the list.**

   The Change Sounds and Alerts screen appears.

3. **Select Profile Management.**

   The Profile Management screen appears.

4. **Press the Menu key, and then select New from the menu that appears.**

   A New Custom Profile screen appears, prompting you to name your profile.

5. **In the Name field, enter a name for your profile.**

   For example, you can type **MyOwnProfile**.

6. **Configure your new profile.**

   To customize each of the categories of applications, refer to Steps 4 through 7 in the preceding section.

7. **Press the Menu key, and then select Save from the menu that appears.**

   Your newly created profile appears in the Profile Management screen.

8. **Select My Profile.**

   Your newly created profile is active, so you can now start to use it.

You can switch between your current profile and the Quiet profile by pressing and holding the # key.

Regardless of whether you use a different ringtone for an incoming call or an incoming e-mail, you can download more ringtones to personalize your BlackBerry. Additionally, you can use any MP3 file in your Media application as your personalized ringtone. Follow these steps:

1. **From the Home screen, press the Menu key twice, and then select Media folder.**

2. **In the Media folder, select the Music category.**

   Various music classifications, such as Artist, Album, and Genres, appear onscreen.

3. **Highlight the music file that you want to use for your ringtone.**

4. **Press the Menu key, and then select Set as Phone Tune from the menu that appears.**

   The music file is set as your new phone tune.

5. **Press and hold the Escape key to return to the Home screen.**

Keeping Your BlackBerry Safe

The folks at RIM take security seriously, and so should you. If someone ever steals your BlackBerry, you might not get the physical BlackBerry back, but if you set up a password, you can make sure the thief can't access the data on your BlackBerry.

Setting a password for your BlackBerry

To prevent anyone from reading your BlackBerry content while you're away from your BlackBerry, set up a password. In an enterprise environment (if your employer handed you a BlackBerry), your BlackBerry may prompt you to set up a password automatically, but if it doesn't, follow these steps:

1. **From the Home screen, press the Menu key twice, and then select Options.**

   The Options screen appears.

2. **Select Security, and then select Password from the screen that appears.**

   The Password screen appears.

3. **From the Password pop-up menu, select Enabled.**

   This step enables the Password feature. Your BlackBerry doesn't prompt you to type a password until you save the changes you just made.

4. **Select Set Password.**

   An Enter Password pop-up screen appears, prompting you to enter a new password, as shown in Figure 3-6.

   If you've set a password before, the option is Change Password (like in Figure 3-6).

5. **Type a password in the Enter Password field, and then type it again in the confirmation field for verification.**

   From this point on, whenever you lock your BlackBerry and want to use it again, you have to type the password.

Figure 3-6:
It's time to
enter a new
password.

Locking your BlackBerry

Setting up your password is a good first step, but just having a password can't help much if you don't take the further step of locking your BlackBerry when you aren't using it. (You don't want people at the office or at the table next to you at the coffee shop checking out your e-mails or phone history when you take a bathroom break, do you?) So, how do you lock your BlackBerry? Let us count the ways. . . . We came up with two.

To simply password-lock your BlackBerry at any given moment, press and hold the asterisk (*) key.

Or you can go the Autolock-after-Timeout (also known as Security Timeout) route by following these steps:

1. **From the Home screen, press the Menu key twice, and then select Options.**

   The Options screen appears.

2. **Select Security, and then select Password from the screen that appears.**

   The Password screen appears.

3. **From the Lock After pop-up menu, select the desired minutes.**

   The preset times range from 1 minute to 1 hour.

4. **Press the Menu key, and then select Save from the menu that appears.**

Blocking That Spam

With your BlackBerry, you can prevent certain e-mails, SMS numbers, or BlackBerry PINs from getting to your inbox. It's like having your own spam blocker on your BlackBerry!

To set up your personal spam blocker, follow these steps:

1. **From the Home screen, press the Menu key twice, and then select Options.**

   The Options screen appears.

2. **Select Security Options.**

   The Security Options screen appears.

3. **Select the Firewall option.**

   The Firewall screen appears.

4. **Select the Enable check box.**

   This setting turns on the spam blocker.

5. **Below Block Incoming Message, make sure that what you want to block is selected.**

   You can select any of these check boxes:

   - *Text Message:* Blocks text messages

   - *PIN:* Blocks BlackBerry PIN messages

   - *Personal Email:* Blocks e-mail messages (for example, the e-mails you receive through the account that you set up from Google or Yahoo! Mail)

   - *Enterprise Email:* Blocks enterprise e-mail (if you're in a corporate e-mail network)

6. **Select the desired Exception check boxes.**

   You can select these check boxes, if you want:

   - *Contact:* Blocks everything except e-mails and calls from e-mail addresses and phone numbers in your Contacts.

   - *Specific Address:* Blocks everything specified by you. (You can set up the list by following Steps 7 and 8.)

7. **Press the Add button below Specific Address.**

   The Firewall Exception screen appears.

8. **Press the Menu key, and then select the desired options from the menu that appears.**

   You can choose these options:

   - *Add Email:* Specify the e-mail address you want to block.

   - *Add PIN:* Specify the BlackBerry PIN you want to block.

   - *Add Phone Number:* Specify the SMS number you want to block.

9. **Press the Menu key, and then select Save from the menu that appears.**

Part II
Organizing with BlackBerry

The 5th Wave   By Rich Tennant

"Well, here's what happened—I forgot to put 'dressing' on my 'To Do' list."

In this part . . .

Find out how to use your BlackBerry to its fullest to get — and remain — organized. Peruse the chapters in this part to find out how to use Contacts, keep appointments, set alarms, use the timer and Bedside mode through the Clock application, keep your passwords safe and easy to retrieve, and take advantage of the many features of BlackBerry Phone.

Chapter 4

Remembering and Locating Your Acquaintances

Address books were around long before the BlackBerry was conceived. And BlackBerry Contacts serves the same function as any address book: It's a place where you record and organize information about people. However, Contacts also affords you a central place to reach your contacts in myriad ways: by landline phone; cellphone; e-mail; or the speedy messaging of PIN, SMS, MMS, or BlackBerry Messenger. Contacts also can give you a central place to find your connections from a variety of social networking sites to which you belong.

In today's connected world, you need an address book like BlackBerry Contacts. This chapter explains all the possible ways that you can use Contacts to help you manage your busy lifestyle.

Accessing Contacts

The Contacts icon looks like an address book with a representation of a person on the cover. You can see it highlighted in Figure 4-1. Opening Contacts couldn't be simpler: From the Home screen, press the Menu key twice, and then select the Contacts icon.

Figure 4-1:
The
Contacts
icon.

You can also access Contacts from Phone, Messages, Messenger, and Calendar. For example, say you're in Calendar and you want to invite people to one of your meetings. Look no further — Contacts shows up when you press the Menu key and then select Invite Attendee from the menu that appears; and it's ready to lend a helping hand.

Another way to get to Contacts is by pressing A while on the Home screen. Go to Chapter 2 for more on how to enable Home screen shortcuts.

Working with Contacts

Getting a new gizmo is always exciting because you just know that your newest toy is chock-full of features you're dying to try out. We bet you feel that way about your BlackBerry. The first thing you want to do is try to call or e-mail someone, right? But wait a sec. You don't have any contact information yet, which means you have to type in someone's e-mail address each time you send an e-mail — what a hassle.

It's time to get with the plan. Most of us humans — social creatures that we are — maintain a list of contacts somewhere, such as in an e-mail program or from a social networking site such as Facebook. We're pretty sure you have some kind of list somewhere. The trick is getting that list into your BlackBerry so that you can access your info more efficiently. Here's some good news: You can easily get that contact info into your BlackBerry.

Often, you can most simply get contact information into your BlackBerry by entering it manually. However, if you've invested a lot of time and energy in maintaining some type of Contacts application on your desktop computer, you may want to hot-sync that data into your BlackBerry. For more on synchronizing data, check out Chapter 18.

Creating a contact

Imagine that you just ran into Jane Doe, an old high school friend whom you haven't seen in years. Jane is about to give you her number, but you don't have a pen or pencil handy to write down her information. Are you then forced to chant her phone number to yourself until you can scare up a writing implement? Not if you have your handy BlackBerry with you.

With BlackBerry in hand, follow these steps to create a new contact:

1. **On the BlackBerry Home screen, press the Menu key twice, and then select the Contacts application.**

   You also can access Contacts from different applications. For example, see Chapter 8 to find out how to access Contacts from Messages.

2. **In the Contacts screen that appears, select Add Contact.**

   The New Contact screen appears, as shown in Figure 4-2.

New Contact ▭ 🗇 ⚡ ⁝⁝ △ EDGE ⅂⒩⒧
Title:
First: |
Last:
Company:
Add Field
Email Addresses ▾

Figure 4-2: Create a new contact in the New Contact screen.

3. **Enter the contact information in the appropriate fields.**

   Use your BlackBerry keyboard to enter this information and scroll down to see additional fields. The New Contact screen is organized into multiple sections. The following section gives you a complete explanation about how to fill out this screen.

   We don't think you can overdo it when entering a person's contact information. Enter as much info as you possibly can. Maybe the benefit isn't obvious now, but when your memory fails you or your boss needs a critical piece of info that you happen to have, you'll thank us for this advice.

4. **Click the Escape key, and then select Save from the confirmation screen that appears.**

Your new contact is added to the list, as shown in Figure 4-3.

Spend a little bit of time creating your own contact record(s). Add at least one record for your business contact info and one for your personal contact info to save yourself from having to type your own contact information every time you want to give it to someone. You can share your contact record by sending it as an attachment to an e-mail. (See the section "Sharing a Contact," later in this chapter.)

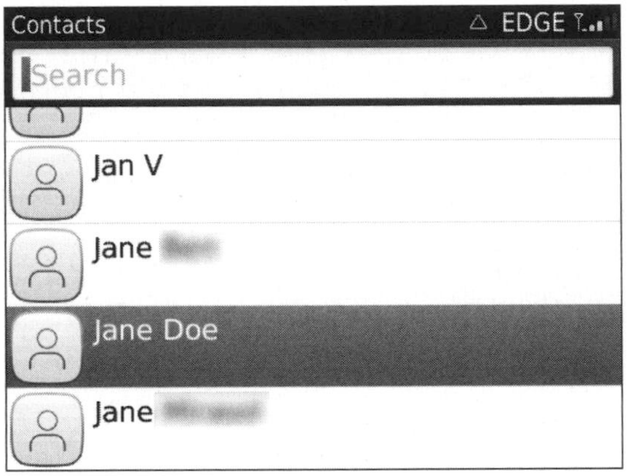

Figure 4-3:
The
Contacts
screen after
you add
contacts.

Contacts	△ EDGE T..ıl
Search	
Jan V	
Jane ▮▮▮	
Jane Doe	
Jane ▮▮▮▮▮	

Completing a contact record

The only field you have to fill in to create a contact is either the Last Name field or the Company field, both of which appear in the first section of the New Contact screen. Filling in these fields is pretty straightforward: Simply move the cursor to the appropriate field and type in the name. Because we encourage you to enter as much information as you can get for your contacts, in the following sections, we describe how to enter each piece of information.

Adding a picture for a contact

Like most cellphones, your BlackBerry can display a picture of the caller. Follow these steps to add a photo for a contact:

1. **Select the person icon in the top-left of the New Contact screen (shown in Figure 4-2).**

The Select Picture screen appears, allowing you to navigate to the folder that contains the picture file you want to use.

2. **Select either Camera Pictures, Picture Library, or Avatars.**

3. **In the folder that opens, scroll to the picture you want to use.**

4. **Select the picture.**

   The picture you choose appears onscreen, including a selection rectangle, as shown in Figure 4-4.

5. **Scroll to position the rectangle on the face.**

   Contacts uses a tiny image for each contact, and this rectangle indicates how the application crops the image.

6. **Press the Menu key, and then select Crop and Save from the menu that appears.**

   You're all set. Just save this contact (as discussed in the section "Creating a contact," earlier in this chapter) to keep your changes.

Figure 4-4: Crop your contact's picture.

You can acquire photos in your BlackBerry in two ways:

✔ **Use the BlackBerry's camera to take a picture of the person.** See Chapter 14 for more about taking photos with your BlackBerry.

✔ **Copy a photo file into your BlackBerry.** You can send it via e-mail (which we explain in Chapter 8), copy it to the microSD card (discussed in Chapter 16), or copy it to the built-in memory of BlackBerry.

Adding a title and nickname

By default, the Job Title and Nickname fields don't appear in the New Contact screen. But you can add them quickly by using the Add Field button. Follow these steps to add a job title or nickname to one of your contacts:

1. **Select the Add Field button, which appears below the Company field of the New Contact screen.**

   The Add Field screen, where you can select either Job Title or Nickname, appears.

2. **Select the option you want to add.**

   The New Contact screen reappears, displaying the Job Title or Nickname field below the Company field.

3. **Select the new field and enter the appropriate information.**

   Save the contact (as discussed in the section "Creating a contact," earlier in this chapter) to keep your changes.

Adding e-mail addresses

To find the Email Addresses section of the New Contact screen, scroll down (it appears directly below the Add Field button). You can enter an e-mail address for this contact in the Email field.

As soon as you type a character in the Email field, a new Email field is added below the existing one. BlackBerry uses this clever feature for contact fields that often have more than one entry, such as phone numbers and e-mail addresses. You can have up to three e-mail addresses per contact.

When you enter an e-mail address, press the Space key to insert the *at* symbol (@) or a period (.). BlackBerry is smart enough to figure out whether you need the @ or a period.

Adding phone numbers

Below the Email Addresses section on the New Contact screen, the Phone Numbers section appears. A Work button appears next to a blank field in which you can enter the phone number. The Work button is actually a pop-up menu from which you can choose Work, Home, Mobile, Work 2, Home 2, Mobile 2, Pager, Work Fax, Home Fax, or Other. Just like the Email field, after you start typing a phone number, another phone number field is added.

Here's something slick to know when you're entering phone information for a contact: BlackBerry can also dial an extra number after the initial phone number. That extra number can be someone's extension, a participant code on a conference number, or simply your voicemail PIN. When you enter the contact's phone number, type the primary phone number, press Alt+X, and then type the extension number. Say you enter 11112345678X1111; when you tell your BlackBerry to call that number, it dials 11112345678 first. Then, a prompt appears, asking you whether you want to continue or skip dialing the extension.

Adding a BlackBerry PIN

Every BlackBerry smartphone has a unique identifier, called a BlackBerry PIN (personal identification number). You need a BlackBerry PIN if you want to communicate with a contact through BlackBerry Messenger (see Chapter 10 to get the complete scoop on BlackBerry Messenger). You can enter this information in the PIN field of the BlackBerry PIN section of the New Contact screen, which appears directly below the Phone Numbers section.

A BlackBerry PIN is always eight characters long, so confirm that you've entered all the characters in the PIN field.

Assigning a tone

Oh, no — your ringing BlackBerry has woken you! Ringtones help you decide whether to ignore the call, or wake up and answer it. (We hope you can easily switch your body back to sleep mode if you decide to ignore the call.)

You can customize the ringtone when you receive a call or have a new message from this contact in the Custom Ring Tones/Alerts section of the New Contact screen, which appears below the PIN field when you scroll down from the top of this screen. To set a custom ringtone for a contact, follow these steps:

1. **In the Custom Ring Tones/Alerts section of the New Contact screen, select Phone, and then customize the ringtone on the screen that appears.**

   You can change the following options:

   - *Ring Tone:* Select a ring tone from the list of tones.

   - *Volume:* Allows you to control the volume. By default, it's set to use the Active Profile settings (see Chapter 3 for more about profiles), which means it follows the volume setting in the profile to which your BlackBerry is currently set. You can change this setting to a value from 1 to 10 (10 is the loudest).

   - *Play Sound:* Lets you control whether you want your BlackBerry to play the tone when you get a phone call. You can choose Active Profile (the default setting; the assigned tone plays if the current profile isn't set to Vibrate Only or Silent), In Holster (plays the assigned tone if the BlackBerry's in a case), and Out of Holster (plays the assigned tone if the BlackBerry isn't in a case).

     A small magnet is embedded in the case that comes with your BlackBerry. The smartphone uses this magnet to detect whether the device is in the case. If you plan to buy a new case, make sure that it's designed for your BlackBerry model so that all the features related to holstering keep working.

- *LED:* Allows you to use LED to indicate a call.

- *Vibration:* Allows you to enable vibration as a way of notifying you about a call. The default setting is Active Profile, which follows the Vibration setting on the profile to which your BlackBerry is currently set. You can override the profile by changing this option to Off, On, or Custom. Choosing Custom is the same as setting Vibration to On, but you can control how long you want the vibration to last.

- *Vibrate with Ring Tone:* Allows you to have your BlackBerry both vibrate and play the tone when you receive a call. You can choose Active Profile, On, and Off. The default value is Active Profile, which means it follows the Vibrate with Ring Tone settings in the profile to which your BlackBerry is currently set.

2. **Press the Escape key.**

   The New Contact screen reappears.

3. **In the Custom Ring Tones/Alerts section of the New Contact screen, select Messages.**

   This section appears below the Phone field.

   The Messages screen, where you can customize the ringtone when you receive a message, appears. You can do all the customizations listed in Step 1, as well as setting Notify Me During Calls. If you want to receive a notification while you're actively on a call, choose Yes. The default is No.

4. **Press the Escape key.**

   You return to the New Contact screen.

Adding addresses

The New Contact screen doesn't show address-related fields by default. However, in the Address section, you can add Home and Work addresses by using the Add Address button. Follow these steps to go about adding an address:

1. **In the Address section of New Contact screen, select Add Address.**

   Address fields appear in the Address section, with Work selected by default. If you want to add a Work address, skip to Step 3.

2. **Select Work, and then select Home from the pop-up menu that opens.**

3. **Type the appropriate address information into the address fields.**

4. **Repeat Steps 1 through 3, selecting the other address type, if you want to add both Home and Work addresses for this contact.**

Customizing with your own fields

Perhaps you want to add contact information that doesn't fit into any of the available fields. Although you can't really create additional fields from scratch, you can commandeer one of the Custom fields for your own purposes.

The Custom Fields section is located near the bottom of the screen, above the Notes section, so you have to scroll down to see it. To use a Custom field, follow these steps:

1. **In the Custom Fields section of the New Contact screen, select Add Custom Field.**

   A list of custom fields, labeled as Custom 1 to Custom 4, appears.

2. **Select any one of the custom fields.**

   The New Contact screen reappears, with the custom field you selected added to the Custom Fields section of the screen.

Basically, you can use custom fields any way you want, and you can even change the field's name. (Face it; *Custom 1* doesn't really help as a descriptive title.) For example, you can use a custom field to record titles that follow a name (such as MD, PhD, and so on) and name it something like Suffix. Or how about profession, hobbies, or school? You decide what information you need to record about your contacts.

Changing a custom field's name for this particular contact changes it for all your contacts.

To rename a custom field, follow these steps:

1. **Scroll to the bottom of the screen and navigate to one of the custom fields.**

2. **Press the Menu key, and then select Change Field Name from the menu that appears.**

   The Change Field Name option appears on the menu only if the cursor is in a custom field.

3. **Enter the new custom field name in the screen that appears, and then press the trackpad.**

   The custom field now displays the name you entered.

Adding notes

At the bottom of the New Contact screen, the Notes field allows you to add a unique description of your contact. For example, you can add info to the field that refreshes your memory with tidbits such as **Knows somebody at ABC Corporation** or **Can provide introduction to a Broadway agent.** Or perhaps your note is something personal, such as **Likes golf; has 2 children: boy, 7 & girl, 3; husband's name is Ray.** The more relevant the information you include is to your relationship with this contact, the more useful you may find it.

Adding contacts from other BlackBerry applications

When you get an e-mail message or a call, that person's contact information is in Messages or Phone. It's just logical to add the information to your Contacts. You can view previous incoming and outgoing phone calls by simply pressing the Call button. A screen appears that lists the phone numbers in order, based on the time you made or received the call. If you already have a number associated with a Contact record, the name of the contact appears; otherwise, you see only a phone number.

A phone log entry stays only as long as you have free space on your BlackBerry. When your BlackBerry runs out of space (which could take years, depending on how you use it), it deletes read e-mails and phone logs, starting from the oldest.

Checking free memory on your BlackBerry

You can view your device memory information by following these steps:

1. **From the Home screen, press the Menu key twice, and then select Options.**

2. **From Options screen that appears, select Device.**

3. **Select Storage from the Device screen that appears.**

    The Storage screen appears, showing you two types of storage: application and media card storage.

In the Free Space field below the Application Storage section, you can see the memory used by the installed applications, including data from out-of-the-box applications such as Contacts, Messages, and Calendar. Your BlackBerry has a limited amount of application storage, and you can see how much is free on this screen. If free Application Storage drops below 10MB, your device might slow down a bit, and if it approaches 0MB, you may experience lag. At this point, you need to free some space:

✔ Pull the battery out to immediately net some space because applications that are currently running and using memory close when you remove the battery.

✔ Delete unused applications.

✔ Remove unnecessary bloatware that comes preloaded on the device (such as movie trailers and sample photos).

Adding contacts from Messages

To create a contact from an existing e-mail address or phone number in Messages, follow these steps:

1. **On the BlackBerry Home screen, press the Menu key twice, and then select Messages.**

2. **In the Messages screen that appears, select the e-mail address or the phone number.**

3. **Select Add to Contacts from the pop-up screen that appears.**

   A New Contact screen appears, filled with that particular piece of information.

4. **Enter the rest of the information that you know in the appropriate fields.**

5. **Press the Menu key, and then select Save from the menu that appears.**

The best solution for capturing contact information from e-mail is an application called gwabbit. The app can detect contact information, and it gives you a quick and easy way to add that contact information to Contacts. You can purchase gwabbit for $9.99 a year and download the app from BlackBerry App World.

Viewing a contact

Okay, you just entered your friend Jane's name into your BlackBerry, but you have this nagging feeling that you entered the wrong phone number. You want to quickly view Jane's information. Follow these steps:

1. **On the BlackBerry Home screen, press the Menu key twice, and then select Contacts.**

2. **In the Contacts screen that appears, scroll to find and select the contact name that you want to see.**

Selecting a name is the same as opening the menu and choosing View — just faster.

View mode displays only information that you've filled in, as shown in Figure 4-5. It doesn't bother showing blank fields.

Jane Doe	▭ 📶 ⁂ △ EDGE ⌐.₁
Jane Doe	
Phone Numbers	
Work:	2121112222
Email Addresses	
Email: jane.doe@blackberryfordummies.com	
Recent Activity	
No recent activity.	

Figure 4-5:
View mode
for a
contact.

View mode also displays the recent communications you've had with the contact in the Recent Activity section. Communications such as e-mail, text messages, and phone calls are listed in this section, with the most recent communications at the top of the list.

Editing a contact

Change is an inevitable part of life. Given that fact, your contact information is sure to change, as well. To keep current the information you diligently put in Contacts, you have to do some updating now and then.

To update a contact, follow these steps:

1. **On the BlackBerry Home screen, press the Menu key twice, and then select Contacts.**

2. **In the Contacts screen that appears, scroll to and highlight a contact name, press the Menu key, and then select Edit from the menu that opens.**

   The Edit Contact screen for that contact makes an appearance. The only difference between the Edit Contact and New Contact screen is the title.

In Contacts (or any BlackBerry application, for that matter), displaying a menu involves a simple press of the Menu key. The Edit option appears on the menu right below View.

3. **Scroll through the various fields of the Edit Contact screen, editing the contact information however you see fit.**

   See the section "Completing a contact record," earlier in this chapter, for a detailed explanation of how to fill in the fields.

If you want to edit only a few words or letters in a field (instead of replacing all the text), use the trackpad while pressing and holding the Alt key (located to the left of the Z key) to position your cursor precisely on the text you want to change. Then, make your desired changes.

4. **Press the Escape key, and then select Save from the confirmation screen that appears.**

   The edits you made for this contact are saved.

When you're editing information and want to replace an entry with a new one, it's much faster to first clear the field's contents, especially if you have a lot of old data. When you're in an editable field (as opposed to a selectable field), just press the Menu key, and then select Clear Field from the menu that appears. This feature is available in all text-entry fields and for most BlackBerry applications.

Deleting a contact

It's time to get rid of somebody's contact information in your Contacts. Maybe it's a case of duplication or a bit of bad blood. Either way, BlackBerry makes it easy to delete a contact. Just follow these steps:

1. **On the BlackBerry Home screen, press the Menu key twice, and then select Contacts.**

2. **In the Contacts screen that appears, scroll to and highlight a contact name that you want to delete, press the Menu key, and then select Delete from the menu that opens.**

   A confirmation screen appears, as shown in Figure 4-6.

3. **Select Delete.**

   The contact you selected is deleted and disappears from your Contacts list.

Figure 4-6:
The
confirmation
screen
when you're
about to
delete a
contact.

You may find dealing with the confirmation screen a pain if you want to delete several contacts in a row. If you're 100-percent sure that you want to ditch a number of contacts, you can suspend the Confirmation feature by removing the check mark on the Confirm Delete option in the Contacts Options screen. See the "Setting preferences" section, later in this chapter, for more on Contacts options.

Looking for Someone?

Somehow — usually through a combination of typing skills and the shuttling of data between various electronic devices — you've created a nice, long list of contacts in Contacts. Nice enough, we suppose, but useless unless you can find the phone number of Rufus T. Firefly at the drop of a hat.

That's where the Search field comes in. In fact, the first thing you see in Contacts when you open it is the Search field, as shown in Figure 4-7.

You can conveniently search through your contacts by following these steps:

1. **In the Search field, enter the first letters of the name you want to search for.**

   Your search criterion is the name of the person. You can enter the last name or first name, or both, although the list is usually sorted by first name and then last name. While you type the letters, the list shrinks based on the matches. Figure 4-8 illustrates how this list refinement works.

Figure 4-7:
Your search
starts at the
Contacts
screen's
Search field.

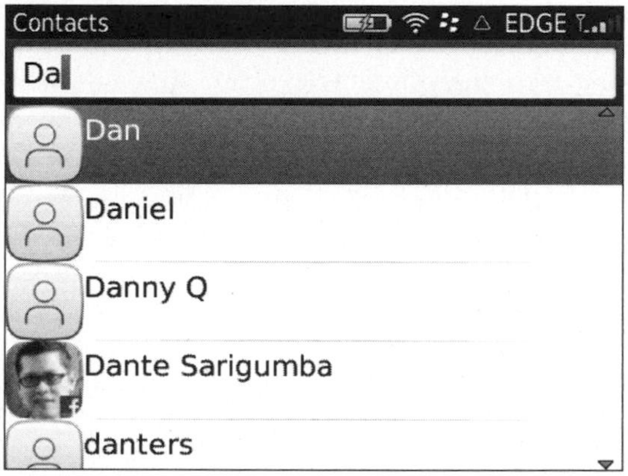

Figure 4-8:
Enter more
letters to
shorten the
potential
contacts in
your search.

2. **Using the trackpad, scroll to and highlight the name you want from the list of matches.**

If your BlackBerry comes with a keypad and you have a long list in Contacts, you can scroll down a page at a time. Just hold down the Alt key (it's located to the left of the Z key) and scroll. You get where you need to go a lot faster.

3. **Press the Menu key, and then select from the possible actions listed on the menu that appears.**

After you find the person you want, you can select among these options, as shown in Figure 4-9:

- *Send Contact Card:* Allows you to forward this contact by using e-mail, a PIN message, a text message, or BlackBerry Messenger.

- *Add to Home Screen:* Creates a shortcut icon for this contact on your Home screen.

- *View Work on Map:* Appears only if you've filled in the work address information. You can map the location by using Maps.

- *Email:* Starts a new e-mail message to the contact. See Chapter 8 for more information about e-mail.

- *Call:* Uses Phone to dial the contact's number. If the contact has more than one number, a pop-up screen appears, listing all the contact's numbers so that you can choose which number you want to call.

- *Text:* Appears only if you've filled in the contact's Mobile field. Starts a new SMS or MMS message. (SMS stands for Short Messaging Service, which is used in cellphones. MMS is short for Multimedia Messaging Service, an evolution from SMS that supports voice and video clips.) See Chapter 9 for more details about SMS and MMS.

- *PIN:* Starts a new PIN-to-PIN message, which is a messaging feature unique to BlackBerry. With PIN-to-PIN, you can send a quick message to someone who has a BlackBerry. See Chapter 9 for more details about PIN-to-PIN messaging.

- *SIM Phone Book:* This menu option enables you to view contacts saved on the SIM card. A SIM card has a very limited storage capacity, and we don't recommend you store anything on one. It can store only names and phone numbers.

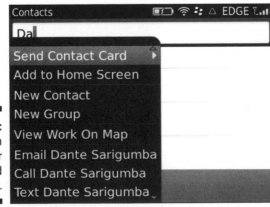

Figure 4-9:
Action options for the selected contact.

If you have a finger-fumble and press a letter key in error, press the Escape key to return to the original list (the one that shows all your contacts), or click the trackpad and then select View All from the menu that appears.

You aren't hallucinating: Sometimes Email <Contact Name> or Call <Contact Name> appears on the menu, and sometimes it doesn't. Contacts knows when to show those menu options. If a contact has a phone number, Call <Contact Name> and Text <Contact Name> show up, and the same is true for e-mail and the personal identification number (PIN). In fact, this list of actions is a convenient way to find out whether you have particular information — a phone number or an e-mail address — for a particular contact.

In a corporate environment, your BlackBerry Enterprise server administrator may disable PIN-to-PIN messaging because it doesn't go to the corporate e-mail servers and, therefore, can't be monitored. If this is the case, the menu option PIN <Contact Name> doesn't appear, even though you entered PIN information for your contacts. You still can receive a PIN-to-PIN message, but you can't send one.

Organizing Your Contacts

You've diligently added your contacts to Contacts, and your list has been growing at a pretty good clip. It now has all the contact information for your business colleagues, clients, and (of course) family and friends. In fact, Contacts has grown so much that it holds hundreds of contacts, and it takes quite some time to find someone.

Imagine that you just saw an old acquaintance, and you want to greet the person by name. You know that if you saw the name, you'd recognize it. The trouble is that your list has 300-plus names, which would take you a long time to scroll through — so long, in fact, that this acquaintance would surely come right up to you in the meantime, forcing you to hide the fact that you can't remember his name. (How embarrassing.) In this scenario, the tried-and-true Search feature can't give you much help. What you need is a smaller pool of names to search.

Organizing your contacts isn't rocket science. You want to do one of the following:

✔ **Organize your contacts into groups.** If you use groups (as every kindergarten teacher can tell you), you can arrange something (in your case, contacts) to make them more manageable. How you arrange your groups is up to you. Base your organization principle on whatever makes sense to you and fits the groups you set up. For example, you can place all your customer contacts in a Clients group and family members in a Family group.

✔ **Set up your contacts so that you can filter them.** Use the Filter feature in combination with BlackBerry's Categories. (By using Categories, you can label your contacts to make it easy to filter them.) The Filter feature can narrow the Contacts list to such an extent that you only have to scroll down and find your contact — no need to type search keywords, in other words.

Whether you use the Group or Filter feature is up to you. You can find out how to use both methods in the following sections.

Creating a group

A BlackBerry *group* in Contacts — as opposed to any other kind of group you can imagine — is just a simple filter or category. In other words, using a group just arranges your contacts into subsets without affecting the contact entries themselves. In Contacts, a group shows up in the Contacts list just like any other contact. The only wrinkle here is that when you select the group, the contacts associated with that group — and only the contacts associated with that group — appear onscreen.

Need some help visualizing how this works? Go ahead and create a group by following these steps:

1. **On the BlackBerry Home screen, press the Menu key twice, and then select Contacts.**

2. **In the Contacts screen that appears, press the Menu key, and then select New Group from the menu that opens.**

   A screen similar to that shown in Figure 4-10 appears. In the top portion of the screen, type the group name, and in the bottom portion, add your list of group members.

3. **Type the name of the group in the New Group field.**

   You can name it anything. For this example, we name it Poker Buddies.

4. **Click the trackpad, and then select Add Member from the menu that appears.**

   The main Contacts list shows up in all its glory, ready to be pilfered.

Figure 4-10:
An empty
screen
ready to
create a
group.

6. **Repeat Steps 4 and 5 to add more contacts to your list.**

5. **Select the contact you want to add to your new group list, click the trackpad, and then select Continue from the menu that appears.**

   Everybody knows a Rob Kao, so select him. Doing so places Rob Kao in your Poker Buddies group list, as shown in Figure 4-11.

   If you simply want to group your contacts and not necessarily use the group as a distribution list, you still must follow a rule: Each contact needs to have at least an e-mail address or a phone number before you can add that contact as a member of a group. (BlackBerry Contacts is strict on this point.) If you need to skirt this roadblock, edit that contact's information and put in a fake (and clearly inactive) e-mail address, such as `notareal@emailaddress.no`.

Figure 4-11:
Your new
group has
one
member.

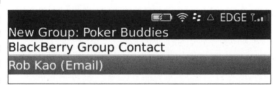

6. **Repeat Steps 4 and 5 to add more contacts to your list.**

   After you're satisfied, move on to Step 7.

7. **Click the trackpad, and then select Save Group from the menu that appears.**

   Your Poker Buddies group is duly saved, and you can now see Poker Buddies in your main Contacts list.

Groups is a valuable tool for creating an e-mail distribution list. When you add members to a group, make sure that you select an e-mail address field for your members, rather than a phone number. Also, use a naming convention to easily distinguish your group in the list. Appending **-DL** or **-Distribution List** to the group name can quickly indicate a distribution list.

Using the Filter feature on your contacts

Are you a left-brainer or a right-brainer? Yankees fan or Red Sox fan? Innie or outie? Dividing up the world into categories is something everyone does (no divisions there), so it should come as no surprise that BlackBerry divides your contacts into distinct categories, as well.

By default, two categories are set for you on the BlackBerry:

- ✔ Business
- ✔ Personal

Why stop at two? BlackBerry makes it easy to create more categories. In the following sections, you can find out how to categorize a contact and filter your Contacts list. Also, you can find out how to create categories.

Categorizing your contacts

Whether you're creating a contact or editing one, you can categorize a particular contact, as long as you're in Edit mode.

If the trick is getting into Edit mode, it's a pretty simple one. Just follow these steps to switch to Edit mode and get categorizing:

1. **On the BlackBerry Home screen, press the Menu key twice, and then select Contacts.**

2. **In the Contacts screen that appears, highlight the contact, press the Menu key, and then select Edit from the menu that opens.**

   Contacts is now in Edit mode for this particular contact, which is exactly where you want to be.

3. **Scroll down to the Categories section, and then select Edit.**

   A Categories list appears, as shown in Figure 4-12. By default, you see only the Business and the Personal categories.

Figure 4-12: Your BlackBerry Contacts default categories.

Select Categories

☐ Business

☐ Personal

4. **Click the trackpad to select the check box next to Personal.**

5. **Press the Escape key, and then select Save from the confirmation screen that appears.**

   You're brought back to the Edit Contact screen for this particular contact.

6. **Press the Escape key, and then select Save (again) from the menu that appears.**

Filtering your contacts

You now have one — count 'em, one — contact that has Personal as its category, which means you can filter your Contacts list by using a category. Follow these steps:

1. **On the BlackBerry Home screen, press the Menu key twice, and then select Contacts.**

2. **Press the Menu key, and then select Filter from the menu that appears.**

   Your Categories list appears.

   If you haven't added any categories in the meantime, you see only the default Business and Personal categories.

3. **Select the Personal check box.**

   Your Contacts list shrinks to just the contacts assigned to the Personal category, as shown in Figure 4-13.

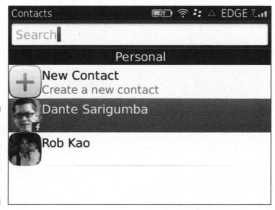

Figure 4-13: The Contacts list after a filter is applied.

When you add contacts to a category, you can use Search within that Contacts list. Enter the first few letters of the name in the Search field to further narrow the contact search. If you need a refresher on how Search works, see the "Looking for Someone?" section, earlier in this chapter.

Adding a category

Whoever thought the default categories (Business and Personal) were enough for the complexities of the real world probably didn't know many people. BlackBerry makes it easy to add categories, so you can divide your world as much as you like. Follow these steps:

1. **On the BlackBerry Home screen, press the Menu key twice, and then select Contacts.**

2. **In the Contacts screen that appears, press the Menu key, and then select Filter from the menu that opens.**

   You get a view of the default categories (refer to Figure 4-12).

3. **Press the Menu key (again), and then select New from the menu that appears.**

   A pop-up screen asks you to name the new category.

4. **Type the name of the category in the Name field, and then press Enter.**

   The category is automatically saved. The Filter screen lists all the categories, including the one you just created. Just press the Escape key to get back to the Contacts main screen.

Setting preferences

Vanilla, anyone? Some days, you may wish that you'd sorted your Contacts list differently — for example, on the day when you need to find the guy who works for ABC Company and who has a foreign name that you can hardly pronounce, let alone spell. What's a body to do?

You're in luck. Contacts Options navigates some out-of-the-ordinary situations. To get to the Contact Options screen, follow these steps:

1. **On the BlackBerry Home screen, press the Menu key twice, and then select the Contacts application.**

2. **In the Contacts screen that appears, press the Menu key, and then select Options from the menu that opens.**

   A screen like the one shown in Figure 4-14 appears. On this screen, you can access a variety of options, which we describe in the following sections.

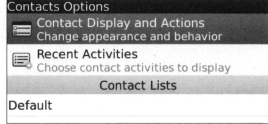

Figure 4-14:
The main
Contacts
Options
screen.

Setting Contact Display and Actions preferences

The first option in the Contact Options screen is Contact Display and Actions. Select this option to open yet another Contact Options screen. Despite its simplicity, it provides you with four important options that change Contacts' behavior:

- **Sort By:** Changes how the list is sorted. You can use First Name, Last Name, or Company. Use the Space key to toggle among the choices (you can see the menu options in Figure 4-15). Remember that guy from ABC Company? You can use the Sort By option to sort by company. By doing that, all contacts from ABC Company appear together, and with any luck, the guy's name will jump out at you.

- **Separators:** Changes the dividers in the Contacts list. It's purely an aesthetic change, but check it out — you may like the stripes.

- **Allow Duplicate Names:** Self-explanatory. If you turn this option on, you can have multiple people who happen to share the same name in your Contacts. If you disable this option, you get a warning when you try to add a name that matches one already on your list: Maybe you're just tired and are mistakenly trying to add the same person twice. Then again, sometimes people just have the same name. We recommend keeping the default value of Yes, which allows you to have contacts with the same names; otherwise, you can't add your BFF John Smith after you add John Smith from ABC Corporation.

Figure 4-15:
Choose the
Sort By field
option that
you want
to use.

Contacts Options		
Views		
Sort By:	First Name	▼
Separators:	Last Name	▼
	Company	
Actions		
Allow Duplicate Names:		✓
Confirm Delete:		✓

REMEMBER

✔ **Confirm Delete:** Displays a confirmation screen for all contact deletions.

Always keep this option turned on for normal usage. Because you could delete someone from your Contacts in many ways, this feature can help you minimize accidents.

How do you change any of these options? The fields behave like any other on a BlackBerry application. Simply highlight the field, and then click the trackpad to bring up a menu from which you can select the option's possible values. For example, Figure 4-15 shows the possible Sort By fields.

Setting Recent Activities preferences

Below the Contact Display and Actions option on the main Contact Options screen, you can find Recent Activities. Selecting this link opens a screen like the one shown in Figure 4-16. Choose the recent activities that you want to appear when you view a contact's details by selecting a contact to view it. The types of activities that can be displayed include BlackBerry Messenger, Phone, MMS, SMS, PIN, Email, and Facebook. We don't see any reason not to display all activity types, so we suggest you leave all the options selected, which is the default.

Figure 4-16:
Choose recent activities that you want to see when you view a contact.

Recent Activities	
Display these items in the recent activity list for your contacts:	
BlackBerry Messenger	✓
Phone	✓
MMS	✓
SMS	✓
PIN	✓
Email	✓
Facebook	✓

Knowing how many contacts you have

Below the options on the Contact Options screen, the Contact List section appears, displaying Default. Selecting Default displays the Contact List Properties informational screen, which tells you the number of contact entries in Contacts.

Sharing a Contact

Suppose that you want to share your contact information with a friend who also has a BlackBerry. A *vCard* — virtual (business) card — is your answer and can make your life a lot easier. In BlackBerry-land, a vCard is a contact in Contacts that you send to someone as an attachment to an e-mail.

At the receiving end, the BlackBerry (being the smart device that it is) recognizes the attachment and informs the BlackBerry owner that he or she has the option of saving it, making it available for his or her viewing pleasure in Contacts.

Sending a vCard

Because a vCard is nothing more than a Contacts contact attached to an e-mail, sending a vCard is a piece of cake. (Of course, you do need to make sure that your recipient has a BlackBerry device to receive the information.)

Follow these steps to go about sending a vCard:

1. **On the BlackBerry Home screen, press the Menu key twice, and then select the Messages application.**

2. **In the Messages screen that appears, press the Menu key, and then select Compose Email from the menu that opens.**

   A screen where you can compose a new e-mail appears.

3. **In the To field, start typing the name of the person to whom you want to send this vCard.**

   A pop-up menu appears, displaying all your contacts that include those letters.

4. **When you see the name you want in the pop-up menu, select it.**

   The e-mail screen reloads, now displaying the name you just selected as the To recipient.

5. **Type the subject and message in the appropriate fields.**

6. **Press the Menu key, and then select Attach from the menu that appears.**

7. **On the submenu that appears, select Contact.**

   The Contacts screen opens.

8. **Scroll to find the name of the person whose contact information you want to attach to the e-mail, and then select the name.**

   The e-mail screen reappears, and an icon that looks like a book indicates that the e-mail now contains your attachment. Now, you just have to send your e-mail.

9. **Click the trackpad, and then select Send from the pop-up menu that appears.**

   You just shared the specified contact information. (Don't you feel right neighborly now?)

Receiving a vCard

If you get an e-mail that includes a contact attachment, follow these steps to save it to your Contacts:

1. **On the BlackBerry Home screen, select Messages.**

   The Messages screen appears.

2. **Select the e-mail that contains the vCard.**

   The e-mail that has the vCard attachment opens.

3. **Scroll down to the attachment and, when the cursor is hovering over the attachment, click the trackpad, and then select View Attachment from the menu that appears.**

   The vCard makes an appearance onscreen. Now, you can save the contact in Contacts.

4. **Press the Menu key, and then select Add to Contacts from the menu that appears.**

   The vCard is saved and available in Contacts.

Searching for Someone outside Your Contacts

Does your employer provide your BlackBerry? Do you use Outlook or Lotus Notes on your desktop machine at work? If you answer yes to both questions, this section is for you.

BlackBerry Contacts allows you to search for people in your organization, basically by using any of the following software that contains employee databases:

- ✔ Microsoft Exchange (for Outlook)
- ✔ IBM Domino (for Lotus Notes)
- ✔ Novell GroupWise

Exchange, Domino, and GroupWise serve the same purposes:

- ✔ Facilitate e-mail delivery in a corporate environment.
- ✔ Enable access to a database of names. The database used depends on the software:
  - • Global Address Lists (GALs) in Exchange
  - • Notes Address Books in Domino
  - • GroupWise Address Books in GroupWise

To search for someone in your organization through a database of names, simply follow these steps:

1. **On the BlackBerry Home screen, press the Menu key twice, and then select Contacts.**

2. **Press the Menu key, and then select Lookup from the menu that appears (see Figure 4-17).**

   Some organizations may not enable the Lookup feature. Please check with your IT department for more information.

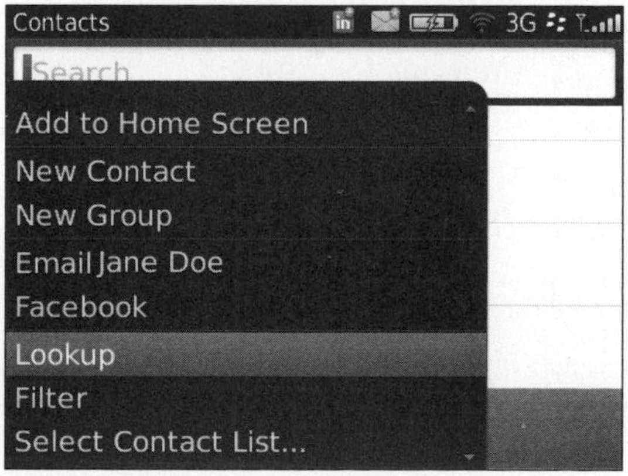

Figure 4-17: Launch Lookup from the Contacts menu.

Contacts

Search

Add to Home Screen
New Contact
New Group
Email Jane Doe
Facebook
Lookup
Filter
Select Contact List...

3. **Type the name you're searching for in the Lookup screen that appears, and then click the trackpad to initiate the search.**

   You can enter the beginning characters of a person's last or first name. You're searching your company's database, not Contacts, so this step may take some time.

   For big organizations, we recommend being very precise when you search. For example, searching for *Rob* yields more hits than searching for *Robert.* The more precise your search criteria, the fewer hits you get and the faster the search.

   After you initiate the search, the Contacts screen reappears. At the bottom of the screen, the criteria that you're searching for are listed, as well as the previous lookup criteria you searched for. After the search is complete, the same screen is updated so that just below the criteria, the number of matches appears, as you can see in Figure 4-18.

4. **From the Contacts screen, select the criteria name.**

   The screen that appears shows your lookup criteria and the lookup results. For example, if you enter *Rob* in Step 3, the top row reads `Lookup: Rob`. After the search is finished, BlackBerry displays the number of *hits,* or matches — for example, `Lookup: Rob (20 of 208 matches)`.

5. **Select the number of matches.**

   The matches appear. A header at the top of this screen details the matches displayed in the current screen, as well as the total hits. For example, if the header reads something like `Lookup: Rob (20 of 130 matches)`, 130 people in your organization have the name *Rob,* and BlackBerry is displaying the first 20. You have the option of seeing more by pressing the Menu key, and then selecting Get More Results from the menu that appears.

   You can add the listed name(s) to your Contacts by using the Add command (for the currently highlighted name) or the Add All command for all the names in the list. (As always, press the Menu key to call up the menu that contains these options.)

6. **Select the person whose information you want to review.**

   The person's contact information appears on a *read-only* screen (you can read but not change it). You may see the person's title; e-mail address; work, mobile, and fax numbers; and snail-mail address at work. Any of that information gives you confirmation about the person you're looking for. Of course, what shows up depends on the availability of this information in your company's database.

Figure 4-18:
See your
lookup
attempts.

Synchronizing Facebook Contacts

Do you network like a social butterfly? You must be using one of the popular social networking BlackBerry applications, such as Facebook. You can copy your social network friends' contact information to your BlackBerry. Individual networking sites have their own unique way to achieve this task. In the following sections, we show you how to get your Facebook contacts into your BlackBerry.

The Facebook application makes it easy to get Facebook contacts to your BlackBerry. The Facebook app also allows you to synchronize information between your BlackBerry and your friend's information in Facebook.

Adding a Facebook friend's info to Contacts

You can easily pull down your friend's information from Facebook by following these steps:

1. **From the Home screen, press the Menu key twice, and then select the Facebook application.**

   The Facebook screen appears.

2. **Press the Menu key, and then press F.**

   Your Friends list shows up on the screen, similar to the one on the left in Figure 4-19.

 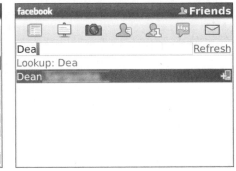

Figure 4-19: Select Facebook friends to add to Contacts.

3. **In the Search field, start typing your friend's name.**

   This input narrows the list, as shown on the right in Figure 4-19.

4. **Highlight the friend you want to add to Contacts, press the Menu key, and select Connect to BlackBerry Contact from the menu that appears.**

   A pop-up screen appears, as shown in Figure 4-20, that allows you to choose whether to connect this Facebook friend to an existing contact or add the friend as a new contact to your BlackBerry. In this case, you want to add.

Figure 4-20: Connect a Facebook friend to an existing contact or add a new contact.

If the same person exists in your BlackBerry and in Facebook, you can simply link the contact here. Also, see the following section to get an automatic update on your BlackBerry whenever your friend changes his or her profile in Facebook.

Connecting in the Facebook application means telling the app which contact is associated with a Facebook friend. After the app records this linkage, it knows which contact to update when information in Facebook changes.

 5. **Select New Contact in the pop-up screen.**

A progress screen appears momentarily, telling you that Contacts is getting the contact information from Facebook. When it's finished, the friend's contact info appears on the screen. This new contact is added to your BlackBerry.

 6. **Press the Escape key.**

The Facebook app displays a prompt, asking you whether you want to request the contact's phone number. This is a default behavior, even if your friend's phone numbers are already in your BlackBerry.

 7. **Select either Yes or No in the prompt to specify whether to request the contact's phone number.**

If you select Yes at this prompt, your Facebook friend receives a Phone Numbers Request notification within Facebook. Your friend needs to reply to that notification with his or her phone numbers before the Facebook app can sync them up.

You're back to the previous Facebook screen, and an Address Book icon has been added to the right of your friend's name, indicating that this friend is now connected, or linked, to a BlackBerry contact.

Automatic syncing between Facebook profiles and Contacts

When you run the Facebook application for the first time, you're asked to enable synchronization. Here are the Facebook and BlackBerry connections that you can choose among:

- **BlackBerry Message application:** You see new Facebook notifications in your Messages application.

- **BlackBerry Calendar application:** A calendar item is automatically created in your BlackBerry whenever you have a new Facebook event.

- **BlackBerry Contacts application:** Your BlackBerry contacts are periodically updated with the latest Facebook information, including the profile pictures. For this update to happen, your BlackBerry sends your contacts to Facebook.

If you opted out of these options the first time you ran Facebook, you can still enable them from the Facebook Options screen. Follow these steps to enable Contacts synchronization:

1. **From the Home screen, press the Menu key twice, and then select the Facebook application.**

   The Facebook screen appears.

2. **Press the Menu key, and then select Options from the menu that appears.**

   The Options screen appears. A lot of information and text are on this screen, and you have to scroll down to see all the options. Feel free to check other options, but for synchronizing contacts, refer to the first two pages of the screen, which look similar to the ones shown in Figure 4-21.

3. **Select BlackBerry Contacts Application to add a check mark.**

   You can read the explanatory text right below this check box. If you scroll down, you see another check box, which allows you to synchronize Facebook profile photos with Contacts photos.

4. **Select the Update Existing Photos in Your BlackBerry Contacts List with Facebook Friend Profile Photos option (as shown on the right of Figure 4-21).**

5. **Press the Escape key, and then select Yes on the Save Changes prompt that appears.**

   Your BlackBerry now periodically updates your Contacts with your Facebook friends.

Figure 4-21:
Enable
Facebook
friends
synchroni-
zation with
Facebook
Options.

facebook ✎ **Options**

You are currently logged in as Dante Sarigumba.

Logout

Run Setup Wizard

Connect your Facebook account with:
✓ BlackBerry Calendar application ❷
✓ BlackBerry Message application ❷
✓ BlackBerry Contacts application ❷
(Enabling this feature will periodically send copies of your BlackBerry device Contacts to Facebook Inc. to match and connect with your Facebook Friends. Profile pictures and information about you and your

facebook ✎ **Options**

to you and your Facebook Friends privacy settings once stored on your BlackBerry device.)
✓ Update existing photos in your BlackBerry contacts list with Facebook friend profile photos

Some Facebook information is stored on the device to improve performance. You can clear the cache to get the most recent information.

Clear Cache

Prompt before refreshing friend list ✓
Check spelling before sending

Chapter 5

Never Miss Another Appointment

In This Chapter

▶ Seeing your schedule from different perspectives

▶ Discovering your Calendar options

▶ Working with appointments in your Calendar

*T*o some folks, the key to being organized and productive is mastering time management and using their time wisely (and we're not just talking about reading this book while you're commuting to work). Many have discovered that they can find no better way to organize their time than to use a calendar — a daily planner tool. Some prefer digital to paper, so they use a planner software program on their PC — either installed on their hard drive or accessed through an Internet portal (such as Yahoo!). The smartest of the bunch, of course, use their BlackBerry handheld because it has the whole planner thing covered in handy form with its Calendar application.

In this chapter, we show you how to keep your life (personal and work) in order by managing your appointments with your BlackBerry Calendar. What's great about managing your time on a BlackBerry versus your computer is that your BlackBerry is always with you to remind you about appointments. Just remember that you won't have excuses anymore for forgetting that important quarterly meeting or Bertha's birthday bash.

Accessing the BlackBerry Calendar

The BlackBerry Calendar is one of the BlackBerry core applications, like Contacts or Phone (read more about the others in Chapter 1), so you can get to it quite easily.

To get cracking with your Calendar, from the Home screen, press the Menu key twice, and then select the Calendar application. *Voilà!* — you have Calendar.

Choosing Your Calendar View

The first time you open Calendar, you likely see the Day view, which is a default setting on the BlackBerry, as shown in Figure 5-1. You can change the Calendar view, however, to a different one that works better for your needs. You have these options:

- **Day:** This view gives you a summary of your appointments for the day. By default, it lists all your appointments from 9 a.m. to 5 p.m.

- **Week:** This view shows you a seven-day summary view of your appointments. By using this view, you can see how busy you are for the week.

- **Month:** The Month view shows you every day of the month. You can't tell how many appointments are in a day, but you can see on which days you have appointments.

- **Agenda:** The Agenda view is a bit different from the other views. It isn't a time-based view like the others; it basically lists your upcoming appointments. And in the list, you can see details of the appointments, such as where and when.

Figure 5-1: Day view in Calendar.

Different views (such as Week view, shown in Figure 5-2) offer you a different focus on your schedule. Select the view that you want based on your scheduling needs and preferences. If your life is kind of complicated, you can even switch between different views for a full grasp of your schedule. Simply follow these steps:

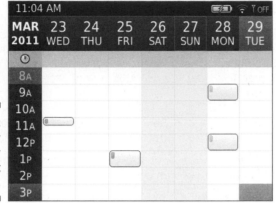

Figure 5-2:
Change your
Calendar
view to fit
your life.

1. **Open Calendar.**

2. **Press the Menu key, and then select the view of your choice from the menu that appears (shown in Figure 5-3).**

   If you start from Day view, your choices are Week, Month, and Agenda.

Figure 5-3:
The
Calendar
menu lets
you select
different
views.

You can always go to today's date, regardless of what Calendar view you're in. Just press the Menu key, and then select Today from the menu that appears.

Furthermore, you can jump to any date of your choosing by pressing the Menu key and then selecting Go to Date from the menu that appears. A handy little pop-up screen appears that lets you choose the date you want. To change the date, scroll the trackpad to the desired day, month, and year, as shown in Figure 5-4.

Figure 5-4:
Go to any
date you
want.

Customizing Your Calendar

To change the initial (default) view in your Calendar — from Day view to Month view, for example — Calendar Options is the answer.

To get to Calendar Options, open Calendar, press the Menu key, select Options from the menu that appears, and then select Calendar Display and Actions. You see choices similar to the ones shown in Table 5-1.

Table 5-1	Calendar Options
Option	*Description*
Initial View	Specifies the Calendar view that you first see when you open Calendar.
Enable Quick Entry	In Day view only, Quick Entry allows you to make a new appointment by typing characters. This way, you don't need to press the trackpad and select New from the menu that appears. *Note:* If you enable this option, Day view shortcuts described on the Cheat Sheet (which you can access at www.dummies.com/cheatsheet/blackberry) don't apply.

Option	Description
Default Reminder	How long before your appointment time your BlackBerry notifies you. The default is 15 minutes.
Snooze	The snooze time when a reminder appears. The default is 5 minutes.
Start of Day	The time of day that defines your Start of Day in Day view. The default is 9 a.m. For example, if you change this option to 8 a.m., your Day view starts at 8 a.m., rather than 9 a.m.
End of Day	The time of the day that defines End of Day in Day view. The default is 5 p.m. If you change this option to 6 p.m., for example, your Day view ends at 6 p.m., rather than 5 p.m.
First Day of Week	The day that first appears in your Week view.
Confirm Delete	This option determines whether the BlackBerry prompts you for confirmation when you delete an appointment.
Show Free Time in Agenda View	If this option is set to Yes, this field allows an appointment-free day's date to appear in the Agenda view. If you select No, the Agenda view doesn't show the date of days on which you don't have an appointment.
Show End Time in Agenda View	If you set this option to Yes, the Agenda view shows the end time of each appointment. If it's set to No, the Agenda view shows only the start time of each appointment.
Show Tasks	Any task appears within your Calendar, just like a Calendar event.
Show Alarms	Enable this option so that the alarms you set appear on your Calendar

All Things Appointments: Adding, Opening, and Deleting

After you master navigating the different Calendar views (and that should take you all of about two minutes) and have Calendar customized to your heart's content (another three minutes, tops), it's time (pun intended) to set up, review, and delete appointments, which we describe in the following sections. We also show you how to set up a meeting with clients or colleagues.

Creating an appointment

You can set up a new appointment easily. You need only one piece of information: when your appointment occurs. Of course, you can easily add related information about the appointment, such as the meeting's purpose, its location, and whatever additional notes are helpful.

In addition to your standard one-time, limited-duration meeting, you can also set all-day appointments. The BlackBerry can assist you in setting recurring meetings, as well as reminders. Sweet!

Creating a one-time appointment

To add a new, one-time appointment, follow these steps:

1. **Open Calendar.**

2. **Press the Menu key, and then select New from the menu that appears.**

   The New Appointment screen appears, as shown in Figure 5-5.

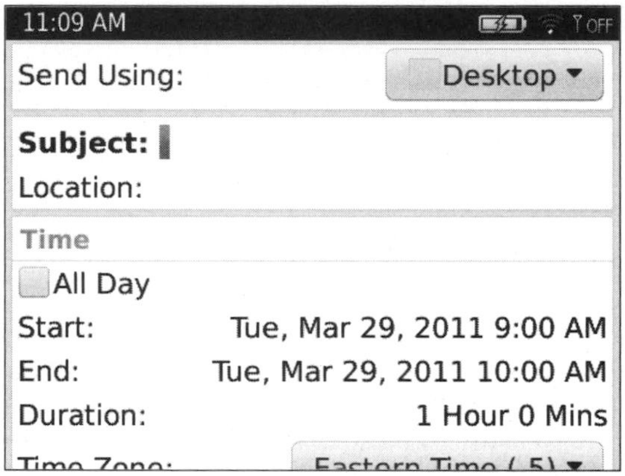

Figure 5-5:
Set an appointment in the New Appointment screen.

11:09 AM	
Send Using:	Desktop ▾
Subject: ▮	
Location:	
Time	
☐ All Day	
Start:	Tue, Mar 29, 2011 9:00 AM
End:	Tue, Mar 29, 2011 10:00 AM
Duration:	1 Hour 0 Mins
Time Zone:	Eastern Time (5) ▾

3. **Fill in the key appointment information.**

   Type all the information regarding your appointment in the appropriate fields. You should at least enter the time and the subject of your appointment.

4. **Press the Menu key, and then select Save from the menu that appears.**

   Your BlackBerry saves your newly created appointment.

Your new appointment is now in Calendar and viewable from any Calendar view. Also, keep in mind that you can have more than one appointment in the same time slot. Why? Well, the BlackBerry Calendar allows conflicts in your schedule and lets you make the hard decision about which appointment you should forgo.

Inviting meeting attendees

You no longer need Microsoft Outlook to create a meeting invite — you can do so right from your BlackBerry. To invite attendees to the appointment that you're creating, simply start adding contact e-mail addresses to the Attendees field, as shown in Figure 5-6.

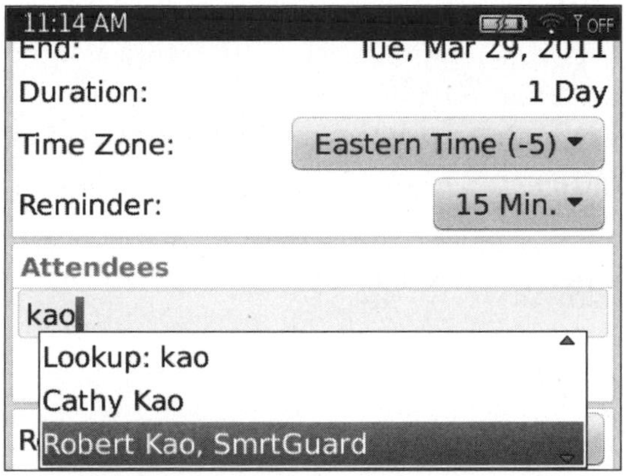

Figure 5-6: Invite e-mail contacts to join your meeting.

Creating an all-day appointment

If your appointment is an all-day event — for example, if you're in corporate training or have an all-day doctor's appointment — mark the All Day Event check box in the New Appointment screen, as shown in Figure 5-7, by scrolling to the check box and pressing the trackpad. When this check box is selected, you can't specify the time of your appointment — just the start date and end date (simply because it doesn't make sense to specify a time for an all-day event).

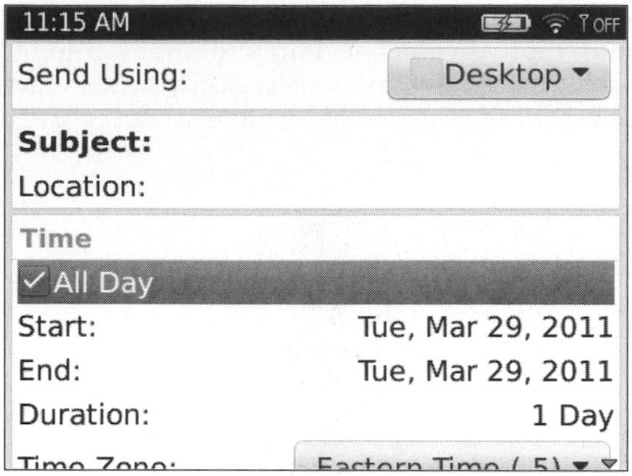

11:15 AM	🔋 📶 📶 OFF
Send Using:	Desktop ▾
Subject:	
Location:	
Time	
✓ All Day	
Start:	Tue, Mar 29, 2011
End:	Tue, Mar 29, 2011
Duration:	1 Day
Time Zone:	Eastern Time (5) ▾ ▿

Figure 5-7:
Set an all-
day event.

Setting your appointment reminder time

You can associate any appointment that you enter in Calendar with a reminder alert — either a vibration or a beep, depending on how you set things up in your profile. (For more on profiles, see Chapter 3.) You can also choose to have no reminder for an appointment. From the New Appointment screen, simply scroll to the Reminder field and select a Reminder time anywhere from None to 1 Week before your appointment time.

Profile is simply another useful BlackBerry feature that allows you to customize how your BlackBerry alerts you when an event occurs. Examples of events include an e-mail, a phone call, or a reminder for an appointment.

By default, whatever reminder alert you set goes off 15 minutes before the event. But you don't have to stick with the default. You can choose your own default reminder time. Follow these steps:

1. **Open Calendar.**

2. **Press the Menu key, select Options from the menu that appears, and then select Calendar Display and Actions.**

   The Calendar Options screen appears.

3. **Select Default Reminder.**

   You can set a reminder for up to one week before the appointment, or you can select None if you don't want a reminder.

4. **From the Reminder pop-up menu, choose a default reminder time.**

So, from now on, any new appointment has a default reminder time of what you just set up. Assuming that you have a reminder time other than None, the next time you have an appointment coming up, you see a pop-up screen like the one shown in Figure 5-8, reminding you of an upcoming appointment.

Figure 5-8:
You get a
reminder
pop-up
screen, if
you want.

Creating a recurring appointment

You can set up recurring appointments based on daily, weekly, monthly, or yearly recurrences. Everyone has some appointments that repeat, such as birthdays or anniversaries (or taking out the trash every Thursday at 7:30 a.m. — ugh).

For all recurrence types, you can define an Every field. For example, say that you have an appointment that recurs every nine days. Just set the Recurrence field to Daily and the Every field to 9, as shown in Figure 5-9.

Depending on what you select in the Recurrence field, you have the option to fill in other fields. If you enter Weekly in the Recurrence field, for example, you have the option of filling in the Day of the Week field. (It basically allows you to select the day of the week on which your appointment recurs.)

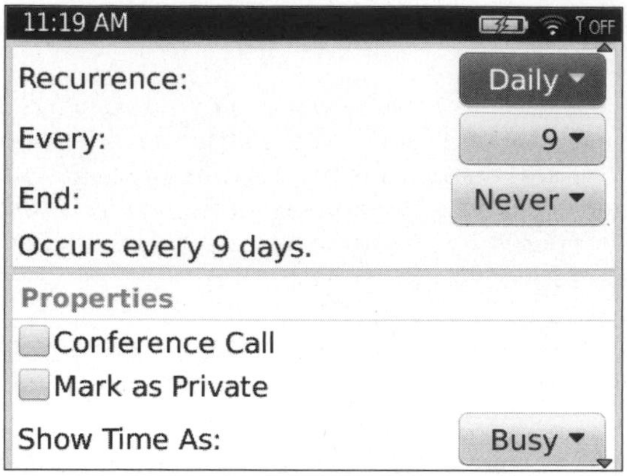

Figure 5-9:
An
appointment
recurring
every nine
days.

If you enter Monthly or Yearly in the Recurrence field, the Relative Date check box is available. If you select this check box, you can ensure that your appointment recurs relative to today's date. For example, if you choose the following, your appointment occurs every two months on the third Sunday until July 31, 2018:

> **Start:** Sunday, June 18, 2017 at 12 p.m.
>
> **End:** Sunday, June 18, 2017 at 1 p.m.
>
> **Recurrence:** Monthly
>
> **Every:** 2
>
> **Relative Date:** Selected
>
> **End:** Tuesday, July 31, 2018

On the other hand, if all options in our example remain the same, except Relative Date isn't selected, your appointment occurs every two months on the 18th of the month until July 31, 2018.

If all this "relative" talk has you dizzy, don't worry: The majority of your appointments won't be as complicated as this example.

Opening an appointment

After you set an appointment, you can view it in a couple of ways. If you've set up reminders for your appointment and the little reminder pop-up screen appears onscreen at the designated time before your appointment, you can view your appointment by clicking the pop-up screen's Open button (refer to Figure 5-8). Or you can open the appointment from Calendar by going to the exact time of your appointment and viewing it there.

While looking at an appointment, you have the option of making changes (a new appointment time and new appointment location) and then saving those changes.

Deleting an appointment

Deleting an appointment is straightforward. When in Day or Week view, simply scroll to the appointment that you want to delete, press the Menu key, and then select Delete from the menu that appears.

If the appointment that you're deleting is part of a recurring appointment, a pop-up screen pops up asking whether you want to delete all occurrences of this appointment or just this particular occurrence, as shown in Figure 5-10. After you make your choice, your appointment is history.

Figure 5-10: You can delete all occurrences or just the single instance of a recurring appointment.

Setting your meeting dial-in number

You may want to set up conference calls with your colleagues and friends all over the country, or even around the world. For group phone meetings, you may need a

- Dial-in number
- Moderator code (if you're the moderator)
- Participation code

To set your phone conference dial-in details, follow these steps:

1. **Open Calendar.**

2. **Press the Menu key, select Options from the menu that appears, and then select Conference Calling.**

   A screen similar to Figure 5-11 appears.

3. **Enter the appropriate numbers in the Moderator and Participant fields.**

4. **Press the Menu key, and then select Save from the menu that appears.**

   Your conference call number is saved.

Figure 5-11:
Setting up conference-call dial-in details.

```
Conference Calling                    123
─────────────────────────────────────────
Moderator
Phone:
Access Code:
─────────────────────────────────────────
Participant
Phone: 8881513691
Access Code: 3946516
```

The next time you create a new appointment, if you select the Conference Call check box below Properties in the Appointment screen, the conference number appears, as shown in Figure 5-12.

Figure 5-12:
Conference
call
information
appears
in the
Appointment
screen.

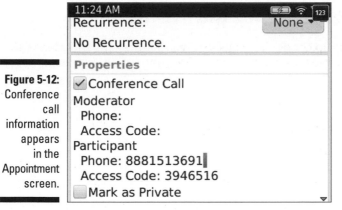

Chapter 6

Setting Alarms and Keeping Your Passwords

*I*n this chapter, we introduce you to the Clock application, which not only tells you the time, but also allows you to set alarms and a timer. Additionally, you can use the application as a stopwatch. And, in keeping with one of the key themes of this book — making your life easier — the Clock app has a feature called Bedside Mode that turns your BlackBerry into a quiet bedside companion.

To add to the theme of making your life a little easier, we make sure that you get the scoop on keeping your passwords in a single location safely by using the Password Keeper application.

Accessing Clock

You can find the Clock application in the All panel of the Home screen, as you can see on the left side of Figure 6-1.

Just look for the icon of an alarm clock. After you find the Clock icon, simply select it to open a screen similar to the one on the right side of Figure 6-1.

Figure 6-1: Launch Clock (left) and view your clock (right).

 If you've changed themes, different icons might appear than the ones shown in Figure 6-1 (refer to Chapter 3 for more on themes). Just remember that the Clock application is always located on the All panel of the Home screen.

Customizing Your Clock

If the default analog clock doesn't fit your taste, you can change it. Customizing your BlackBerry clock is easy and doesn't take much time.

You customize the clock in the Options screen. Follow these steps:

1. **On the BlackBerry Home screen, press the Menu key twice, and then select Clock.**

   The Clock application opens.

2. **Press the Menu key, and then select Options from the menu that appears.**

   The Clock Options screen appears. Figure 6-2 shows the first two pages of this screen.

3. **In each field, choose the option you want.**

   We describe each of these fields in the following list.

4. **Press the Escape key, and then select Save from the prompt that appears.**

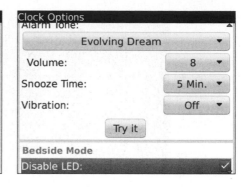

Figure 6-2:
Customize
your clock
on the Clock
Options
screen.

The Clock Options screen is divided into five sections:

⮞ **Clock:** Choose the type of clock, time zone, and time. This section includes these options:

• *Clock Face:* Allows you to set the type of clock. The options are Analog (the default; refer to the right side of Figure 6-1), Digital (shown on the left side of Figure 6-3), Flip Clock (on the right of Figure 6-3), and LCD Digital. The only difference between LCD Digital and Digital is that the numbers on the LCD Digital aren't continuous, meaning they look like the numbers you see in an old-fashioned calculator.

• *Home Time Zone:* Select your time zone from the list.

• *When Charging:* Allows you to control the behavior of the clock when you connect your BlackBerry to the charger. Possible choices include Do Nothing, Display Clock (the default), and Enter Bedside Mode.

• *Set Time:* Select this button to see a Date/Time screen that displays the time in Edit mode, allowing you to change the time. You can also change the time zone and decide whether to synchronize your BlackBerry time to the network carrier's time.

Figure 6-3: Digital (left) and Flip Clock (right) clocks.

✓ **Alarm:** Navigate to this section if you want to customize the behavior of the alarm. You can adjust these options:

- *Alarm Tune:* Choose from a list of ringtones that you want to play. The default tone is Alarm_Antelope.

- *Snooze Time:* Just like with your ordinary alarm clock, you have the option to hit the Snooze. You can choose 30, 15, 10, or 5 (the default) minutes; 1 minute; or None.

- *Volume:* You can set the volume of the tone to Silent, 1 to 10 (10 being loudest; the default is 8), or Escalating. Escalating means that the tone starts quietly and gradually becomes loud.

- *Vibrations:* You can enable or disable vibration. Choose Off, On (the default), or Custom. If you choose Custom, two new fields appear. The first, Length, enables you to choose the duration of the vibration: Short, Medium (the default), or Long. The second field, Count, vibrates your BlackBerry as your alarm. Choices are 1, 2 (the default), 3, 5, and 10 repetitions.

- *Try It:* A button to quickly try the settings you just entered.

✓ **Bedside Mode:** This section allows you to set the behavior of your BlackBerry in Bedside Mode (which we talk about in more detail in the section "Setting and Exiting Bedside Mode," later in this chapter). It offers these options:

- *Disable LED:* Allows you to disable LED notifications during Bedside Mode. Choices are Yes (the default) and No.

- *Disable Radio:* Allows you to disable the radio during Bedside Mode. Choices are Yes and No (the default).

Disabling the radio means that no communication-related applications — e-mail, SMS, MMS, BlackBerry Messenger, Instant Messaging clients, and Phone — can receive incoming signals.

- *Dim Screen:* Choose the Yes (the default) or No option to control the dimming of the screen in Bedside Mode.

- *Sound Profile:* Use for anything that requires sound notification. You have several profiles to choose among: Active Profile (the default), Normal, Loud, Medium, Vibrate Only, Silent, Phone Calls Only, and All Alerts Off. Leaving this setting with the default Active Profile means that your BlackBerry follows the notification settings on the profile to which the BlackBerry is currently set. You can find out more about profiles in Chapter 3.

  You can always add a custom profile (see Chapter 3 for details).

✓ **Stopwatch:** The section to change the face of the stopwatch has only one option, Stopwatch Face. Choose between an Analog (the default) and a Digital stopwatch.

✓ **Countdown Timer:** Navigate to this section if you want to customize the behavior of the timer. You can set these options:

- *Timer Face:* Your choices are Analog (the default) and Digital.

- *Timer Tune:* From a list of ringtones, choose the sound that you want to play when the timer reaches the time you set.

- *Volume:* You can select Mute or set the volume of the tone to Low, Medium, High, or Escalating. The default is Medium.

- *Vibrate:* Choose Yes if you want the BlackBerry to vibrate when the timer reaches the time set; otherwise, choose No (the default).

Setting a Wake-Up Alarm

The Clock application is also your bedside alarm clock. You can set it to wake you up once or regularly.

Follow these steps to tell your wake-up buddy to do the work for you:

1. **On the BlackBerry Home screen, press the Menu key twice, and then select Clock.**

   The Clock appears.

2. **Press the Menu key, and then select Set Alarm from the menu that appears.**

   A Time field appears in the middle of the screen, as shown in Figure 6-4. The time defaults to the previous Set Alarm time or, if you haven't used the alarm before, the current time. If the default time isn't your intended alarm time, proceed to Step 3 to change the time. If it is the time you want the alarm to sound, skip to Step 4.

Figure 6-4:
Set your alarm time in this Time field.

3. **Scroll sideways to select the specific portion of the time that you want to change, and then enter the new values.**

   Any highlighted portion of the time is editable. You can change the hours; minutes; AM/PM; and whether the alarm is On, Off, or only Weekdays. Setting a value doesn't create an entry in Calendar or Tasks. You can either enter the value, or scroll up or down to choose among possible values.

4. **Press the trackpad, and then select Save from the confirmation screen that appears to accept all your changes.**

Setting and Exiting Bedside Mode

You can use a setting in the Clock application called Bedside Mode to minimize disturbances from your BlackBerry. With Bedside Mode, you can dim the screen, disable the LED, and even turn off the radio, all of which pretty much make your BlackBerry behave like a brick. Bear in mind that when you turn off the radio, you can't get incoming phone calls or any type of messaging. If you want a refresher on how to set these options, see the "Customizing Your Clock" section, earlier in this chapter.

If you're concerned about sleeping next to a "live" and connected smartphone, worry no more! You can have the network connection turn off automatically. See the section "Customizing Your Clock," earlier in this chapter, for details on disabling the radio in Bedside Mode.

To set your BlackBerry to Bedside Mode, follow these steps:

1. **On the BlackBerry Home screen, press the Menu key twice, and then select Clock.**

   The Clock appears.

2. **Press the Menu key, and then select Enter Bedside Mode from the menu that appears (see the left side of Figure 6-5).**

   That's it. Your BlackBerry should now behave like a good bedside companion.

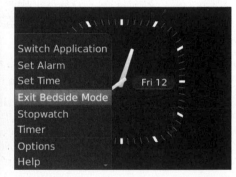

Figure 6-5: Enter and exit Bedside Mode from the Clock menu.

Buy a charging pod from www.shopblackberry.com or http://shop.crackberry.com. Then, you can put your BlackBerry on a bedside table in an upright position while the charging pod adds juice to your device. Make sure that the Clock setting (not just the BlackBerry) is in Bedside Mode when charging by following these steps:

1. **On the BlackBerry Home screen, press the Menu key twice, and then select Clock.**

   The Clock appears.

2. **Press the Menu key, and then select Options from the menu that appears.**

3. **In the Clock section of the Clock Options screen, change the When Charging option to Enter Bedside Mode.**

To exit Bedside Mode, follow these steps:

1. **On the BlackBerry Home screen, press the Menu key twice, and then select Clock.**

   The Clock appears.

2. **Press the Menu key, and then select Exit Bedside Mode from the menu that appears, as shown on the right side of Figure 6-5.**

Using Stopwatch

If you ever need a stopwatch, look no further than your BlackBerry. Follow these steps to run the stopwatch:

1. **On the BlackBerry Home screen, press the Menu key twice, and then select Clock.**

   The Clock appears.

2. **Press the Menu key, and then select Stopwatch from the menu that appears.**

   You see a screen similar to the left side of Figure 6-6. The two buttons on this screen are

   • *Stopwatch:* Select this button to start and stop the stopwatch.

   • *Lap:* The image on this button looks like a circular arrow initially. After you start the stopwatch, the image changes to a connected, oval-shaped arrow (as you can see on the right side of Figure 6-6). You can use this lap button when someone's doing laps in a swimming pool or on a track field, and you want to record how long each lap takes. Select the lap button to record the completion of a lap. The lap and the lap time appear onscreen. Each lap is labeled as Lap 1 for the first lap, Lap 2 for the second lap, and so on.

Figure 6-6:
Start (left)
and stop
(right) your
stopwatch.

3. **To start the stopwatch, select the Stopwatch button.**

4. **To stop the stopwatch, select the Stopwatch button again.**

Using Timer

Have you overcooked something? Not if you have a good timer to warn you. Follow these steps to set up your BlackBerry Timer:

1. **On the BlackBerry Home screen, press the Menu key twice, and then select Clock.**

   The Clock appears.

2. **Press the Menu key, and then select Timer from the menu that appears.**

   A screen similar to the left side of Figure 6-7 appears. The left button that features the stopwatch image is the Start and Pause button. You can use the right button that features the circular arrow image to stop and reset the timer. The default time for your timer is based on what you set the last time you used your timer. If you haven't set a time, proceed to Step 3. If you want to use the default time, you can proceed to Step 5.

3. **Press the Menu key, and then select Set Timer from the menu that appears.**

   A screen similar to the right side of Figure 6-7 appears.

Figure 6-7:
Start and
set the
time for the
Timer.

4. **Enter the time that you want to use.**

   You can either enter the time with numeric keys, or scroll up or down to choose from provided values.

   From left to right, the time component is based on hours, minutes, and seconds. Scroll sideways to choose the time component.

5. **Select Start.**

   Your timer starts ticking. When it reaches the time, it notifies you.

You can customize the timer notification to a tone, a vibration, or both. Just follow these steps:

1. **On the BlackBerry Home screen, press the Menu key twice, and then select Clock.**

   The Clock appears.

2. **Press the Menu key, and then select Options from the menu that appears.**

3. **In the Countdown Timer section of the Clock Options screen, make your selections.**

   In the Countdown Timer section, you can select the tone that you want to play when the timer expires and how loud you want the tone to sound, as well as specify whether to make the BlackBerry vibrate.

Using Password Keeper

Suppose that you're in front of an Internet browser, trying to access an online account. For the life of you, you just can't remember the account password. It's your third login attempt, and if you fail this time, your account will be locked. Then you have to call the customer hotline and wait hours before you can speak to a representative. Argghh! We've all done it. Luckily, BlackBerry gives you an application that can help you avoid this headache.

Password Keeper is the simple yet practical BlackBerry application that makes your life that much easier because you don't have to worry about not remembering a password. Password Keeper is filed in the Applications folder of the All panel of the Home screen (as shown in Figure 6-8).

Figure 6-8: You can find Password Keeper in the Applications folder.

Setting a password for Password Keeper

The first time you access Password Keeper, you're prompted to enter a password. Be sure to remember the password you choose because this is the password to all your passwords. Forgetting this password is like forgetting the combination of your safe. You can't retrieve a forgotten Password Keeper password. You're prompted to enter this master password every time you access the application.

Trust us — one password is much easier to remember than many passwords.

Creating credentials

Okay, so you're ready to fire up your handy-dandy Password Keeper application. When you run Password Keeper, a screen similar to the left side of Figure 6-9 appears. On this screen, you can create a password account — simply select New Password to open a screen similar to the one shown on the right side of Figure 6-9. Now, what does Password Keeper expect you to do in order for it to work its magic? Obviously, you need to collect the pertinent info for all your password-protected accounts so that you can store them in the protected environs of Password Keeper. Therefore, when you create a new password entry, be sure you have the following information for each account that you want to store:

- **Title:** Just come up with a name to describe the password-protected account — My Favorite Shopping Site, for example.

- **Username:** Enter the username for the account.

- **Password:** Enter the password for the account.

- **Website:** Enter the website address (its URL).

- **Notes:** Not exactly crucial, but the Notes field does give you a bit of room to add a comment or two.

Figure 6-9:
Create a
password
account
(left) and
set your
password
on the New
Password
screen
(right).

Password Keeper	⬠ edge ▾.ᵢᵢ
Search	
New Password:	
* No Passwords *	

New Password	🔋 📶 ⁑ △ EDGE ▾.ᵢ
Credentials	
Title:	
Username:	
Password:	
Website:	http://
Notes	

The only required field is Title, but a title alone usually isn't of much use to you. We suggest that you fill in as much other information as possible.

If someone gains access to the information you store in Password Keeper, you can potentially face serious problems, such as that person finding the password to your bank account. So, we recommend that you make sure you enable password security on your BlackBerry. Also, make sure that you have a different password for Password Keeper than your password for your smartphone. See Chapter 3 for the details of enabling password security on your BlackBerry.

Generating random passwords

If you're the kind of person who uses one password for everything but knows deep in your heart that this is just plain wrong, wrong, wrong, random password generation is for you. When you create a new password for yet another online account (or when you change your password for an online account you already have), fire up Password Keeper, press the trackpad, and then select Random Password from the menu that appears, as shown in Figure 6-10. *Voilà!* A new password is automatically generated for you.

Figure 6-10: Generate a random password.

Using random password generation makes sense in conjunction with Password Keeper because you don't have to remember the randomly generated password that Password Keeper came up with for any of your online accounts — that's Password Keeper's job.

Using your password

The whole point of Password Keeper is to let your BlackBerry's electronic brain do your password-remembering for you. So, imagine this scenario: You can no longer live without owning a personal copy of the *A Chipmunk Christmas* CD, so you surf on over to your favorite online music store and attempt to log in. You draw a blank on your password, but instead of seething, you take out your BlackBerry, open Password Keeper, and search. Follow these steps:

1. **Type the first letters of your account title in the Find field to search for the title of your password.**

2. **Select the title when you find it, and then press the trackpad.**

   The screen for your account appears, conveniently listing the password.

3. **Enter the password in the login screen for the online music store.**

   You're in! Alvin, Simon, and Theodore will soon be wending their way to your address, ready to sing "Chipmunk Jingle Bells."

Yes, you *can* copy and paste your password from Password Keeper to another application — BlackBerry Browser, for instance. Just highlight the password name, press the trackpad, and select Copy to Clipboard from the menu that appears. Then, navigate to where you want to enter the password, press the trackpad, and select Paste from the menu. For the copy-and-paste function to work for passwords from Password Keeper, you need to enable the Allow Clipboard Copy option in the Password Keeper options (see Table 6-1). You can copy and paste only one password at a time.

After you paste your password in another application, clear the Clipboard by pressing the trackpad and choosing Clear Clipboard from the menu that appears. The Clipboard keeps your last copied password until you clear it.

Accessing Password Keeper options

Password Keeper's Options menu (accessible by pressing the Menu key while in Password Keeper and selecting Options from the menu that appears) allows you to control how Password Keeper behaves. For example, you can set what characters can make up a randomly generated password. Table 6-1 describes all the options in Password Keeper.

Table 6-1	Password Keeper Options
Option Name	*Description*
Random Password Length	Select a number between 4 and 16 for the length of your randomly generated password.
Random Includes Alpha	If Yes, a randomly generated password includes alphabetic characters.
Random Includes Numbers	If Yes, a randomly generated password includes numbers.

Option Name	Description
Random Includes Symbols	If Yes, a randomly generated password includes symbols.
Confirm Delete	If Yes, all deletions are prompted with a confirmation screen.
Password Attempts	Select 1 to 20 attempts to enter the password to Password Keeper successfully.
Allow Clipboard Copy	If Yes, you can copy and paste passwords from Password Keeper.
Show Password	If Yes, you can see the characters of the password; otherwise, asterisks take the place of the password characters.

Changing your password to Password Keeper

If you want to change your password to Password Keeper — that is, change the master password for opening Password Keeper — follow these steps:

1. **On the BlackBerry Home screen, press the Menu key twice, and then select Applications.**

   The Applications folder of the Home screen appears.

2. **Select Password Keeper.**

   The initial login screen for Password Keeper appears.

3. **Enter your old password in the Enter Password field, and then select OK to access Password Keeper.**

4. **In Password Keeper, press the Menu key, and then select Change Password from the menu that appears.**

   The Password Keeper screen that allows you to enter your new password, as shown in Figure 6-11, appears.

5. **Enter a new password in the Please Choose a New Password field, confirm it by entering it again in the Please Confirm Your New Password field, and then select OK.**

Figure 6-11:
Change your
Password
Keeper
password.

Chapter 7

Calling Your Favorite Person

*P*hone capability has been incorporated into BlackBerry from the very first generations of the device. The great news is that the BlackBerry phone operates no differently than any other phone you've used.

So, why bother with this chapter? Although your BlackBerry phone operates like any other phone, it has capabilities that far outreach those of your run-of-the-mill cellphone. For example, with a standard cellphone, you can't connect a traditional phone to your to-do list or place a call directly from an e-mail. But with your BlackBerry smartphone, you can do these things and more.

In this chapter, we first cover phone basics, and then show you some of the neat ways BlackBerry Phone intertwines with other BlackBerry applications and functions.

Accessing the BlackBerry Phone Application

You can access the Phone application from the BlackBerry easily. To start using Phone, press the green Send button located right below the display screen to open the Phone application. In this chapter, when we tell you to open the Phone application, we simply mean press the green Send key.

The folks at RIM have created an intuitive user interface to all the essential Phone features, including making and receiving calls.

Making a call

To make a call, start from the Home screen and enter the number that you want to dial. As soon as you start entering numbers, the Phone application opens. When you finish typing the destination number, press the green Send key.

Calling from Contacts

Because you can't possibly remember all your friends' and colleagues' phone numbers, you may find calling from the Contacts application convenient and useful.

To call from Contacts, follow these steps:

1. **Open the Phone application.**

2. **Press the Menu key.**

   The Phone menu appears, as shown in Figure 7-1.

   Alternatively, you can enter the contact's name in the Phone field. If you use this method, skip to Step 4.

3. **Select Call from Contacts.**

   Contacts opens.

4. **Highlight the contact you want to call, and then press the trackpad to make the call.**

   BlackBerry Phone makes the call to your contact. *Note:* If the contact you selected has more than one number listed, a pop-up screen appears, asking you to select which number to dial.

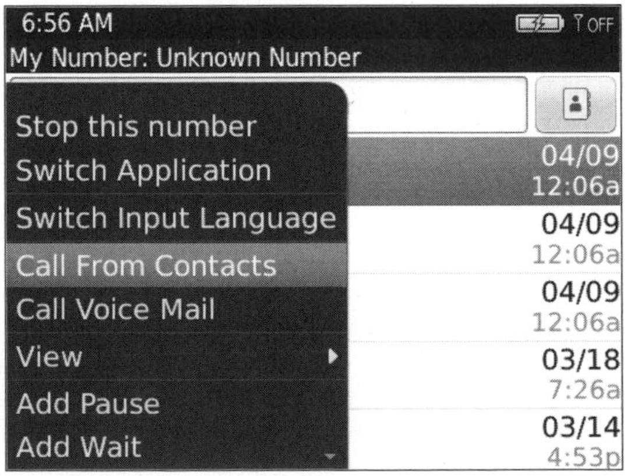

Figure 7-1: The Phone menu.

Dialing letters

One of the nice features of the BlackBerry Phone is that you can dial letters, and BlackBerry figures out the corresponding number. For example, to dial 1-800-11-LEARN, follow these steps:

1. **From the Phone application (or the Home screen), dial 1-8-0-0-1-1.**

   When you type the first number, the Phone application opens (if it isn't open already) and displays the numbers you dial.

2. **Press and hold the Alt key, and then press L-E-A-R-N.**

   The letters appear onscreen while you type.

3. **Press the green Send key.**

   Phone translates the letters into the corresponding numbers that feature those letters on a standard touchtone phone keypad, and then initiates the call.

Receiving a call

You can receive a call on your BlackBerry even more easily than you can make a call. You can receive calls in a couple ways: by using your BlackBerry's automated answering feature and by answering manually.

Automated answering is triggered when you take your BlackBerry out of your holster; in other words, just taking out the BlackBerry forces it to pick up any call, so you can start talking right away. However, you don't have time to see your Caller ID to figure out who's calling you before the phone answers the call.

What's the advantage of disabling autoanswer? Manual answering prompts you to answer or ignore an incoming call (see Figure 7-2). By using manual answering, you can see on your Caller ID who's calling before you decide to pick up or ignore the call.

Follow these steps to turn on autoanswer:

1. **Open the Phone application.**

2. **Press the Menu key.**

   The Phone menu appears (refer to Figure 7-1).

3. **Select Options.**

   The Phone Options screen appears, listing the categories of options.

   4. **Select In-Call Settings.**

      The In-Call Settings Options screen appears.

   5. **In the Auto Answer Calls field, select Out of Holster.**

   6. **Press the Menu key, and then select Save from the menu that appears.**

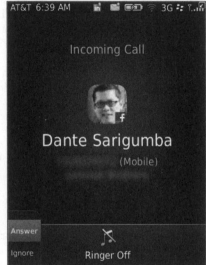

Figure 7-2:
Ignore or answer a call with manual answering.

Let freedom ring

From the Phone application, you can quickly set the general ringtone for the current Sound Profile, which controls how your BlackBerry alerts you to calls, e-mails, and Instant Messages.

To set how you want your phone to ring, follow these steps:

   1. **Open the Phone application.**

   2. **Press the Menu key.**

      The Phone menu appears (refer to Figure 7-1).

   3. **Select Phone Ring Tone.**

      The Phone Settings screen for the current Sound Profile opens. (Chapter 3 explains how to set up alerts in Sound Profile for e-mails and other alerts.)

   4. **In the Ring Tone field, select a ring option.**

      You can also set the volume level, ranging from 10 to 1 (10 being the loudest), or select silent.

   5. **Press Escape to save your settings.**

You can also set personal ring tones for each of your contacts. Chapter 4 shows you how.

Handling missed calls

You missed a call from that important client. What makes it worse is that you didn't notice the missed call because you didn't see the little Missed Call icon; you pay attention only to what's in your e-mail inbox. What can you do to make sure that you know about that call so that you can return it?

You can have your BlackBerry display notifications of missed calls in your e-mail inbox so that you're sure to return those calls (if you choose to, that is).

To have your missed calls appear in your inbox, follow these steps:

1. **Open the Phone application.**

2. **Press the Menu key.**

   The Phone menu appears (refer to Figure 7-1).

3. **Select Options.**

   The Phone Options screen appears, listing the different categories of options.

4. **Select Call Logs and Lists.**

   The Call Logs and Lists screen opens.

5. **Highlight Show These Call Log Types in Message, and then press the trackpad.**

   In the pop-up menu that appears, you can choose between Missed Calls, All Calls, and None. We recommend selecting Missed Calls: If you choose All Calls, then all incoming and outgoing calls appear in your e-mail inbox.

6. **Press the Menu key, and then select Save from the menu that appears.**

You can find out total call time that you've made on your BlackBerry and last call time in the Phone Status screen. You can get to this screen by pressing the Menu key in Phone, and then selecting Status from the menu that appears.

Phone Options while on a Call

When you're on the phone, situations might arise where you want to mute your end of the conversation or change the call volume. No problem. Your BlackBerry makes such adjustments easy.

Muting your call

You might want to use the mute feature while on a conference call (see the section "Arranging Conference Calls," later in this chapter), for example, when you don't need to speak but do need to hear what's being discussed. Maybe you're on the bus or have kids in the background, making your surroundings noisy. When you use mute, all the noises (including yourself) are filtered out from the conference call.

To mute your call, follow these steps:

1. **While in a conversation, press the Menu key.**

   The Phone menu appears in all its glory.

2. **Select Mute.**

   You hear a tone sound, indicating that your call is on mute.

To un-mute your call, follow these steps:

1. **While a call is on mute, press the Menu key.**

   The Phone menu makes another appearance.

2. **Select Turn Mute Off.**

   You hear a tone sound, indicating that your call is now un-muted.

Adjusting the call volume

You can adjust the call volume, a simple yet important action on your BlackBerry phone, by simply pressing the volume up or down key on the side of your BlackBerry.

Customizing the BlackBerry Phone

For your BlackBerry Phone to work the way you like, you have to first set it up the way you want it. In the following sections, we go through some settings that can make you the master of your BlackBerry Phone.

Setting up your voicemail number

This section shows you how to set up your voicemail access number. Unfortunately, the instructions for setting up your voicemail mailbox vary,

depending on your service provider. Fortunately, however, most service providers are more than happy to walk you through the steps to get your mailbox set up in a jiffy.

To set up your voicemail number, follow these steps:

1. **Open the Phone application.**

2. **Press the Menu key, and then select Options from the menu that appears.**

   The Phone Options screen appears, listing the different categories of options.

3. **Select Voice Mail.**

   The Voice Mail Configuration screen appears.

4. **Scroll to the Access Number field and enter your voicemail access number if it doesn't already appear.**

   If this field is empty and you don't know your voicemail access number, contact your service provider.

5. **Press the Menu key, and then select Save from the menu that appears.**

Using call forwarding

On the BlackBerry, you have two types of call forwarding:

- **Forward All Calls:** Any calls to your BlackBerry are forwarded to the number you designate. Another name for this feature is *unconditional forwarding.*

- **Forward Unanswered Calls:** Calls that meet different types of conditions are forwarded to different numbers.

For the unanswered calls type of forwarding, three conditions determine what number to forward to:

- **If Busy:** You don't have call waiting turned on, and you're on the phone.

- **If No Answer:** You don't hear your phone ring or somehow are unable to pick up your phone (perhaps you're in a meeting).

- **If Unreachable:** You're out of network coverage and can't receive any signals.

Out of the box, your BlackBerry forwards any unanswered calls, regardless of conditions, to your voicemail number by default. However, you can add new numbers to which you want to forward a call.

You need to be within network coverage before you can change your call-forwarding option. If you're covered, follow these steps:

1. **Open the Phone application, press the Menu key, and then select Options from the menu that appears.**

   A list of phone options appears.

2. **Select Call Forwarding.**

   Your BlackBerry now attempts to connect with the server. If it's successful, the Call Forwarding screen appears.

   If you don't see the Call Forwarding screen, wait until you have network coverage and try again.

3. **From the Call Forwarding screen, press the Menu key, and then select Edit Numbers from the screen that appears.**

   A list of number(s) appears. If this is the first time you're setting call forwarding, most likely, only your voicemail number is on this list.

4. **To add a new forwarding number, press the Menu key, and then select New Number from the menu that appears.**

   A pop-up window appears, prompting you to enter the new forwarding number.

5. **In the pop-up window, enter the number to which you want to forward the caller, and then press the trackpad.**

   The new number you entered now appears on the call forward number screen. You can add this new number to any call forwarding types or conditions.

6. **Press the Escape key.**

   You return to the Call Forwarding screen.

7. **Scroll to the If Unreachable field and press the trackpad.**

   A pop-up menu appears, listing numbers from the call forwarding number list, including the one you just added.

8. **Select the number to which you want to forward, and then press the trackpad.**

   The selected number goes into the If Unreachable field on the Call Forwarding screen.

9. **Confirm your changes by pressing the Menu key and then selecting Save from the menu that appears.**

Configuring speed dial

Speed dial is a convenient feature on any phone. And after you get used to having it on a phone system, you probably want to use it on other phones, including your BlackBerry.

Viewing your speed dial list

To view your speed dial list, follow these steps:

1. **Open the Phone application.**

2. **Press the Menu key, select View from the menu that appears, and then select Speed Dial List from the submenu.**

   A list of speed dial entries appears, as shown in Figure 7-3. If you haven't set up any speed dials, this list is empty.

Figure 7-3:
The speed
dial list.

Adding a new number to speed dial

Setting up speed dial numbers is as easy as using them. It takes a few seconds to set them up, but you save time whenever you use this feature.

To assign a number to a speed dial slot, follow these steps:

1. **Open the Phone application.**

2. **Press the Menu key, select Options, and then select View Speed Dial List.**

   The list of speed dial numbers that you've assigned appears. If you haven't assigned any speed dial numbers, the list is empty.

3. **Scroll to an empty speed dial slot, press the Menu key, and select New Speed Dial from the menu that appears.**

   The BlackBerry Contacts appears so that you can select a contact's phone number.

4. **Select a contact, and then press the trackpad.**

   The number appears in the speed dial list.

   If more than one number is associated with the selected contact in the Contacts, you're prompted to select which number to add to the speed dial list.

Using speed dial

After you have a few speed-dial entries set up, you can start using them. While at the Home screen or Phone application, press a speed dial key. The call is initiated to the number associated with that particular speed dial key.

Arranging Conference Calls

To get two or more people on the phone with you — the infamous conference call — follow these steps:

1. **Use the Phone application to place a call to the first participant.**

2. **While the first participant is on the phone with you, press the Menu key, and then select Add Participant from the menu that appears.**

   The first call is placed on hold, and a New Call screen appears, as shown in Figure 7-4, prompting you to place another call.

3. **Place a call to the second participant by entering his or her number, pressing the trackpad, and then selecting Call from the menu that appears.**

   You can enter the number either by using the number pad or selecting a frequently dialed number from your call log. To place a call from your Contacts, press the trackpad from the New Call screen and choose Call from Contacts from the menu that appears. Your BlackBerry then prompts you to select a contact to dial from the Contacts.

   This call is just like any other phone call (except that the first participant is still on the other line).

4. **While the second participant is on the phone with you, press the Menu key, and then select Join Conference from the menu that appears, as shown in Figure 7-5.**

   Your BlackBerry reconnects the first participant back with you, along with the second participant. Now, you can discuss away with both participants at the same time.

Another name for having two people on the phone with you is *three-way calling,* which isn't a new concept. If you want to chat with four people — or even ten people — on the phone at the same time, you certainly can. Simply repeat Steps 2 through 4 in the preceding list until you have all the participants connected on the phone conference.

Figure 7-4: With a meeting participant on hold, you can add another call participant.

Figure 7-5: Join two people in a conference call.

If you think the steps to host a phone conference by using your BlackBerry are a bit too much, the folks at RIM rolled out an application called Blackberry Mobile Conferencing, which allows you conduct phone conferences with ease. You can download this app from BlackBerry App World. For more on BlackBerry App World, please refer to Chapter 20.

Talking privately to a conference participant

During a conference call, you might want to talk to one participant privately, which you can do by *splitting* your conference call. Follow these steps:

1. **While on a conference call, press the Menu key, and then select Split from the menu that appears.**

   A pop-up screen appears, listing all the participants of the conference call. (See Figure 7-6.)

Figure 7-6:
All the participants in the conference call appear in a list.

2. **From the pop-up screen, select the participant with whom you want to speak privately.**

   This action places all other participants on hold and connects you to the participant you selected. On the display screen, you can see to whom you're connected — which confirms that you selected the right person to privately chat with.

3. **To talk to all participants again, press the Menu key, and then select Join Conference from the menu that appears.**

   This step brings you back to the conference call with everyone.

Alternate between phone conversations

Whether you're in a private conversation during a conference call or talking to someone while you have someone else on hold, you can switch between the two conversations by swapping them. Follow these steps:

1. **While you talk to someone with another person on hold, press the Menu key, and then select Swap from the menu that appears.**

   You switch from the person with whom you were talking to the person who was on hold.

2. **Repeat Step 1 to go back to the original conversation.**

Dropping that meeting hugger

If you've been on conference calls, you can identify those chatty "meeting huggers" who have to say something about everything. Don't you wish that you could drop them off the call? Well, with your BlackBerry, you can (as long as you're the meeting moderator or the person who initiates the call). Follow these steps to boot a meeting hugger from your conference call:

1. **While on a conference call, press the Menu key, and then select Drop Call from the menu that appears.**

   A pop-up screen appears, listing all the participants of the conference call.

2. **From the pop-up screen, select the meeting hugger you want to drop.**

   Your BlackBerry disconnects him or her from the call.

3. **Conversation can continue as usual.**

Communicating Hands-Free

Because you may need to talk while your hands are occupied, and because more and more places prohibit the use of mobile phones without a hands-free headset while driving, we go through the hands-free options you have on your BlackBerry in the following sections.

Using the speaker phone

The Speaker Phone function is useful in certain situations, such as when you're in a room full of people who want to join in on your phone conversation. Or you might be all by your lonesome in your office but stuck rooting through your files — hard to do with a BlackBerry scrunched up against your ear. (We call such moments *multitasking* — a concept so important that we devote the section "Multitasking while on the Phone," later in this chapter, to it.)

To switch to the Speaker Phone while you're on a phone call, press the P key or the Menu key, and then select Activate Speaker Phone from the menu that appears.

Pairing your BlackBerry with a Bluetooth headset

Because your BlackBerry comes with a wired hands-free headset, you can start using it by simply plugging it into the headset jack on the left side of your BlackBerry. You adjust the volume of the headset by using the volume keys (on the side of the BlackBerry).

Using the wired hands-free headset can help you avoid being a police target, but if you're multitasking on your BlackBerry, the wired headset can get in the way and become inconvenient.

So, enter the whole Bluetooth wireless thing. You can purchase a BlackBerry Bluetooth headset to go with your Bluetooth-enabled BlackBerry. For a list of BlackBerry-compatible Bluetooth headsets, see Chapter 21.

After you purchase a BlackBerry-compatible Bluetooth headset, you can pair it with your BlackBerry. Think of *pairing* a Bluetooth headset with your BlackBerry as registering the headset with your BlackBerry so that it recognizes the headset.

First things first: You need to prep your headset for pairing. Each headset manufacturer has a different take on this procedure, so you need to consult your headset documentation for details. After you prep the headset, you can continue with the pairing by following these steps:

1. **From the Home screen, press the Menu key twice, and then select Manage Connection.**

   The Manage Connection Screen appears.

2. **Select Bluetooth Connection.**

   The Enable Bluetooth screen appears.

3. **If the Bluetooth option doesn't display On, select Bluetooth, and then select On from the pop-up menu that appears.**

   Bluetooth is enabled on your BlackBerry.

4. **Press the Menu key to display the Bluetooth menu, and then select Add Device.**

   The Searching for Devices progress bar, um, progresses, as shown in Figure 7-7 (left). When your BlackBerry discovers the headset, a Select Device pop-up screen appears, featuring the name of the headset, as shown in Figure 7-7 (right).

Figure 7-7:
Searching
for a
headset
(left).
Success!
A headset
located
(right).

5. **From the Select Device pop-up screen, select the Bluetooth headset.**

   Another pop-up screen appears to prompt you for a passkey code to the headset.

6. **Enter the passkey and press the trackpad.**

   Normally, the passkey is 0000, but refer to your headset documentation. After you successfully enter the passkey, your headset appears listed in the Bluetooth screen.

7. **Press the Menu key to display the Bluetooth menu, and then select Connect.**

   Your BlackBerry now attempts to connect to the Bluetooth headset.

8. **When you see a screen like the one shown in Figure 7-8, you can start using your Bluetooth headset.**

Figure 7-8:
You can
begin
using your
Bluetooth
headset.

Using voice dialing

With your headset and the Voice Dialing application, you can truly be hands-free from your BlackBerry. You may be thinking, "How do I activate the Voice Dialing application without touching my BlackBerry?" Good question. The majority of hands-free headsets (Bluetooth or not) come with a multipurpose button.

Usually, a multipurpose button on a hands-free headset can mute, end, and initiate a call. Refer to the operating manual of your hands-free headset for more info.

After your headset is active, press its multipurpose button to activate the Voice Dialing application. You will be greeted with a voice stating, "Say a command." At this point, simply say, "Call," and state the name of a person or say the number. (For example, say, "Call President Obama" or "Call 555-2468.") The Voice Dialing application is good at recognizing the name of the person and the numbers you dictate. However, we strongly suggest that you try the voice dialing feature before you need it so that you're familiar with the voice commands that control the features.

Multitasking while on the Phone

One of the great things about the BlackBerry is that you can use it for other tasks while you're on the phone. For example, you can take notes or make a to-do list. Or you can look up in BlackBerry Contacts a phone number that your caller is requesting. You can even compose an e-mail and receive e-mails while on a call!

When multitasking, you really need to be using a hands-free headset or a speakerphone. Otherwise, your face is stuck to your BlackBerry, and you can't engage in your conversation while multitasking.

Accessing applications while on the phone

After you don your hands-free headset or turn on the speakerphone (by pressing the P key), you can multitask after you follow these steps:

1. **While in a conversation, from the Phone application, press the Menu key, and then select the Home Screen option from the menu that appears.**

   You return to the Home screen without terminating your phone conversation.

   Alternatively, you can simply press the Escape key while in the Phone application to return to the Home screen.

2. **From the Home screen, you can now multitask.**

While on the phone and multitasking, you can still access the Phone menu from other applications. For example, you can end a call or put a call on hold from your to-do list. For example, while you're on a phone call and in the Message application, press the Menu key to display Phone-related menu items, such as Mute and Hold.

Taking notes while on the phone

To take notes during your call, follow these steps:

1. **During a phone conversation, press the Menu key, and then select Notes from the menu that appears.**

   The Notes screen appears.

2. **Type notes for the conversation, as shown in Figure 7-9.**

   When the call ends, the notes are saved for you automatically.

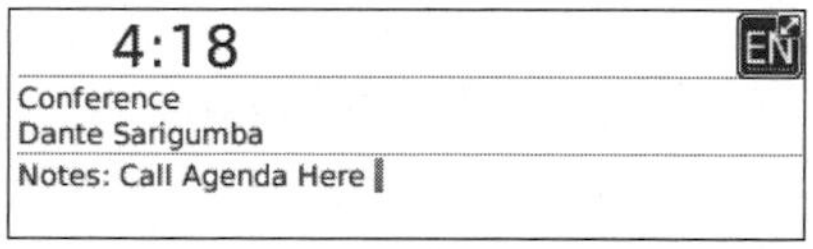

Figure 7-9:
Take notes
while on a
phone call.

```
 4:18                          EN
Conference
Dante Sarigumba
Notes: Call Agenda Here |
```

You can add notes while you're on the phone, but you can also add them afterward. While you're viewing a call's history, press the Menu key, and from the menu that appears, select Add Notes if you have no notes for the call yet or Edit Notes if you already have notes.

You can perform these functions from the Call History list:

✔ **Accessing phone notes:** From the Call History list (see Figure 7-10), you can access notes that you made during a call or a conference call. Additionally, you can edit notes and add new notes. You can get to the Call History list by following these steps:

1. **Open the Phone application.**

2. **Highlight a number for which you want to view the call history.**

3. **Press the Menu key, select View from the menu that appears, and then select Call History from the submenu.**

The Call History list opens, shown in Figure 7-10.

✔ **Forwarding phone notes:** You can forward your phone notes the way you forward an e-mail. While on the Call History screen (refer to Figure 7-10), press the Menu key, and then select Forward from the menu that appears.

Figure 7-10:
The Call History list, where you can access conversation notes.

Part III
Getting Online with Your BlackBerry

The 5th Wave   By Rich Tennant

"I find it so obnoxious when people use their cell phones in public that I'm getting on the web right now to blog about it."

In this part . . .

*H*ere's the good stuff — how to use your BlackBerry for e-mail and text messaging. Get on board the BlackBerry messaging bandwagon by using the BlackBerry Messenger. And we explain how you can always stay online, even while on the go, and keep abreast with your social network friends. Finally, figure out surfing the web on your BlackBerry.

Chapter 8

You've Got (Lots of) E-Mail

Your BlackBerry smartphone brings a fresh new face to the convenience and ease-of-use that you associate with e-mail. You can direct mail to your BlackBerry from up to ten e-mail accounts from the likes of AOL and Yahoo!. You can set up an e-mail signature, configure e-mail filters, and search for e-mails.

In this chapter, we show you how to use and manage the mail capabilities of your BlackBerry to their full potential. From setup to sorts, we have you covered.

Getting Up and Running with E-Mail

Regardless of your network service provider (such as AT&T, Rogers, or Vodafone), you can set up your BlackBerry to receive mail from at least one of your current e-mail accounts. Thus, with whatever address you use to send and receive e-mail from your PC (Yahoo!, Gmail, and so on), you can hook up your BlackBerry to use that same e-mail address. Instead of checking your Gmail at the Google site, for example, you can now get it on your BlackBerry.

Most network service providers allow you to connect up to ten e-mail accounts to your BlackBerry. You can enjoy the ease of one central point from which you get all your e-mail, without having to log into multiple e-mail accounts. Such convenience!

Using the BlackBerry Internet Service client

You can pull together all your e-mail accounts into one by using the BlackBerry Internet Service client (formerly known as the BlackBerry Web client). The BlackBerry Internet Service client allows you to

- **Manage up to ten e-mail accounts.** You can combine up to ten of your e-mail accounts onto your BlackBerry. See the following section for details.

- **Use wireless e-mail reconciliation.** No more trying to match your BlackBerry e-mail against e-mail in your combined account(s). Just turn on wireless e-mail reconciliation, and you're good to go. For more on this feature, check out the section "Enabling wireless reconciliation," later in this chapter.

- **Create e-mail filters.** You can filter e-mails so that you get only those e-mail messages that you truly care about on your BlackBerry. See the section "Filtering your e-mail," later in this chapter, to find out how to use filters.

Think of the BlackBerry Internet Service client (or just the Service client) as an online e-mail account manager. Unlike other online e-mail accounts, the Service client doesn't keep your e-mails. Instead, it routes the e-mails from your other accounts to your BlackBerry (because it's directly connected to your BlackBerry).

Combining your e-mail accounts into one

To start aggregating e-mail accounts (such as Gmail) onto your BlackBerry, you must first run a setup program from the BlackBerry Internet Service client. You can access the Service client from either your BlackBerry or your desktop computer.

To access the Service client from your PC, you need the URL that's specific to your network service. Contact your network service provider for the URL and login information. In this chapter, we will cover setting up the Service client from your BlackBerry.

Accessing e-mail account setup

From the Home screen, press the Menu key twice, and then select Setup. In the Setup screen that appears, select Email Accounts, which prompts you to log in to the Service client.

After you log in to the Service client, an Email Accounts screen, similar to Figure 8-1, appears. If your network provider has activated your BlackBerry, you should see one e-mail address, the default address of your BlackBerry.

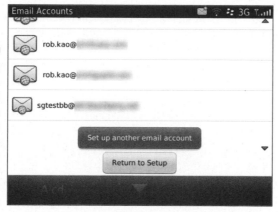

Figure 8-1:
Set up
an e-mail
account on
the Email
Accounts
screen
on your
BlackBerry.

If you press the Menu key while in the Service client, a menu appears, displaying a couple of options:

- ✔ **Email Accounts:** Add, edit, and delete e-mail accounts. In addition, for each e-mail address, you can set up filters and an e-mail signature.

- ✔ **Service Books:** Each service book represents the e-mail account you integrate into your BlackBerry. So, if you have three e-mail accounts integrated into your BlackBerry, the Service client sends three service books to your BlackBerry. You don't really need this option very often, so we don't cover it here.

Adding an e-mail account

You can have up to ten e-mail accounts on your BlackBerry — this is the good stuff right here. To add an e-mail account to your BlackBerry account, follow these steps:

1. **From the BlackBerry Internet Service client (refer to Figure 8-1), select the Set Up Another Email Account button.**

   The Add Email Account screen appears. You can choose Yahoo!, Gmail, AOL, Windows Live, or Other.

2. **Select your e-mail provider.**

    The Email Account screen appears, where you can enter the e-mail address and credentials for the e-mail account you want to add.

3. **Enter the e-mail address and password credentials for that e-mail address.**

    You want to include the e-mail address from which you want to receive mail: for example, `myid@yahoo.com`. The password is the one you use associated with that e-mail's login.

4. **Select the Next button.**

    You're finished. It's that easy!

Configuring your e-mail signature

By default, your e-mail signature is something like Sent via My BlackBerry, which you may find cool in the first week, showing off to people that you're a la mode with your BlackBerry. But sooner or later, you might not want people to know you're out and about while answering e-mail. Or you might want to make your signature something more personal. Follow these steps to configure your e-mail signature by using the Service client:

1. **Log in to the BlackBerry Internet Service client (refer to Figure 8-1).**

2. **Select the Edit icon for the desired e-mail account.**

    The Edit screen appears, as show in Figure 8-2.

3. **In the Signature field, type the desired text for your e-mail signature.**

4. **Press the Menu key, and then select Save from the menu that appears.**

Figure 8-2: The Edit screen of an e-mail account.

Enabling wireless reconciliation

With wireless reconciliation, you don't need to delete the same e-mail in two places: The two e-mail inboxes reconcile with each other, meaning they're in sync — hence the term *wireless reconciliation*. Convenient, huh?

Enabling wireless e-mail synchronization

You can start wireless e-mail synchronization by configuring your BlackBerry. Follow these steps:

1. **From the Home screen, press the Menu key twice, and then select Messages.**

   The Messages application opens, displaying the message list.

2. **In the message list, press the Menu key, and then select Options from the menu that appears.**

   The Message Options screen appears.

3. **Select Email Reconciliation.**

   The Email Reconciliation screen appears, offering the following options:

   - *Delete On:* Configures how BlackBerry handles your e-mail deletion.

   - *Wireless Reconciliation:* Turns on or off the wireless sync function.

   - *On Conflict:* Controls how BlackBerry handles inconsistency between e-mail on your BlackBerry versus e-mail on the BlackBerry Internet Service client.

     You can choose who "wins" via this option: your BlackBerry or the BlackBerry Internet Service client.

4. **Select Delete On, and then select an option from the menu that appears.**

   You have these choices:

   - *Handheld:* A delete on your BlackBerry takes effect on your BlackBerry only.

   - *Mailbox & Handheld:* A delete on your BlackBerry takes effect on both your BlackBerry and your inbox on the BlackBerry Internet Service client.

   - *Prompt:* Prompts your BlackBerry to ask for confirmation at the time of deletion.

5. **Select Wireless Reconciliation, and then select On from the menu that appears.**

6. **Select On Conflict, and then make a selection from the menu that appears.**

   You can choose Handheld Wins or Mailbox Wins. If you choose Handheld Wins, the e-mail messages in your online e-mail account match the ones on the handheld; so if e-mails on your BlackBerry are out of sync with your online e-mail account, then the reconciliation makes your e-mail account match what you see on your BlackBerry. If you select Mailbox Wins, the sync works in the opposite way (with your BlackBerry changed to match your e-mail account).

Unfortunately, some e-mail accounts might not work well with the e-mail reconciliation feature of the BlackBerry. So, you might have to delete an e-mail twice.

Permanently deleting e-mail from your BlackBerry

When deleting e-mail on your BlackBerry, the same message in that e-mail account is moved to the Deleted folder. You can set up your BlackBerry to permanently delete e-mail, but use this option with caution — after that e-mail is gone, it's gone.

To permanently delete e-mail on your Service client from your BlackBerry, follow these steps:

1. **From the Home screen, press the Menu key twice, and then select Messages.**

2. **In the message list, press the Menu key, and then select Options from the menu that appears.**

3. **In the Options screen, select Email Reconciliation.**

4. **In the Email Reconciliation screen that appears, press the Menu key, and then select Purge Deleted Items from the menu that opens.**

   A pop-up menu appears, listing all your e-mail accounts.

5. **From the pop-up menu, choose the e-mail account from which you want to purge deleted items.**

   A pop-up message appears, confirming that you're about to purge deleted e-mails on your Service client.

6. **Select Yes.**

   Deleted e-mails in the selected e-mail account are purged.

Unfortunately, the Purge Deleted Items feature may not work with some e-mail accounts.

Accessing Messages

From Messages, you can send and receive your e-mails, and also configure wireless e-mail reconciliation with your e-mail account(s).

From the Home screen, press the Menu key twice, and then select Messages. The first thing you see after opening Messages is the message list. Your message list can contain e-mail, voicemail messages, missed phone call notices, Short Messaging Service (SMS) messages, Multimedia Message Service (MMS) messages, and even saved web pages.

Receiving e-mails

Whether you're concerned about security or speed of delivery, with BlackBerry's up-to-date secured network, you're in good hands when receiving e-mail on your BlackBerry.

And whether you've aggregated accounts or just use the plain-vanilla BlackBerry e-mail account, you receive your e-mail the same way. When you receive an e-mail, your BlackBerry notifies you by displaying a numeral next to a mail icon (an envelope) at the top of the screen. This number represents how many new (unread) e-mails you have (see Figure 8-3). The asterisk next to the envelope indicates that you have new mail and haven't opened the Messages application yet.

Your BlackBerry can also notify you of new e-mail by vibration or a sound alert, or both. You can customize this from Profile, as we detail in Chapter 3.

Figure 8-3:
You've
got (333)
e-mails!

Retrieving e-mail

Retrieving your e-mail is simple. Just follow these steps:

1. **From the Home screen, press the Menu key twice, and then select Messages.**

   Your message list appears.

2. **In the message list, scroll to any e-mail, and then press the trackpad.**

   You can tell whether an e-mail is unopened by the small unopened envelope icon on the left side of the e-mail. A read e-mail bears an opened envelope icon, a sent e-mail has a check mark as its icon, and a draft e-mail is represented by a document icon.

3. **After you finish reading the message, press the Escape key to return to the message list.**

Saving a message to the saved folder

You can save any important e-mail into a folder so that you can find it without sorting through tons of e-mail. Simply scroll to the e-mail you want to save, press the Menu key, and select Save from the menu that appears. A pop-up message confirms that your e-mail has been saved. *Note:* Your saved e-mail still remains in the message list.

To retrieve or view a saved e-mail, follow these steps:

1. **From the Home screen, press the Menu key twice, and then select Messages.**

2. **In the message list, press the Menu key, and then select View Saved Messages from the menu that appears.**

   The list of all the messages you saved appears.

3. **Select the message that you want, and then press the trackpad to open it.**

Viewing attachments

Your BlackBerry is so versatile that you can view most e-mail attachments just like you can on a desktop PC. And we're talking sizeable attachments, too, such as JPEGs (photos), Word documents, PowerPoint slides, and Excel spreadsheets. Table 8-1 has a list of supported attachments that you can view from your BlackBerry.

Table 8-1	BlackBerry-Supported Attachments
Supported Attachment Extension	*Description*
`.zip`	Compressed file format
`.htm`	HTML web page
`.html`	HTML web page
`.doc, docx`	MS Word document
`.dot`	MS Word document template
`.ppt, .pptx`	MS PowerPoint document
`.pdf`	Adobe PDF document
`.wpd`	Corel WordPerfect document
`.txt`	Text file
`.xls, xlsx`	MS Excel document
`.bmp`	BMP image file format
`.gif`	GIF image file format
`.jpg`	JPEG image file format
`.png`	PNG image file format
`.tif`	TIFF image file format

You can also create documents by using the Documents To Go application that comes with your BlackBerry. Although you can view and edit documents from e-mails by using this app, you have to pay (around $15 a copy) for the app to create documents from scratch. As for images, you can attach pictures that are stored on your BlackBerry without the need for third-party software. See Chapter 14 for details.

To tell whether an e-mail has an attachment, look for the standard paper-clip icon next to your e-mail in the message list.

You retrieve all the different types of attachments the same way, which makes retrieving attachments an easy task. To open an attachment, follow these steps:

1. **While reading an e-mail, press the Menu key, and then select Open Attachment from the menu that appears.**

   An Option pop-up screen appears, where you can select to View or Edit with Documents To Go.

   2. **From the pop-up screen, select View.**

     Your BlackBerry attempts to contact the BlackBerry server to retrieve your attachment. Initially, your BlackBerry retrieves only part of your attachment. It retrieves more, as necessary, while you scroll through the attachment. When you're retrieving a picture, all parts of the attachment appear.

     Alternatively, if you select Edit in this pop-up screen, Documents To Go downloads the whole attachment, and then opens it for editing.

Sending e-mail

The first thing you probably want to do when you get your BlackBerry is write an e-mail to let your friends know that you've just gotten a BlackBerry. Follow these steps:

   1. **From the Home screen, press the Menu key twice, and then select Messages.**

   2. **In the message list that appears, press the Menu key, and then select Compose Email from the menu that opens.**

     A blank e-mail form appears. You just need to fill it out like you do on your PC.

   3. **In the To field, type your recipient's name or e-mail address.**

     While you type, a list of contacts from your Contacts, matching the name or address that you're typing, appears.

   4. **Type your message subject and body in the appropriate fields.**

   5. **When you're finished, press the Menu key, and then select Send from the menu that appears.**

     Your message has wings.

Forwarding e-mail

When you need to share an important e-mail with a colleague or a friend, you can forward that e-mail. Simply follow these steps:

   1. **Open the e-mail.**

     For information on opening e-mail, see the section "Retrieving e-mail," earlier in this chapter.

   2. **Press the Menu key, and then select Forward from the menu that appears.**

3. **Type the recipient's name or e-mail address in the appropriate field, then add a message body, if needed.**

   When you start typing your recipient's name, a list of your contacts whose names include those letters appears, and you can choose the recipient from that list.

4. **Press the Menu key, and then select Send from the menu that appears.**

   Your message is on its way to your recipient.

Saving a draft e-mail

Sometimes the most skillful wordsmiths find themselves lost for words to express the message they want. Don't fret, fellow wordsmith, you can save that e-mail composition as a draft until your words come back to you. You only need to press the Menu key, and then select Save Draft from the menu that appears to save your e-mail as a draft.

When you're ready to send your message, choose the draft from the message list. You can tell which messages are drafts because they sport a tiny document icon; finished messages have an envelope icon.

Adding a sender to your Contacts

You can add a message-sender's contact info to your BlackBerry Contacts directly from Messages. You don't ever have to copy or write down the person's name and e-mail address on paper.

To add a sender to your Contacts, follow these steps:

1. **From the Home screen, press the Menu key twice, and then select Messages.**

2. **In the message list that appears, scroll to an e-mail, and then press the trackpad.**

3. **From the open e-mail, scroll to the sender's name, press the trackpad, and then choose Add to Contacts from the menu that appears.**

   The New Address screen opens. The sender's first name, last name, and e-mail address are automatically transferred to your Contacts.

4. **If needed, add any additional information (such as a phone number and a mailing address).**

5. **Press the Menu key, and then select Save from the menu that appears.**

Filtering your e-mail

Most of us get some e-mail that either isn't urgent or doesn't really concern us. Instead of receiving those messages on your BlackBerry — and wasting both time and effort to check them — you can filter them out. While in the BlackBerry Internet Service client, set up filters to make your BlackBerry mailbox receive only those e-mails that you care about. (Don't worry; you'll still receive all your messages on your computer.)

To create a simple filter that treats work-related messages as urgent and forwards them to your BlackBerry, follow these steps:

1. **From the Home screen, press the Menu key twice, and then select Setup.**

   The Setup screen appears.

2. **Select Email Accounts.**

   The BlackBerry Internet Service client opens and prompts you for your username and password.

3. **Log into the BlackBerry Internet Service client (refer to Figure 8-1).**

4. **Highlight an e-mail account, press the Menu key, and then select Filters from the menu that appears.**

   The Filters screen that appears shows a list of filters that have been created. If you haven't created any yet, the screen says No Filters Configured, as shown in Figure 8-4.

5. **Select the Add Filter button.**

   The Add Filter screen appears, as shown in Figure 8-5.

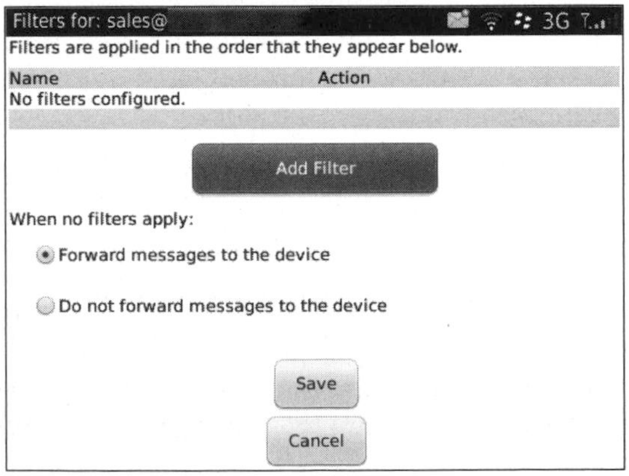

Figure 8-4: The Filters screen.

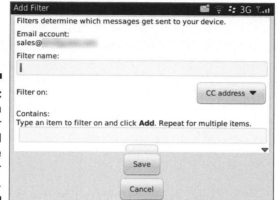

Figure 8-5:
Create a
filter for
your e-mail
on the
Add Filter
screen.

6. **Enter a filter name in the Filter Name field.**

   The filter name can be anything you want.

7. **In the Filter On menu, choose the condition to place on the filter.**

   The list offers these options:

   • *A High-Priority Mail Arrives:* Select this option if the filter applies only to urgent e-mail.

   • *Subject Field Contains:* When you select this option, the Contains field is enabled (you can type text in it). You can specify what keywords you want the filter to look for in the Subject field. Separate each entry with a semicolon (;).

   • *From Field Contains:* When you select this option, the Contains field is enabled (you can type text in it). You can type in full addresses or part of an address. For example, you can type **rob@robkao.com** or just **kao**. Separate each entry with a semicolon (;).

   • *To Field Contains:* Works like the From Field Contains option, except the text you enter applies to the To field.

   • *CC Field Contains:* Works like the From Field Contains option, except the filter looks for the text in the CC field.

   In our example, we selected From Field Contains.

8. **Enter text in the Contains field, unless you selected A High-Priority Mail Arrives in Step 7.**

   In our example, you'd type the domain of your work e-mail address. For example, if your work e-mail address is myname@XYZCo.com, enter **XYZCo.com**.

9. **In the Action section, select the Forward Message to Handheld option or the Do Not Forward Message to Handheld option.**

   If you select Forward Messages to Handheld, you can select either or both of these check boxes:

   • *Header Only:* Choose this option if you want only the header of the e-mails that meet the condition(s) you set in Steps 7 through 9 to be sent to you. (A *header* doesn't contain the body of the e-mail — just who sent it, the subject, and the time it was sent.) Select this check box if you get automated alerts, for which you need to receive only the subject.

   • *Level 1 Notification:* Another way of saying *urgent e-mail.* When you receive a Level 1 e-mail, it appears bold in the list of messages.

   If you select the Do Not Forward Message to Handheld option, any e-mail that meets the conditions you set in Steps 7 through 9 isn't sent to your BlackBerry.

10. **Confirm your filter by selecting the Save button.**

    You return to the Filters screen, where you can see your newly created filter in the list.

If you have a hard time setting the criteria for a filter, just take a best guess, and then test it by having a friend send you an e-mail. If the test e-mail isn't filtered correctly, set the conditions and test again until you get them right.

Searching through Your Messages Like a Pro

You probably won't use your BlackBerry's Search function every day — but when you do run a search, you usually need the information fast. The following sections help you familiarize yourself with BlackBerry Message's search options.

Doing a quick search

If you need to quickly locate an e-mail by searching for the To, From, or Subject field, you can do a quick search. Follow these steps:

1. **From the Home screen, press the Menu key twice, and then select Messages.**

2. **In the messages list that appears, press the Menu key, and then select Search from the menu that opens.**

   A Search field appears at the top of your messages.

3. **Type search criteria into the Search field.**

   By default, the message's To, From, and Subject fields are searched. While you type, the message list shows results that match your search.

Running an advanced search

If you can't find the message you're looking for by using quick search, you can do an advanced search, which performs a keyword search of your messages.

To run an advanced search, follow these steps:

1. **From the Home screen, press the Menu key twice, and then select Messages.**

2. **In the messages list that appears, press the Menu key, select Search By from the menu that appears, and then select Advanced from the submenu.**

3. **In the Advanced Search screen that appears, fill in your search criteria (see Figure 8-6).**

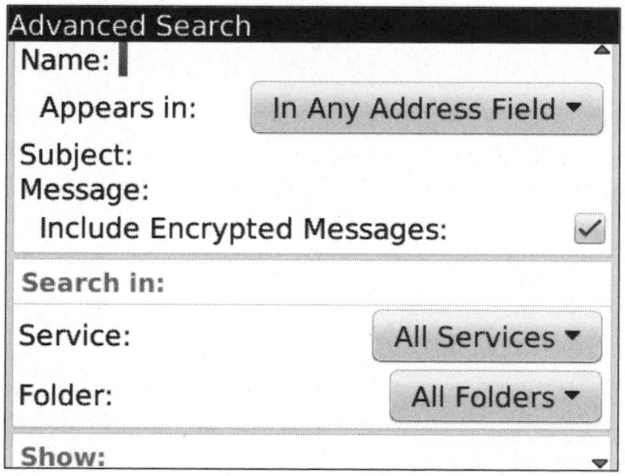

Figure 8-6:
The
Advanced
Search
screen in
Messages.

Advanced Search

Name:	
Appears in:	In Any Address Field ▼
Subject:	
Message:	
Include Encrypted Messages:	✓

Search in:

| Service: | All Services ▼ |
| Folder: | All Folders ▼ |

Show:

The search criteria for an advanced search include

- *Name:* The name of the sender or recipient that you want to search for.

- *Appears In:* Related to the Name criterion. From this menu, select an option that indicates where the name might appear, such as in the To or CC field. Your choices are From, To, CC, BCC, or Any Address Fields.

- *Subject:* Some or all of the keywords that appear in the subject.

- *Message:* Keywords that appear in the message.

- *Service:* If you set up your BlackBerry to receive e-mail from more than one e-mail account, you can specify which e-mail account received the message you're looking for.

- *Folder:* The folder in which you want to perform the search. Generally, search all folders. Although all e-mails come into the Inbox folder, you might have saved some emails into a different folder or folders.

- *Show:* How the search result will appear: for example, whether you want to see only e-mails that you sent or e-mails that you received. Your choices in this menu are Sent and Received, Received Only, Sent Only, Saved Only, Draft Only, and Unopened Only.

- *Type:* The type of message that you're trying to search for: e-mail, text message, or voicemail. The menu offers these choices: All, Email, Email with Attachments, Meeting Requests, PIN, Text Message, Phone, Voice Mail.

In the Search screen shown in Figure 8-6, you can enter multiple search criteria or just a single one (you get to decide).

4. **Press the Menu key, and then select Search from the menu that appears to launch your search.**

The search results appear onscreen.

You can narrow the search results by performing a second search on the initial results. For example, you can search by sender and then narrow those hits by performing a second search by subject.

You can quickly search by subject when you're looking for a specific e-mail that has a specific subject that you already know. Just scroll to an e-mail bearing the same specific subject you're searching for, press the Menu key, and then select Search Subject from the menu that appears.

You can also do a quick search by sender or recipient when you're looking for a message from a specific person. To do so, scroll to an e-mail bearing the specific sender or recipient. Press the Menu key, and then select Search Sender or Search Recipient from the menu that appears. If the e-mail that you highlighted is an incoming e-mail, you see Search Sender in the menu. On the other hand, if the e-mail is outgoing, you see Search Recipient.

Saving search criteria

If you find yourself re-searching by using the same criteria over and over, you might want to save the search options and then reuse them to get latest search results.

By saving the search options, you're not saving the results of the search, merely the different options that you used to perform the search.

Follow these steps to save search criteria for reuse:

1. **Follow Steps 1 through 3 in the preceding section for an outgoing e-mail search.**

2. **In the Advanced Search screen, press the Menu key, and then select Save from the menu that appears.**

   The Save Search screen appears, from which you can name your search and assign it a shortcut key. See Figure 8-7.

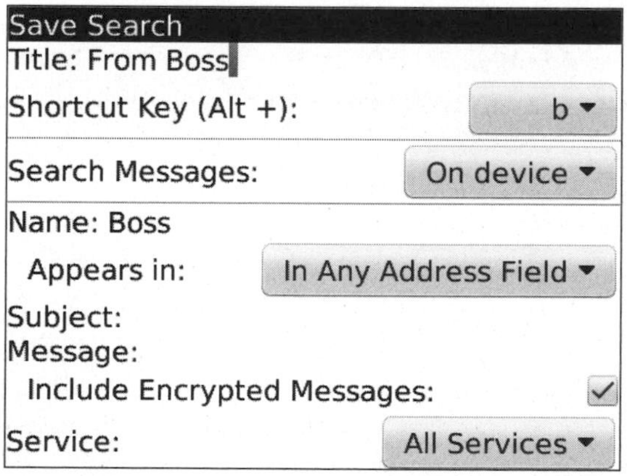

Figure 8-7:
Name your
search and
assign a
shortcut
key.

Save Search
Title: From Boss
Shortcut Key (Alt +):   b ▼
Search Messages: On device ▼
Name: Boss
Appears in: In Any Address Field ▼
Subject:
Message:
Include Encrypted Messages: ✓
Service: All Services ▼

3. **In the Title field, enter a name.**

   The title is the name of your search, which appears in the Search Result screen.

4. **Scroll to the Shortcut Key field, press the trackpad, and select a letter from the menu that opens.**

   You have ten letters to choose from.

5. **Confirm your saved search by pressing the Menu key, and then selecting Save from the menu that appears.**

Reusing saved search results

Right out of the box, your BlackBerry comes with five saved search results. Any new saved result can make your search that much more robust.

To see all the saved search results, follow these steps:

1. **From the Home screen, press the Menu key twice and then select Messages.**

2. **In the messages list that appears, press the Menu key, select Search By from the menu that opens, and then select Advanced from the submenu.**

3. **Press the Menu key, and then select Recall from the menu that appears.**

   The Recall screen opens. You can see all the the preloaded search shortcuts (the letters in parentheses in Figure 8-8), which indicate you're in the Recall screen.

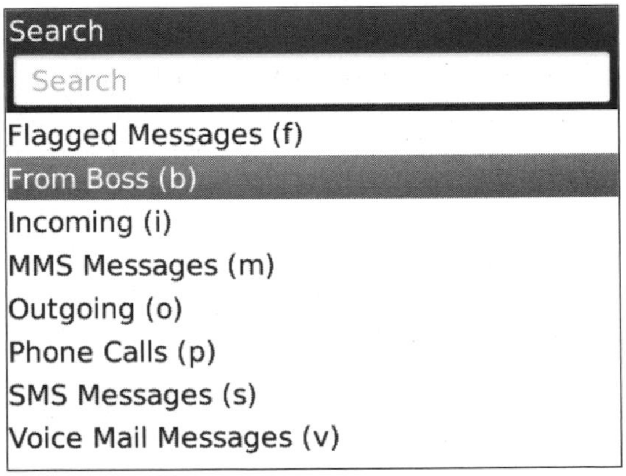

Figure 8-8: The Recall screen, showing default search shortcuts.

Search

Search

Flagged Messages (f)

From Boss (b)

Incoming (i)

MMS Messages (m)

Outgoing (o)

Phone Calls (p)

SMS Messages (s)

Voice Mail Messages (v)

To reuse one of the saved search results, simply select a search from the list in Figure 8-8, press the Menu key, and select Search from the menu that appears. Alternatively, you can invoke the saved search by pressing Alt in combination with the shortcut key (the key for the letter in parentheses).

Long Live E-Mail

No closet has unlimited space, and your BlackBerry e-mail storage has limits, too. You've likely pondered how long your e-mails are kept in your BlackBerry smartphone. (The default is 30 days. Pshew.) You can choose several options: from 15 days to forever (well, for as long as your BlackBerry has enough space for them).

Because any message you save is kept for as long as you want, you can save an important message to make sure that you don't lose it.

To change how long your e-mails live on your BlackBerry, follow these steps:

1. **From the Home screen, press the Menu key twice, and then select Messages.**

2. **Press the Menu key, and then select Options from the menu that appears.**

3. **Select Message Display and Actions.**

   The Display and Actions screen opens.

4. **Scroll to the Days to Keep Messages option and press the trackpad.**

5. **From the menu that appears, select the time frame that you want.**

   The menu includes these options:

   • *Forever:* If you choose Forever, you'll seldom need to worry about your e-mails being automatically deleted. On the downside, though, you'll eventually run out of memory on your BlackBerry. At that point, you must manually delete some e-mail so that you have space to accept new e-mail.

   You can archive your e-mail by backing up your e-mails, using BlackBerry Desktop Software. See Chapter 19 for more on backing up your BlackBerry on your computer.

- *Time:* If you choose a set-time option, any message older than that time frame is automatically deleted from your BlackBerry the next time you reboot it. However, that message is deleted only on your BlackBerry — even if you turn on e-mail reconciliation — because you don't manually complete these deletions.

6. **Confirm your changes by pressing the Menu key and selecting Save from the menu that appears.**

Chapter 9

Too Cool for E-Mail

*Y*our BlackBerry is primarily a communication tool, with e-mail messages and phone conversations as the major drivers. It's a wonderful technology, but sometimes, another means of communication is more appropriate. For instance, e-mail isn't the tool of choice for Instant Messaging — most people would find that method slow and cumbersome. Nor is e-mail the best tool to use when you want to alert someone to something.

Your BlackBerry offers some less-obvious ways to communicate — ways that may serve as the perfect fit for a special situation. In this chapter, you can get the scoop on PIN-to-PIN messaging and text messaging. We also give you tips on how to turn your BlackBerry into a lean (and not-so-mean) Instant Messaging (IM) machine.

Sending and Receiving PIN-to-PIN Messages

What actually happens when you use PIN-to-PIN messaging? First and foremost, *PIN* stands for *personal identification number* (familiar to anyone who's ever used an ATM) and refers to a system for uniquely identifying your device. *PIN-to-PIN*, then, is another way of saying *one BlackBerry to another BlackBerry*.

As for the other details, they're straightforward. PIN-to-PIN messaging is based on the technology that underpins two-way pager systems, which is fast. When you send a PIN-to-PIN message, unlike a standard e-mail message, the message doesn't venture outside the Research in Motion (RIM) infrastructure in search of an e-mail server and (eventually) an e-mail inbox. Instead, it stays solidly in the RIM world, where it's shunted through the recipient's network provider until it ends up on the recipient's BlackBerry. Trust us when we say it's fast. You have to try it to see the difference.

So, when you use PIN-to-PIN messaging, that's another way of saying *sending a message from one BlackBerry to another BlackBerry.*

Here's the neat part. According to RIM, the message isn't saved anywhere in this universe *except* on the one device that sends the PIN message and the other device that receives it. Compare that with an e-mail, which is saved in at least four separate locations (the mail clients and e-mail servers of both sender and recipient), not to mention all the system redundancies and the backups employed by the server. Think of it this way: If you whisper a little secret in someone's ear, only you and that special someone know what was said. In a way, PIN-to-PIN messaging is the same thing, with one BlackBerry whispering to another BlackBerry. Now, that's discreet.

If you read the financial newspapers — especially the ones that cover corporate lawsuits extensively — you know that there's no such thing as privacy in e-mail. PIN-to-PIN messaging — in theory, at least — is as good as the old Code of Silence. Now, is such privacy really an advantage? You can argue both sides of the issue, depending on what you want to use PIN-to-PIN messaging for.

A little bit of RIM history

Sometime during the last millennium, Research in Motion (RIM) wasn't even in the phone business. Before BlackBerry became all the rage with smartphone features, RIM was doing a tidy little business with its wireless e-mail.

Back then, RIM's primitive wireless e-mail service was served by network service providers on a radio bandwidth: DataTAC and Mobitex networks. These networks were separate from a typical cellphone infrastructure's bandwidth.

RIM devices at that time already had PIN-to-PIN messaging. This type of messaging is akin to a pager; a message doesn't live in a mailbox but is sent directly to the BlackBerry with no delay. (No one wants a paging system that moves at turtle speed when you can get one that moves like a jackrabbit, right?)

Several interesting facts followed from RIM's initial decision. Of note, most cellphone users in New York City were left without service during the 9/11 disaster. The entire cellphone infrastructure in New York and surrounding areas was overwhelmed when faced with too many people trying to use the bandwidth available. However, one communication device continued to work during that stressful time: RIM's PIN-to-PIN messaging kept the information flow going.

Basically, if you like the idea that you can keep your communications discreet, PIN-to-PIN messaging has great curb appeal. If you don't care about privacy issues, you still may be impressed by PIN-to-PIN messaging's zippy nature. (It really is the Ferrari of wireless communication — way faster than e-mail.)

The Code of Silence has always been a thorny issue in companies that have strict regulatory requirements. As expected, RIM addressed this issue, allowing BlackBerry Enterprise Server administrators to flip a flag, forcing the device to forward all PIN-to-PIN messages to the BlackBerry Enterprise Server. A company can also install on the device third-party applications that report PIN-to-PIN messages.

Getting a BlackBerry PIN

When you try to call someone on the telephone, you can't get far without a telephone number. As you may expect, the same principle applies to PIN-to-PIN messaging: no PIN, no PIN-to-PIN messaging.

In practical terms, you need the PIN of any BlackBerry to which you want to send a PIN message. (You also need to find out your own PIN so that you can hand it out to folks who want to PIN-message you.)

The cautious side of you may wonder why on Earth you'd give your PIN to someone. Here's the difference: Unlike a PIN for an ATM account, this PIN isn't your password. In fact, this PIN doesn't give anyone access to your BlackBerry or do anything to compromise security. It's simply an ID; think of it like a phone number.

Here are a couple quick paths to PIN enlightenment:

✔ **From the Message screen:** Send your PIN from the Message screen with the help of a keyword. When you type a preset word, your BlackBerry replaces what you type with a bit of information specific to your device.

Sound wacky? It's easier than it sounds. Follow these steps:

a. *Compose a new message.*

If you need a refresher on the whole e-mail message and messaging thing, visit Chapter 8.

b. *In the subject or body of your message, type **mypin** and add a space.*

See the left side of Figure 9-1. As soon as you type the space, mypin is miraculously transformed into your PIN in the format pin:*your-pin-number*, as shown on the right side of Figure 9-1. Isn't that neat? *Note:* Case doesn't matter here.

mypin isn't the only keyword that RIM predefines for you. mynumber and myver give you the phone number and OS version, respectively, of your BlackBerry.

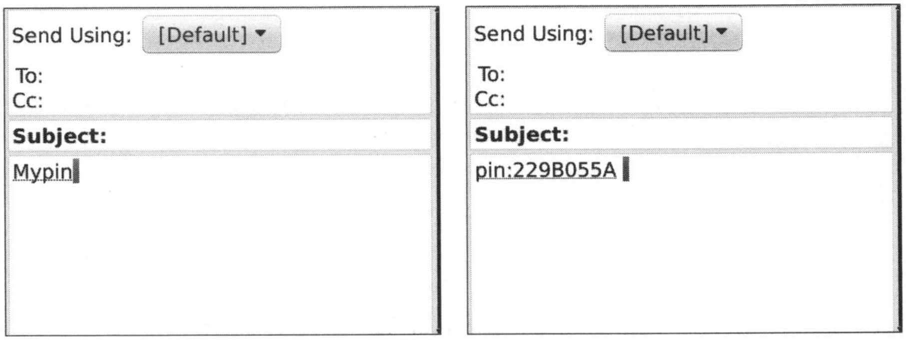

Figure 9-1:
Type a key-
word (left)
and add
a space,
and your
BlackBerry
translates
the keyword
(right).

Send Using: [Default] ▾
To:
Cc:
Subject:
Mypin|

Send Using: [Default] ▾
To:
Cc:
Subject:
pin:229B055A|

✔ **From the Device and Status Information screen:** You can also find your PIN on the Device and Status Information screen. Display the Device and Status Information screen by selecting the following links in succession from the All panel of the Home screen: Options, Device, and Device and Status Information. Figure 9-2 shows a typical Device and Status Information screen.

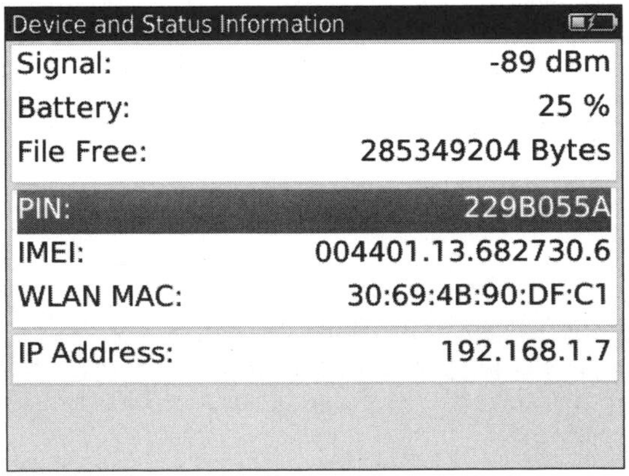

Figure 9-2:
Find your
PIN on the
Device
and Status
Information
screen.

Device and Status Information	
Signal:	-89 dBm
Battery:	25 %
File Free:	285349204 Bytes
PIN:	229B055A
IMEI:	004401.13.682730.6
WLAN MAC:	30:69:4B:90:DF:C1
IP Address:	192.168.1.7

Assigning PINs to names

So, you convince your BlackBerry-wielding buddies to go to the trouble of finding out their PINs and passing said PINs to you. Now, the trick is finding a convenient place to store your PINs so that you can use them. Luckily for you, you have an obvious choice: BlackBerry Contacts. And RIM, in its infinite wisdom, makes storing such info a snap. To add a PIN to someone's contact info in Contacts, follow these steps:

1. **From the BlackBerry Home screen, press the Menu key twice, and then select Contacts.**

   Contacts opens.

2. **Highlight a contact name, press the Menu key, and then select Edit from the menu that appears.**

   The Edit Contact screen for the contact name you selected makes an appearance.

3. **On the Edit Contact screen, scroll down to the PIN field (as shown in Figure 9-3) and type the PIN.**

4. **Press the Escape key, and then select Save from the menu that appears.**

   The edit you made for this contact is saved.

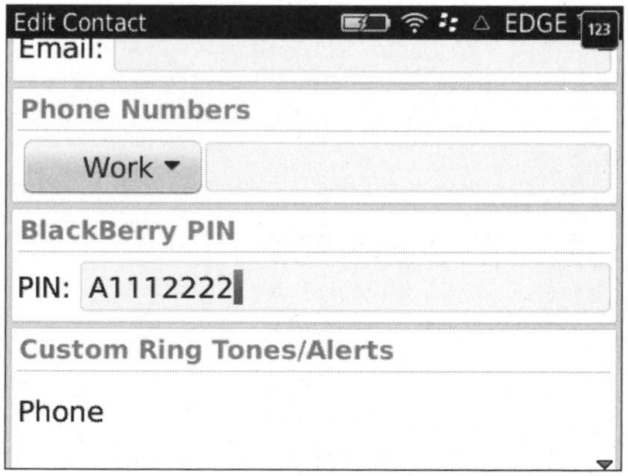

Figure 9-3: Add a contact's PIN info on the Edit Contact screen.

It's that simple. Of course, it's even easier if you think ahead and enter the PIN information you have when you set up your initial contact info (by using the New Contact screen), but we understand that a PIN isn't the kind of information people carry around.

If all this talk about New Contact screens and Edit Contact screens doesn't sound familiar, check out Chapter 4, which covers the Contacts application in more detail.

Sending a PIN-to-PIN message

PIN-to-PIN just means from one BlackBerry to another.

Sending a PIN-to-PIN message is no different than sending an e-mail. Follow these steps:

1. **From the BlackBerry Home screen, press the Menu key twice, and then select Contacts.**

2. **In Contacts, highlight a contact name, and then press the Menu key.**

   If a contact has a PIN, you see a menu item titled PIN *<Contact Name>* in the menu that appears. Say, for example, you have a contact named Dante Sarigumba. When you highlight Dante Sarigumba in the list and then press the Menu key, the menu item PIN Dante Sarigumba appears as an option, as shown in Figure 9-4.

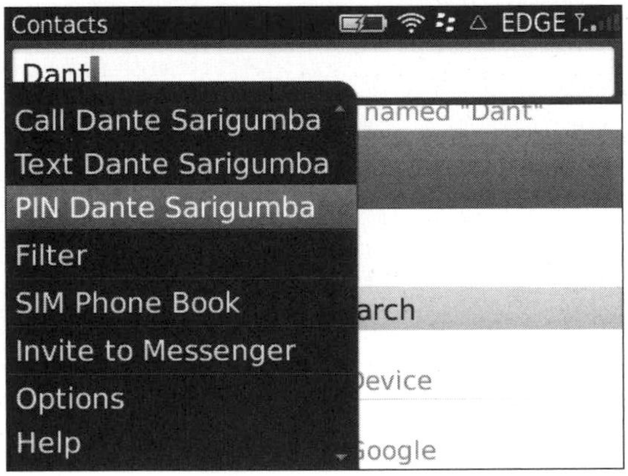

Figure 9-4:
Send a PIN
message
via your
Contacts.

> Contacts   🔋 📶 🔀 △ EDGE ❶.
>
> Dant
>
> Call Dante Sarigumba   named "Dant"
> Text Dante Sarigumba
> PIN Dante Sarigumba
> Filter
> SIM Phone Book   arch
> Invite to Messenger
> Options   Device
> Help   oogle

3. **Select PIN *<Contact Name>* from the menu.**

   You see the ever-familiar New Message screen, with the PIN of your buddy already entered as an address.

4. **Enter the rest of the text fields — subject, message, and signature text — just as you would with an e-mail.**

5. **Click the folder image on the right corner of the screen to send the PIN message.**

Alternatively, if you know the PIN, you can type it directly. Follow these steps:

1. **From the BlackBerry Home screen, press the Menu key twice, and then select Messages.**

   The Messages application opens.

2. **Press the Menu key, and then select Compose Other from the menu that appears.**

3. **In the submenu that appears, select Compose PIN.**

   The New Message screen makes an appearance.

4. **In the To field, enter the PIN, and then press the trackpad.**

   You just added a recipient in the To field.

5. **Add a subject line, the message, and then the signature text, just like you would in an e-mail.**

6. **Click the folder icon on the right corner of the screen to send the PIN message.**

Unlike e-mails, when you send a PIN-to-PIN message, you can tell almost instantly whether the recipient got your message. Viewing the message list, you see the letter D — which means *delivered* — beside the check mark next to the PIN-to-PIN message you sent.

Because of the nature of PIN-to-PIN messaging (and the conspicuous lack of a paper trail), companies can disable PIN-to-PIN messaging on your BlackBerry device. (No paper trail can mean legal problems down the road — can you say *Sarbanes-Oxley?*)

Receiving a PIN-to-PIN message

Receiving a PIN-to-PIN message is no different than receiving a standard e-mail. You get the same entry in your messages list for the PIN-to-PIN message, and the same screen appears when you open the message.

By default, your BlackBerry vibrates to alert you, but you can change this setting in Profiles. (Check out Chapter 3 for more details on changing your profile.) When you reply to the message, the reply is a PIN-to-PIN message, as well.

Keeping in Touch, the Text-Messaging Way

Short Messaging Service (also known as *SMS,* or *text messaging*) is so popular that you've probably seen TV shows asking for your feedback via SMS. Multimedia Messaging Service (MMS) is a much later evolution of SMS. Instead of just sending a simple text message, you can also send someone an audio or a video clip.

How short is *short?* The industry-standard maximum size per message is 160 characters. But network carriers control the length of texts, and some carriers (such as Telus in Canada) allow only 140 characters on BlackBerry smartphones.

Sending a text message

Get your fingers pumped up and ready for action: It's message-sending time! Whether you're sending an SMS or MMS message, follow these steps:

1. **From the BlackBerry Home screen, press the Menu key twice, and then select Contacts.**

2. **In the Contacts menu that appears, highlight a contact who has a cell-phone number, press the Menu key, and select Text *<Contact Name>* from the menu that appears.**

    SMS and MMS work only on mobile phones.

    The menu item for Text is intelligent enough to display the name of the contact. For example, if you choose Dante Sarigumba, the menu item reads Text Dante Sarigumba, as shown in Figure 9-5.

    A chat-like screen appears.

3. **(Optional) Press the Menu key, and then select Attach from the menu that appears.**

4. **Select the type of files you want to attach in the submenu that appears.**

    When you want to include an attachment to your text, this extra step allows you to choose the file to attach. This process also makes your message an MMS, rather than a simple SMS. You can choose from the following attachments:

Figure 9-5:
Select the
Text option
in the
Contacts
menu to
send a text
message.

- Picture
- Video
- Location
- Audio
- Voice Note
- Contact
- Appointment

5. **Type your message in the text field of the chat screen.**

6. **Press the trackpad, and then select Send on the screen that appears.**

   Your message is sent on its merry way.

Viewing a message you receive

If you have an incoming SMS or MMS message, you get a notification, just like you do when you receive an e-mail. Also, like with e-mail, the e-mail icon at the top of the Home screen indicates a new message. You also view an SMS or MMS message in the same way that you read an e-mail. Follow these steps:

1. **From the BlackBerry Home screen, press the Menu key twice, and then select Messages.**

   The Messages screen appears.

2. **Scroll to and select the unread message.**

Bob's your uncle: The message appears onscreen.

Customize how your BlackBerry notifies you when you receive an SMS message. Check out Chapter 3 for more details.

Always Online Using Instant Messaging

You can have *real-time* (as-they-happen) conversations with your friends over the Internet easily by using IM (Instant Messaging). IM enables two or more people to send and receive messages over the Internet. It all started with pure text messages and evolved into a rich medium involving voice and even video conversation in real time.

IM may not be available on your BlackBerry. Service providers choose whether to include it. (Most providers, however, do support it for the BlackBerry.) You can add IM to your BlackBerry, even if it didn't come with it. Simply search and download the IM app from BlackBerry App World. See Chapter 20 for more details on BlackBerry App World.

Instant Messaging on your BlackBerry

Most network providers dish out the three most popular IM services to their BlackBerry customers:

- Google Talk
- Yahoo! Messenger
- Windows Live Messenger

Those three IM programs aren't the only popular ones. Here are a few more:

- AOL Instant Messenger (AIM)
- ICQ Instant Messenger
- iChat AV (on the Mac)
- Jabber (open source)

IM basics: What you need

Assuming that you have the IM application that you want to use available on your BlackBerry, you need just two things to start using the standard five IM programs:

✔ User ID

✔ Password

Getting a user ID/password combo is a breeze. Just go to the appropriate registration web page (from the following list) for the IM application(s) you want to use. *Note:* You can more quickly and easily use your desktop or laptop to sign up, rather than your BlackBerry. Choose from the following links to sign up for the most popular IM services:

✔ **AOL Instant Messenger (AIM):** AOL has the habit of changing their signup link, so your best bet is to look for *AIM signup* in a major search engine.

✔ **Google Talk:** www.google.com/talk.

✔ **ICQ Instant Messenger:** www.icq.com/register.

✔ **Windows Live Messenger:** https://signup.live.com.

✔ **Yahoo! Messenger:** http://messenger.yahoo.com.

Given the many IM network choices available, your friends have probably signed up on a bunch of different networks. You might end up having to sign up for multiple networks if you want to reach them all via IM.

Going online with IM

After you obtain the user ID/password combo for one (or more) of the IM services, you can use your BlackBerry to start chatting with your buddies by following these steps:

1. **From the BlackBerry Home screen, select the IM application of your choice.**

   In our example, we use Google Talk. An application-specific login screen appears where you sign on, similar to the one shown in Figure 9-6. It's straightforward, regardless of which application you use, with the standard screen name (also called a username or ID) field and password field.

2. **Enter your screen name/ID and password in the appropriate fields.**

3. **(Optional) Select the Remember Password check box and the Automatically Sign Me In check box.**

   When the Remember Password check box is enabled, the ID/password information is pre-entered the next time you come back to this screen. (So, you don't have to type this stuff every time you want to IM.)

   We recommend that you select the Remember Password check box to save time but also set your handheld password to Enabled so that you don't compromise the security of your BlackBerry and your IM accounts. Refer to Chapter 3 if you need a refresher on how to enable passwords on your BlackBerry.

Google Talk

Google
ta|k

Username:

Password:

Sign In

Remember password

Automatically sign me in

Need an account?

Figure 9-6:
The login
screen for
Google Talk.

The Automatically Sign Me In check box determines whether you're automatically signed in when you power up your BlackBerry. You may want to select this check box if you have a habit of turning off your BlackBerry periodically.

4. **Click the Sign In button.**

At this point, IM tries to log you on. This process can take a few seconds, during which time the screen reads Sending Request to AOL or something similar. After you're logged on, a simple listing of your contacts, or buddies, appears onscreen.

5. **Select the person with whom you want to chat.**

A chat screen appears, where you can start your conversation with your friend.

You can highlight a contact's name in your IM list of contacts and press the Menu key to open a menu that lists the options or actions related to this contact. Features differ a little bit for each IM application, but for Google Talk, you can select Start Chat, Send File, Add a Friend, Rename, Remove, and Block.

Adding a contact/buddy

Before you can start chatting with your buddies, you need to know their user IDs (see Table 9-1).

Table 9-1	How to Obtain Your Friend's Credentials
Provider	**Where You Get Someone's User ID**
AOL Instant Messenger	Ask your friend or search AOL's directory.
Google Talk	The text before the @ sign in his or her Google e-mail address.
ICQ Instant Messenger	Use your friend's e-mail or search the ICQ Global Directory.
MSN Live Messenger	Your friend's MSN Passport ID or Hotmail ID.
Yahoo! Messenger	The text before the @ sign in his or her Yahoo! e-mail address.

Luckily for you, you don't need to search around for IDs every time you want to IM someone. You can store IDs as part of a contacts list. Follow these steps:

1. **In the IM service of your choice, press the Menu key.**

2. **Select Add a Friend from the menu that appears, as shown in Figure 9-7.**

   The Add a Friend screen appears.

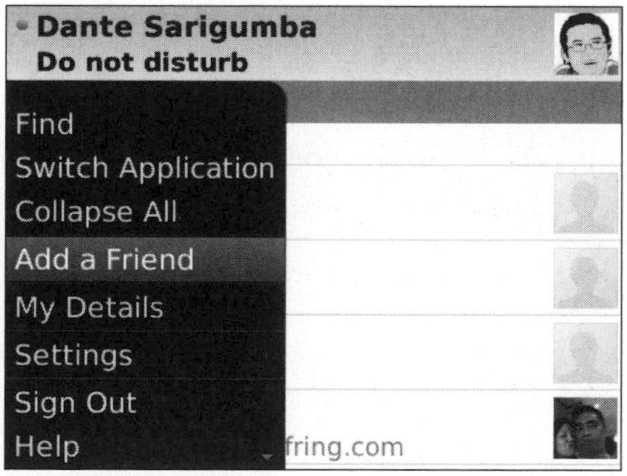

Figure 9-7:
Adding a friend to a Google Talk account.

3. **Enter the user ID of your contact in the Username field.**

4. **Press the trackpad.**

   IM is smart enough to figure out whether this contact has a valid user ID. If the ID is valid, the application adds the ID to your list of contacts. The buddy goes either to the Online or Offline section of your list, depending on whether he or she is logged on. If the ID you entered isn't valid, a pop-up screen appears telling you so.

Doing the chat thing

Suppose that you want to start a conversation with one of your contacts (a safe assumption, we think). When you send a message within the IM application, you're initiating a conversation. Follow these steps:

1. **Log on to the IM application of your choice.**

2. **Select the person you want to contact from your contacts list.**

   A typical online chat screen appears. The top portion lists old messages sent to and received from this contact. You can type your message in the bottom part of the screen.

3. **Type your message, and then press the Enter key.**

   Your user ID and the message you just sent show up in the topmost (History) section of the chat screen. When you get a message, it's added to the History section so that you can see both sides of your conversation.

Sending your smile

You can quickly add emoticons to your message. Follow these steps:

1. **While you're typing your message, press the Menu key.**

2. **From the menu that appears, select Show Symbols.**

   All the icons available appear, as shown in Figure 9-8.

3. **Select the emoticon you want to use.**

   The emoticon is added to your message.

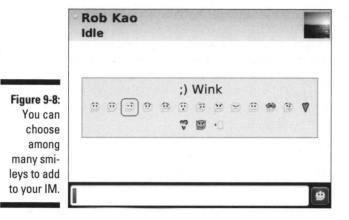

Figure 9-8:
You can
choose
among
many smi-
leys to add
to your IM.

Taking control of your IM app

If you use IM frequently — and you tend to chat with many contacts at the same time — your BlackBerry's physical limitations may cramp your IM style. No matter whether you use AIM, Yahoo! Messenger, ICQ Instant Messenger, MSN Live Messenger, or BlackBerry Messenger (see Chapter 10), you still have to type words on the tiny keypad more slowly than you can type on your computer.

Do you just give up on the dream of IM on the go? Not necessarily. The following sections show how you can power up your BlackBerry IM technique.

Use a custom status

If you can't keep up with all your buddies, your best bet is to limit your exposure. You can set up a custom message on your profile that lets your friends know whether you're able to respond to a message. For example, if your profile displays a Do Not Disturb message, your friends likely don't bother you with a "whazzup?" query. Each IM app has its own way of creating a custom status. For example, in Google Talk, follow these steps:

1. **From the Home screen, press the Menu key twice, and then select Instant Messaging.**

   The Instant Messaging folder opens.

2. **Select Google Talk.**

3. **In the Google Talk screen that appears, select your name.**

   The My Details screen appears.

4. **Select the Status field.**

   The My Status screen appears.

5. **Select the Custom Status option.**

   The New Status screen appears, allowing you to enter your custom status.

6. **Enter your custom status in the blank text field, and then select OK.**

   You return to the My Details screen. Your newly created status now appears in the list of Status options on the My Status screen. You just need to use it.

7. **Select the Status field, and then select your newly created status on the My Status screen that appears.**

8. **Press the Escape key, and then select Save from the confirmation screen that appears.**

   Your main Google Talk screen appears, displaying your new status below your name, as shown in Figure 9-9.

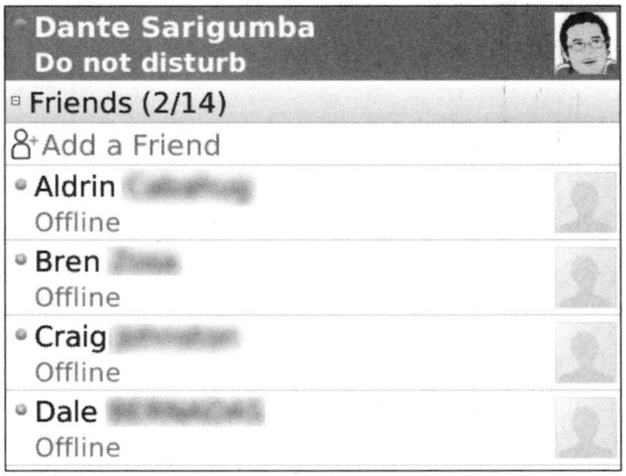

Figure 9-9:
The main
Google Talk
screen,
showing
a custom
message.

Dante Sarigumba
Do not disturb

Friends (2/14)
Add a Friend

Aldrin
Offline

Bren
Offline

Craig
Offline

Dale
Offline

SMS versus connecting via the web

SMS messages are short messages designed for cellphones. IM is a step up, evolving from the Internet, where bandwidth is no longer a concern. It provides a better real-time conversation experience across distances. These two technologies evolved in parallel. While more people use IM, it becomes apparent that this technology has a place in handheld devices, where mobility is an advantage. Some of the IM programs developed and used in the BlackBerry in the past use SMS behind the scenes. And because your BlackBerry can connect to the Internet, other programs use the Internet directly. These differences can affect your monthly bill, as well as your messaging experience.

If you don't have unlimited SMS but have an unlimited data plan, be careful with any third-party IM software. Make sure that it uses the Internet, rather than SMS. If it uses SMS, you incur charges for every message sent and received. Most network providers charge 20 cents for every SMS message, which can add up quickly and lead to a nasty surprise on your monthly bill.

Chapter 10

Instant Messaging on BlackBerry Messenger

● ●

In This Chapter

▶ Getting familiar with BlackBerry Messenger

▶ Inviting your friends to join the IM party

▶ Having Messenger conversations

▶ Creating a group and adding members

▶ Broadcasting a message to your contacts

● ●

In Chapter 9, you can find a slew of ways to send messages on your BlackBerry. In this chapter, you get the scoop on another way to send messages, using a special application known and loved by BlackBerry users: BlackBerry Messenger. This application is based on BlackBerry's PIN-to-PIN messaging technology (refer to Chapter 9), which means that it's mucho fast and quite reliable.

With BlackBerry Messenger, you can chat with those buddies who have a BlackBerry and have PIN-to-PIN messaging enabled. The application supports IM features common to many other applications, such as group chatting and the capability to monitor the availability of other IM buddies. In addition, you can integrate text messaging into BlackBerry Messenger, so you don't have to use multiple apps.

Using BlackBerry Messenger

You can access BlackBerry Messenger in the All panel of the Home screen, as shown in Figure 10-1. The first time you run BlackBerry Messenger, a welcome screen appears, asking you to enter your display name. This display name is the one you want other people to see on their BlackBerry Messengers when you send them a message.

Figure 10-1: Launch BlackBerry Messenger from the All panel of the Home screen.

A Contacts list appears the next time you open the application, as shown on the left in Figure 10-2. (Okay, the picture in this figure displays some contacts, but your list is initially empty; we show you how to populate the list in the following section.)

 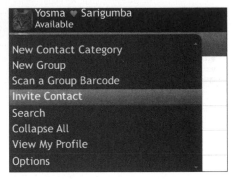

Figure 10-2: The Contacts list (left) and menu (right).

Pressing the Menu key opens a menu featuring these options, some of which are shown on the right side of Figure 10-2 (scroll to see all the options in the menu):

- ✔ **Start Chat:** Initiate a conversation with the highlighted contact.
- ✔ **View Contact Profile:** Open a screen that shows the information of the highlighted contact.
- ✔ **Contact <*Contact Name*>:** Selecting this option opens the familiar Messages screen, where you can compose a PIN message to the contact.
- ✔ **Move Contact:** Move the highlighted contact to a different category.
- ✔ **Delete Contact:** Delete the highlighted contact.

✓ **Show on Home Screen:** Creates an icon in the Home screen as a shortcut with the name of the contact. Selecting the icon displays the Messenger chat screen for the highlighted contact.

✓ **Link with BlackBerry Contact:** If you have an entry on your Contacts for the highlighted BlackBerry Messenger contact, you can link the information you have in both locations.

✓ **Remove Contacts Link:** This option appears in the place of the Link with BlackBerry Contact option when the highlighted contact is already linked to Contacts.

✓ **Forward to Messenger Contact:** Send the highlighted contact information to your other BlackBerry Messenger contacts. A Forward To pop-up screen appears where you can choose to whom the information gets forwarded from a list of your Messenger contacts.

✓ **New Multiperson Chat:** Similar to conference calling, but for chat. This option allows you to start a chat session with more than one contact.

✓ **Broadcast Message:** Send a message to multiple contacts in your BlackBerry Messenger. The message appears as a conversation in the recipients' BlackBerry Messengers.

✓ **New Contact Category:** Create a custom category for your contacts within BlackBerry Messenger.

You can use this option to organize your contacts if you have several contacts in BlackBerry Messenger. When you select this menu item, a New Contact Category screen appears, where you can enter a category name.

✓ **New Group:** Create a group of your contacts. Groups are listed in the same way as your contacts, but groups appear towards the bottom of the screen. This option allows members of the group to chat with each other. See the section "Grouping Your Messenger Contacts," later in this chapter, for the scoop on groups.

✓ **Invite Contact:** Add a new contact to BlackBerry Messenger (which we discuss in the following section).

✓ **View My Profile:** Customize your personal information and control how others see you in their BlackBerry Messenger Contacts list. You can do the following (see Figure 10-3):

- Change your picture.

- Change your display name.

- Display your barcode (which you need to display if you want someone to scan your BlackBerry's barcode).

- Enter a personal message that others can see in your Contacts profile.

- Allow others to see the title of the song you're currently listening to.

- Allow others to see your location and time zone information.

✓ **Options:** Customize the behavior of your BlackBerry Messenger.

Although some of the items in the preceding list don't appear on the right side of Figure 10-2, scroll up or down the menu to see them.

My Profile

Display Name:

Yosma ♥ Sarigumba

PIN:

PIN Barcode: [Show]

Personal Message:

Status: [Available ▼]

☐ Show What I'm Listening To

Figure 10-3: Set your personal information on the My Profile screen.

Inviting a Contact

With no one in your Contacts list, BlackBerry Messenger is a pretty useless item. So, you need to add a contact to your list. Ideally, you'd use BlackBerry Messenger with someone who also has BlackBerry Messenger. But you can also integrate text messaging if you have contacts who aren't into the BlackBerry Messenger addiction.

Inviting someone with BlackBerry Messenger

To add someone who has BlackBerry Messenger into your BlackBerry Messenger, you need his or her permission first. To start the process, invite your friend, meaning someone you know who

✔ Has a BlackBerry

✔ Has PIN-to-PIN messaging enabled

✔ Has a copy of BlackBerry Messenger installed on his or her device

If you know someone who fits these criteria, you can invite that person to appear in your list, which you can do in a couple of ways. If you want to send a PIN or e-mail invite, follow these steps:

1. **In BlackBerry Messenger, press the Menu key, and then select Invite Contact from the menu that appears.**

   The Invite Contact screen appears, listing actions related to inviting a contact, as shown in Figure 10-4.

2. **Select the first option, Invite by Sending a PIN or Email Message.**

   An Invite Contact screen appears that allows you to enter a PIN or an e-mail address in the To field.

3. **Start typing the name of the contact in the To field, and then select the name that you want to add from the list of contacts that appears.**

   The To field works with Contacts, so when you start to enter the person's name in this field, a pop-up screen appears, displaying a list of your contacts whose names start with the letters you typed.

4. **(Optional) Type a personal message in the text field just below the To field.**

   A default message is provided, but you can edit this message, which the contact receives after you finish Step 5.

5. **Select Send.**

   The application sends your request. As long as the person hasn't responded to your request, his or her name appears as part of the Pending group, as shown in Figure 10-5. When your contact responds positively to your request, that name goes to your official Contacts list.

Figure 10-4:
Add a contact to your Blackberry Messenger.

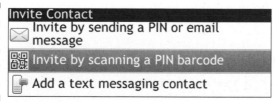

Figure 10-5:
To-be-approved contacts appear in the Pending group.

Alternatively, if you are beside your friend, you can add him or her to your BlackBerry Messenger app right away by using his or her BlackBerry barcode. Just follow these steps:

1. **In BlackBerry Messenger, press the Menu key, and then select Invite Contact from the menu that appears.**

   The Invite Contact screen appears (see Figure 10-4).

2. **In your friend's BlackBerry's Messenger app, press the Menu key, and then select View My Profile.**

   The My Profile screen appears.

3. **Select Show next to PIN Barcode.**

   A barcode image similar to Figure 10-6 appears on your friend's BlackBerry.

Figure 10-6:
A
Black-
Berry's
invitation
barcode.

4. **On your BlackBerry, select the Invite by Scanning a PIN Barcode option.**

   The Camera application appears.

5. **Position both BlackBerry devices so that your BlackBerry fully displays the other BlackBerry's barcode on the camera screen and wait until you hear the shutter sound.**

   Until your BlackBerry's camera recognizes the barcode, you can't get it to actually take the picture.

   That BlackBerry's contact information is added to your BlackBerry Messenger Contacts list.

Adding a text-messaging contact

If you want to use BlackBerry Messenger to communicate with someone who doesn't have a BlackBerry but does use text messaging, you can add that person directly into BlackBerry Messenger by following these steps:

1. **In BlackBerry Messenger, press the Menu key, and then select Invite Contact from the menu that appears.**

   The Invite Contact screen appears, listing actions related to inviting a contact, as shown in Figure 10-4.

2. **Select the Add a Text Messaging Contact option.**

   The Add Contact screen appears.

3. **Start typing your contact's phone number in the Phone field, and then select the name that you want to add from the list that appears.**

   The Phone field works with Contacts, so when you start typing the person's number on this field, a pop-up screen appears, featuring a list of contacts whose cellphone number starts with the numbers you typed.

4. **Select Add Contact.**

   The BlackBerry Messenger main screen reappears, with the contact added. Any chat conversation you initiate with this contact happens through text messaging.

Having Conversations

The whole reason you want BlackBerry Messenger is so that you can chat with your friends by using it. The following sections give you a quick rundown on how to start individual or group conversations, how to share files, and ways to save your conversation history.

Starting a conversation

You can easily start a conversation with any of your contacts. Follow these steps:

1. **On the BlackBerry Messenger screen, select the name in your Contacts list.**

   A traditional chat interface opens, with a list of old messages at the top and a field for typing messages at the bottom.

2. **Type your message.**

3. **Press the Enter key.**

   Any messages you send (as well as any responses you get) appear at the bottom of the history list.

Starting a group conversation

You can easily invite others to your BlackBerry Messenger conversation by following these steps:

1. **During a conversation, press the Menu key, and then select Invite Others from the menu that appears.**

   The Select Contacts pop-up screen opens, listing your BlackBerry Messenger contacts who are available (see Figure 10-7). You can select the check box next to each contact's name to indicate that you want to invite that person to the chat.

2. **Select the check boxes for the people you want to invite.**

   You can choose any number of people.

3. **Select OK.**

   The conversation screen reappears, with the history list showing the contacts you added to the conversation.

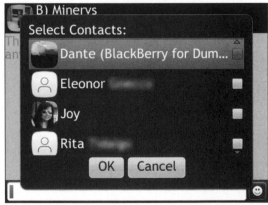

Figure 10-7: See your available contacts in the Select Contacts pop-up screen.

Sprucing up your conversations

You can set a subject for your message, which can be the topic or main agenda during a group conversation. To add a subject to a conversation, follow these simple steps:

1. **While the conversation screen is open, press the Menu key, and then select Set Subject.**

   You can add a subject to an individual conversation or a conference.

2. **In the Set Chat Subject pop-up screen that appears (as shown in Figure 10-8), enter the subject, and then select OK.**

   The subject appears as a header of the conversation screen.

Figure 10-8:
Add a
subject to
your
conversation
in the
Set Chat
Subject
pop-up
screen.

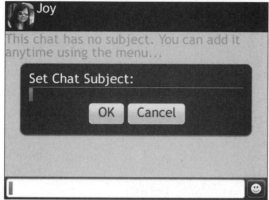

You can make your name appear snazzy by adding symbols, such as Dante☺ (see Figure 10-9 for the symbols you can choose from). Just follow these steps:

1. **On the BlackBerry Messenger screen, press the Menu key, and then select My Profile from the menu that appears.**

   The My Profile screen opens.

2. **Press the Menu key, and then select Add Smiley.**

   The Smile pop-up screen appears.

3. **Select the symbol you want to attach to your name.**

   The pop-up screen closes, and the smiley you selected is now appended to your name.

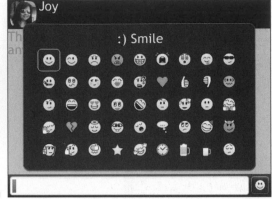

Figure 10-9:
Choose
symbols to
add to your
name in the
Smile pop-
up screen.

Sending a file or contact information

By using BlackBerry Messenger, like any other IM application, you can send files. During a conversation, just press the Menu key, and then select Send to open a submenu of items that allow you to share a file or contact info:

✔ **Picture:** Selecting this option shows a screen similar to Figure 10-10, where you can either launch the Camera application by selecting Camera to take a picture or select the picture file you want to send (you can navigate to a specific folder, if necessary).

✔ **Voice Note:** Selecting this option displays the Voice Note screen, shown in the left of Figure 10-11, and starts recording sound. Speak the voice message you want to send, and then follow these steps:

 a. *When you finish speaking your message, select Stop.*

 A screen similar to the right side of Figure 10-11 appears. You can play the message to review what you said, send the message if you're satisfied, or cancel sending the voice note.

 b. *Select Send.*

 A request to transfer the file is sent, and your friend needs to accept it in his or her BlackBerry Messenger for the transmission to begin.

✔ **File:** Displays a screen that allows you to locate the file you want to send. When you select this option, the screen displays the Media Card and Device folders. You can navigate to the location of the file you want to send.

Figure 10-10: Send a picture from the Select Picture screen.

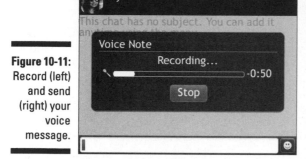
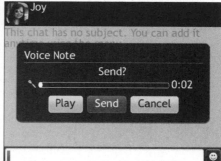

Figure 10-11: Record (left) and send (right) your voice message.

✔ **Messenger Contact:** Choose a contact from your list of BlackBerry Messenger contacts whose information you want to send.

✔ **BlackBerry Contact:** Sends a vCard (see Chapter 4 for details on the vCard) on the current conversation. When you select this option, Contacts appears where you can select the contact that you want to send as a vCard.

Saving the conversation history

While you're on the conversation screen, you can save your chat history in two ways. You can access both methods by simply pressing the Menu key:

✔ **Copy Chat:** Copies the existing chat history to the Clipboard. Then, you can paste it into the application where you want it saved, such as Calendar or MemoPad.

✔ **Email Chat:** Displays the Compose Message screen, shown in Figure 10-12, with the Subject field pre-populated with `Chat with <Contact>` on `<Date>` and the body of the message pre-populated with the chat history.

| Send Using: [Default] ▼ |
| To: | |
| Cc: |
| **Subject: Chat: Mirasols: Virtual Drinking Session** |
| From Group: Mirasols |
| ** May 21 Sat 06:13 ** Aleli Haberday, Dan! Kampai! ** May 21 Sat 06:18 ** Joy Happy Birthday! :) |

Figure 10-12: E-mail your BlackBerry Messenger chat history.

Grouping Your Messenger Contacts

The new Group feature of the BlackBerry Messenger allows you to create a permanent group. All the members of the group can see that group listed on their BlackBerry Messengers. When you use groups, you can start a group chat quickly with the same set of people.

Creating a group

To create a group, follow these steps:

1. **On the BlackBerry Messenger screen, select the Create New Group option (shown in Figure 10-13).**

   A Create New Group screen appears.

2. **Enter the group's name in the Group Name field; enter a description, if you want, in the Description field; and then select Create Group.**

   The BlackBerry Messenger main screen reappears, listing the newly created group towards the bottom of the screen. Now, you need to add members to your group.

3. **Select the newly created group.**

Figure 10-13:
Create
a new
group in
BlackBerry
Messenger.

4. **Press the Menu key, and then select Invite New Member from the menu that appears.**

   The Add Member screen appears, listing actions related to inviting a member, as shown in Figure 10-14.

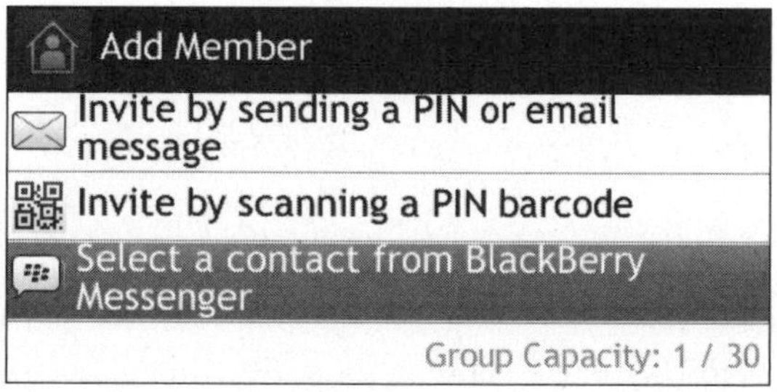

Figure 10-14:
Invite mem-
bers to your
new group.

5. **Select the option Select a Contact from BlackBerry Messenger.**

   The Select Contacts screen appears, where you can choose from your existing BlackBerry Messenger contacts.

6. **Select the contacts you want to be members of your group.**

   A checkmark appears next to each contact's name.

7. **Select Send.**

After your buddies accept your invitation, they appear in the list of members when you select Members. Anyone who's a member of the group can now initiate a chat by selecting the group and selecting Chat on the group's screen.

Navigating a group

Groups you create or belong to appear listed toward the bottom of the BlackBerry Messenger main screen. Select a group's name to open a screen like the one shown in Figure 10-15.

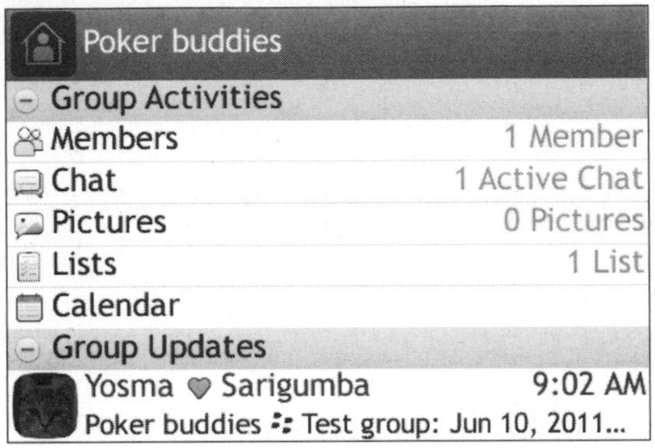

Figure 10-15:
Navigating
the group
screen.

Poker buddies	
Group Activities	
Members	1 Member
Chat	1 Active Chat
Pictures	0 Pictures
Lists	1 List
Calendar	
Group Updates	
Yosma ♥ Sarigumba	9:02 AM
Poker buddies ∷ Test group: Jun 10, 2011...	

This screen features two collapsible sections. The Group Activities section includes

- ✓ **Members:** Opens a screen listing the members of this group. To add a member, select Invite a New Member to make the Add Member screen appear. (The Add Member screen is the same as the Invite Contact screen, which we discuss in the section "Inviting a Contact," earlier in this chapter.)

- ✓ **Chat:** Opens the Group Chat screen, where you can start a group chat. Just select Start New Chat to make a new chat screen appear. If you have an ongoing chat, selecting this option opens a chat screen that displays the earlier exchange of messages.

- ✓ **Pictures:** Displays the Group Pictures screen, listing the pictures that any of the members shared. To share a picture, select Share Picture on this screen, and then navigate to and select the picture you want to share on the Select Picture screen that appears.

- ✓ **List:** Displays the Group Lists screen. Select Start New List on this screen to create a to-do list that every member of the group can see.

- ✓ **Calendar:** Displays the Calendars screen, where you can create a calendar item by selecting New Appointment, which opens the New Appointment screen. See Chapter 5 if you need a refresher on how to create and save an appointment. After you save the appointment item, it appears in the Calendar of every member of the group.

In the Group Updates section of the screen, all the updates to the group appear (such as when new members are added or removed, a new picture is shared, or a new list is added).

Broadcasting a Message

Do you feel the need to start a conversation on the same subject with several people? You can always use a group chat (we discuss creating groups in the preceding sections), but what if you want to get a personal opinion from each individual, something that each person isn't comfortable saying in front of the crowd? You can most easily get a lot of personal opinions by broadcasting a message to multiple recipients. Follow these steps:

1. **On the BlackBerry Messenger screen, press the Menu key, and then select New Broadcast Message from the menu that appears (as shown in Figure 10-16).**

   The New Broadcast Message screen appears, allowing you to enter your message and select the recipients.

Figure 10-16: Broadcast a message to your BlackBerry Messenger contacts.

2. **Enter your message in the Message field.**
3. **Select the recipients from the contacts listed on the bottom half of the screen.**
4. **Select Send.**

Chapter 11

Networking Like a Social Butterfly

In This Chapter

▶ Using Facebook on your BlackBerry

▶ Posting tweets to Twitter with your BlackBerry

▶ Grouping your social network accounts with Social Feeds

▶ Shopping on BlackBerry App World for social networking apps

Social networking is one of the biggest success stories in communications brought about by the sudden explosion of the Internet. Today's social networking venues help people stay in touch with their longtime friends. They've also become popular venues for doing everything from getting a date, to promoting business, to simply sharing thoughts and ideas. Facebook and Twitter also provide timely sources of information during natural disasters. These sites have even helped when a country's people decide to transform its mode of government. So, you're probably not surprised that many people immediately log in to Facebook or tweet through Twitter when they first get their BlackBerries.

In this chapter, we introduce you to a few applications whose sole purpose is to keep you connected with your network buddies in the wonderful world of social networking, as well as explain how to find any social networking apps you may need.

Gearing Up for Facebook

More than half a billion people use Facebook; the platform is definitely the number one social networking choice for most people. Because you're reading this section, we're going to assume that you're on a quest to enjoy Facebook from your BlackBerry.

In most BlackBerry devices, the Facebook app should be preinstalled, so you can find it in the All panel of the Home screen. The app has the same icon that you see on their website, as you can see in Figure 11-1.

Figure 11-1: Launch Facebook from your BlackBerry's All panel.

 If you can't find the Facebook icon in the All panel of the Home screen, don't panic. You can always download the app from the BlackBerry App World. See the section "Finding Social Networking Apps in BlackBerry App World," later in this chapter, to find out how to find the Facebook app. Chapter 20 describes how to install it.

Using Facebook on your BlackBerry

To run Facebook on your BlackBerry, follow these steps:

1. **From the All panel of the BlackBerry Home screen, press the Menu key twice, and then select the Facebook application.**

   The first time you run Facebook, a login screen appears, like the one shown in Figure 11-2. After you log in, Facebook runs behind the scenes all the time, so you don't have to face this login screen again unless you reset your BlackBerry or choose to manually log out.

2. **In the Email and Password fields, enter the e-mail address and password, respectively, that you used when you set up your account with Facebook.**

3. **Select Login.**

   Facebook verifies your e-mail address and password, and after you're validated, you're on your way to Facebook adventure-land.

Figure 11-2:
Logging in to
Facebook.

The first screen you see after you log in to the Facebook app allows you to update your status right then and there, as shown in Figure 11-3. Enter your status in the What's on Your Mind text field and select Share. That's it. Your new status is now posted on your Facebook wall.

News Feed   Add a Friend

Notifications   Friends   Send a Message

Upload a Photo   Messages

Figure 11-3:
The
Facebook
screen,
displaying
News Feed
view.

What do you want to see — the latest photos, the latest status updates, or the latest links posted by your buddies? The Facebook screen displays a list of your friends' updates in chronological order, starting from the most recent. You can hone in on the type of feeds you want to see by using one of the four views:

> ✔ News Feed
> ✔ Status Updates
> ✔ Photos
> ✔ Links

To change the view, select News Feed to open a pop-up menu, and then select the view you want from that menu.

Working with Facebook notifications

Facebook notifications are one of those special messages you get from the system that requires an action from you. You might receive a friend request from a long-lost high school chum or a help request from a friend who's playing Facebook's farming game.

You can respond to notifications by using your BlackBerry in the same way you do by using your computer. When you're logged into your Facebook account on your BlackBerry, simply select Notifications at the top of the screen. (It's second from the left, featuring an icon that resembles an easel with lines on it, as you can see in Figure 11-3.)

Sharing your pictures with your Facebook friends

You no longer need to wait until you get home from a vacation to post pictures to Facebook. Having a BlackBerry, which includes a camera, conveniently allows you to post pictures instantly when events unfold.

Posting a photo with the Facebook app

Just captured a cool picture of your best friend by using your BlackBerry? Why wait? Post it now.

You can post a picture right from the Facebook app by following these steps:

1. **From the All panel of the Home screen, press the Menu key twice, and then select Facebook.**

2. **On the top of the Facebook screen that appears, select Upload a Photo.**

   The Upload a Photo icon is third from the right on the top of the screen (it looks like a camera).

   The Select Picture screen appears, allowing you to choose a picture to post, as shown in Figure 11-4.

Figure 11-4:
On the
Select
Picture
screen,
choose a
picture to
post on
Facebook.

3. **On the Select Picture screen, navigate to the folder that contains the photo you want to post, and then select the photo.**

   Facebook's Upload a Photo screen reappears (see Figure 11-5), displaying these options:

   • *Caption:* Enter a brief description of the picture.

   • *Album:* Choose the album to which you want to post this picture. The default folder is Mobile Uploads.

   • *Tag This Photo:* Tagging a photo allows you to highlight people from your Facebook friends in the photo so that others can identify who's in the picture (plus, it adds a link users can select to go to that friend's Facebook page).

Figure 11-5:
Enter a
caption for
the photo,
choose
in which
album you
want to
store it, and
tag your
friends who
appear in
the photo.

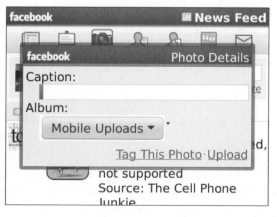

4. **In the Caption field, enter the caption for this photo.**

5. **(Optional) Select Mobile Uploads and, from the menu that appears, choose the album in which you want to post this photo.**

   If you want to post the photo to your Mobile Uploads folder, skip this step.

6. **(Optional) Select Tag This Photo and, on the Tags screen that appears, add tags by selecting Add and typing the name of the person whom you want to tag.**

7. **Select Upload to upload your photo.**

   Your picture is posted to your Facebook wall and filed in the album you selected in Step 5.

Make sure that the pictures you post are appropriate. You can't delete pictures from your BlackBerry. If you need to delete a picture, you need to log into Facebook from your computer.

Posting a photo from Pictures

You can also post a picture to Facebook through Pictures. If you find a cool image in Pictures that you want to share, you can easily upload it to Facebook by following these steps:

1. **From the All panel of the Home screen, press the Menu key twice, and then select Pictures.**

   The Pictures screen appears, listing picture folders.

2. **Navigate to the folder that contains your photo.**

3. **Select the photo, press the Menu key, and then select Send from the menu that appears.**

4. **Select Facebook from the Send submenu (see Figure 11-6).**

   The screen shown in Figure 11-5 appears.

5. **Follow Steps 5 through 7 in the preceding section to finish uploading your photo.**

Figure 11-6: Upload your photo to Facebook.

Finding and posting to a friend's Facebook wall

You may have hundreds of friends in Facebook whose updates whiz by you. With the onslaught of minute-by-minute updates, you likely miss some of the most interesting tidbits. And at some point, you may wonder what's going on with a particular friend. You can go to his or her Facebook wall to get the latest scoop.

To view a friend's wall and post a comment there in your BlackBerry's Facebook app, follow these steps:

1. **From the All panel of the Home screen, press the Menu key twice, and then select Facebook.**

2. **At the top of the Facebook screen that appears, select Friends.**

   The Friends icon (which appears fourth from the right) resembles a person's head.

   The Friends screen appears, listing all your Facebook friends.

3. **Enter your friend's name in the Search field.**

   While you type your friend's name, the list of options shrinks, displaying only names that start with what you've typed.

4. **Select your friend's name when you see it.**

   Your friend's wall appears, displaying all his or her recent updates.

5. **In the Write Something field, enter a comment that you want to post to your friend's wall, and then select Share.**

   Your comment appears at the top of your friend's wall, as well as in both of yours and your friend's News Feed.

Inviting a friend to Facebook

Do you have a friend who has yet to join the rest of the world in Facebook? You can send him or her an invitation to join by following these steps:

1. **From the All panel of the Home screen, press the Menu key twice, and then select Facebook.**

2. **On the top of Facebook screen that opens, select Add a Friend.**

   The Add a Friend icon is the third from the right on top of the screen, and it resembles a person's head with a plus one (+1).

   The Add a Friend screen appears.

3. **Enter your friend's e-mail address in the Email field.**

4. **(Optional) Enter a message in the Message field.**

5. **Select Invite.**

   An invitation is on the way to your friend's e-mail inbox.

Sending a private message to a Facebook friend

Sometimes, you want to send a message to your friend without the whole virtual neighborhood peeking in. If you want to keep things private, send a message in Facebook. Follow these steps:

1. **From the All panel of the Home screen, press the Menu key twice, and then select Facebook.**

2. **On the top of Facebook screen, select Friends.**

   The Friends icon is the fourth from the right and resembles a person's head.

   The Friends screen appears, listing all your Facebook friends.

3. **(Optional) Enter your friend's name in the Search field.**

   While you're typing the name of your friend, the list of names on the screen narrows down to the names that start with what you've entered.

4. **Highlight your friend's name, press the Menu key, and then select Send *<Your Friend's Name>* a Message from the menu that appears.**

   The Message screen appears, where you can enter your message.

5. **(Optional) Enter additional message recipients by entering a name in the To field and selecting the friend's name from the list of names that appears.**

6. **Write the subject and body of your message in the Subject and Message fields, respectively.**

7. **Select Send.**

   Your private message is sent to your friend's Facebook Messages inbox (or friends' inboxes, if you sent it to more than one person).

Viewing your own profile

You may not think you need to go to your own profile often, but from time to time, Facebook makes adjustments on privacy settings, so you want to make sure you stay on top of who can view your profile. Also, you can go to your profile to make sure your information appears the way you want it to.

To view your profile by using the BlackBerry Facebook app, follow these steps:

1. **From the All panel of the Home screen, press the Menu key twice, and then select Facebook.**

2. **On the Facebook screen that appears, press the Menu key, and then select View My Profile from the menu that appears.**

   Your profile page opens.

Using Twitter

Twitter is a microblogging site where you can post a short message or blog post, referred to as a *tweet.* How short is a tweet? The maximum tweet is 140 characters long. Millions of people are tweeting. Whatever your reasons for using Twitter, you probably want to be able to do it on your BlackBerry. Happily, your BlackBerry can absolutely fulfill your tweeting needs.

Using Twitter from your BlackBerry

In most cases, your BlackBerry comes with the Twitter app already installed, and you can find it in the All panel of the Home screen. The Twitter app's icon is a letter *t,* as you can see in Figure 11-7.

Figure 11-7: Launch the Twitter app from your BlackBerry's All panel.

If you can't find the Twitter app, it may not be installed on your BlackBerry. You can find it in BlackBerry App World. Check out the section "Finding Social Networking Apps in BlackBerry App World," later in this chapter, for details about locating the social networking apps you want to download. Flip to Chapter 20 for the scoop on installing those apps.

Follow these steps to log into your Twitter account:

1. **From the All panel of the Home screen, press the Menu key twice, and then select Twitter.**

   The first time you launch the Twitter app, a login screen appears, as shown in Figure 11-8. After you log in, though, Twitter runs in the background, so this screen reappears only if you log out or reset your BlackBerry.

Figure 11-8:
Log in to
your Twitter
account.

2. **On the login screen, enter your Twitter username and password in the appropriate fields.**

3. **(Optional) Select the Remember Me check box.**

   When you select this check box, the app automatically logs you in the next time you open it, even if you reset your BlackBerry.

4. **Select Sign In.**

   The Twitter Home screen, like you see in Figure 11-9, appears. In this screen, you can see a list of recent tweets from the people you follow.

5. **In the What's Happening? field, enter your message.**

   The number below this field, right next to the Tweet button, tells you how many characters you have left in your tweet, starting from 140.

6. **After you finish entering your message, select the Tweet button.**

   Your BlackBerry tweet is posted to the world of Twitter.

Twitter allows you to exchange private messages with another Twitter user. On the Twitter app, you can view your messages simply by selecting the Direct Messages icon (which resembles an envelope) on the top of the Twitter Home screen. If you want to compose a new message or reply to a message, just press the Menu key, and then select either Compose Message or Reply from the menu that appears.

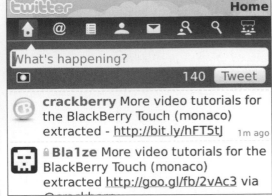

Figure 11-9:
On the Twitter Home screen, view recent tweets and post a tweet.

Finding out what people are tweeting about

Twitter has evolved so that now people direct messages to each other, kind of like a conversation. By adding an @ symbol plus a Twitter user's name, you indicate that you're directing that message to or talking about that user.

In the Twitter app, you can easily see all the tweets that have your username by simply clicking the @ symbol at the top of the Twitter Home screen. A list of those tweets appears on a screen labeled @*<yourusername>*. From this screen, you also can choose to reply to a tweet by highlighting the tweet, pressing the Menu key, and then selecting Reply from the menu that appears.

One of the most popular features of Twitter displays what's trending at the moment. *Trending* refers to when many recent tweets have included a word or combinations of words. You can access the list of latest trending keyword(s) from the Popular Topics screen. Select Popular Topics (the right-most icon) to make the Popular Topics screen appear, displaying current and recent list of trends on separate tabs, like the screen shown in Figure 11-10.

Viewing your Twitter lists

A *list* in Twitter is simply a grouping of Twitter users you follow. Twitter doesn't offer any lists; you have to create them yourself, based on how you want to group the people you follow. For example, if you want quickly to view any finance-related tweets, you can create a list called Finance and add to this list all the Twitter users who tweet about finance. Then, you can filter your Tweets screen to display only the tweets from people in the Finance list by selecting Finance on the Lists screen.

Figure 11-10:
View what's trending on the Popular Topics screen.

To create a list or view your lists, follow these steps:

1. **From the All panel of the Home screen, press the Menu key twice, and then select Twitter.**

2. **Select the Lists icon at the top of the Twitter Home screen.**

   The Lists icon is the third from the left.

   The Lists screen appears, displaying all your existing lists. If you haven't created any lists yet, this screen is empty.

3. **To create a new list, select Create New List.**

   A New List pop-up screen appears.

4. **Enter the name of the list and a description in the appropriate fields, and then select Create.**

   You're back to the List screen, where the list you just created appears.

To add someone to or remove someone from one of your lists, follow these steps:

1. **From the All panel of the Home screen, press the Menu key twice, and then select Twitter.**

   The Twitter Home screen appears.

2. **Highlight a tweet from the person you want to add to or remove from a list.**

3. **Press the Menu key, and then select Add *<Twitter User>* to List or Remove *<Twitter User>* from List.**

   A pop-up message appears, featuring options for adding or removing a user from the list, depending on which option you select.

4. **Select the Select a List field, and then select a list from the pop-up menu that appears.**

5. **Select Add or Remove, depending on which action you want to take.**

   The user is added or removed from the list, depending on the action you take, and the Twitter Home screen reappears.

Viewing and updating your Twitter profile

On the Twitter Home screen, selecting the fourth icon from the left, which resembles a person's head, takes you to your Twitter Profile screen, similar to Figure 11-11.

Figure 11-11:
View your Twitter Profile page.

This screen displays the last tweet you posted. Your profile page also displays the information you entered on your Twitter profile, such as your bio, your websites, the date that you signed up for Twitter, and your location.

If the information about you on your page becomes stale, you can easily edit it by pressing the Menu key, and then selecting Edit My Profile from the menu that appears. The Edit Profile screen shows up, letting you update the information.

When you select any of these options on your profile page, you're taken to a related screen:

- ✔ **Tweets:** A screen listing your previous tweets
- ✔ **Followers:** A list of Twitter users who follow you
- ✔ **Following:** A list of Twitter users whom you follow
- ✔ **Favorites:** A list of tweets that you've marked as favorites
- ✔ **Lists:** A screen showing all your lists

Using Social Feeds for Social Networking

You might feel overwhelmed looking for each individual social network app in your BlackBerry if you've subscribed to a slew of social networking sites. No problem. Research in Motion (RIM) created an app called Social Feeds. In a single app, you can see updates from your Facebook, Twitter, and Instant Message accounts, as well as subscribe to RSS feeds. And when you post a message by using Social Feeds, you post that message into all your social networking accounts and Instant Messaging networks in one go.

Setting up Social Feeds

The Social Feeds app comes preinstalled on your BlackBerry, and you can find it in the All panel of the Home screen. To integrate Social Feeds to your social networking accounts, you need to tell it what social networks you belong to and provide credentials for each of your social networking accounts.

Follow these steps to tell Social Feeds which social networking accounts you want integrated:

1. **From the All panel of the Home screen, press the Menu key twice, and then select Social Feeds.**

   The app's icon looks like the one on the left of Figure 11-12. Selecting this icon opens the Social Feeds screen, similar to right of Figure 11-12, which displays a Getting Started message the first time you open it.

2. **Press the Menu key, and then select Options from the menu that appears.**

   The Social Feeds Options screen appears, listing Display, Software Update, and RSS Options.

Figure 11-12:
The Social
Feeds
app's icon
(left) and
the Social
Feeds
screen
(right).

3. **Select Display.**

    The Display screen shows up, similar to the one in Figure 11-13, showing a list of social networking sites, as well as Instant Messaging networks, it supports.

4. **Select the social networking sites that you want to include.**

    A check mark appears next to each site you select.

5. **Press the Escape key, and then select Save from the confirmation screen that appears.**

    The Social Feeds Options screen reappears.

6. **Press the Escape key again to get back to the Social Feeds screen.**

7. **On the Social Feeds screen, select Social Filter.**

    Social Filter is the top scrollable bar. This bar behaves like a tab.

    A pop-up menu like the one on the left of Figure 11-14 appears.

Figure 11-13:
Choose
the social
networking
sites that
you want
to integrate
to Social
Feeds.

8. **Scroll in the top bar to display a specific network, and then select that network.**

   For example, we selected the Facebook icon. A pop-up screen similar to the right of Figure 11-14 appears.

9. **Select Log In.**

   The social network's login screen appears.

10. **Enter your username and password for that network in the appropriate fields.**

11. **Select Log In.**

    While Social Feeds logs in to your social network account, a status screen appears. After you're logged in, the main Social Feeds screen reappears, with the tab for the social network you signed into displaying the latest updates.

Figure 11-14: Filter a social network (left) and log into that social network (right).

Posting a status update by using Social Feeds

If you like to use a full-featured social networking app, don't fully discount Social Feeds. Social Feeds also allows you to post status updates across multiple networks in one go.

To post a status update to multiple networks by using Social Feeds, follow these steps:

1. **From the All panel of the Home screen, press the Menu key twice, and then select Social Feeds.**

2. **Press the Menu key, and then select New Post from the menu that appears (shown in the left of Figure 11-15).**

   The Post screen makes an appearance, similar to the right of Figure 11-15. This screen displays the icons of all the social networks you've integrated to Social Feeds. Each icon includes a check box.

Figure 11-15: Posting a status update to multiple social networks.

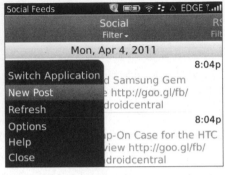

3. **Select the social network icons from the networks on which you want to update your status.**

   Selecting an icon marks the check box.

4. **Enter your status update in the Post field.**

5. **Select Post, located at the bottom of the screen.**

   You just made a status update to multiple social networks.

Finding Social Networking Apps in BlackBerry App World

With so many social networks, the app that you need may not be preinstalled on your BlackBerry. You can find any BlackBerry app in BlackBerry App World.

BlackBerry App World has over 30,000 apps, and thankfully, it offers ways to quickly find the apps you need (if you know the names of those apps). However, if you don't know the names, all isn't lost: You can locate a social networking app by browsing through the App World categories.

Follow these steps to browse through the list of social networking apps in BlackBerry App World:

1. **From the All panel of the Home screen, press the Menu key twice, and then select BlackBerry App World.**

   The icon for BlackBerry App World shows seven white dots with a circle around them.

   BlackBerry App World appears, displaying the Featured Items screen.

2. **Select Categories (which looks like a stack of folders) on the bottom of the screen.**

   The Categories screen appears, listing all the main app categories.

3. **From the list of categories, select IM & Social Networking.**

   In the IM & Social Networking screen that appears, Blogs, Instant Messaging, and Social Networking are listed.

4. **Select Social Networking.**

   A Social Networking screen appears, listing all the available apps related to social networking, as you can see in Figure 11-16.

5. **After you find the app you're looking for, select that app, and then follow the instructions to download and install the app.**

   If you need a rundown on how to install an app from BlackBerry App World, jump to Chapter 20.

Figure 11-16: Choose your social networking app in BlackBerry App World.

Chapter 12

Surfing the Internet Wave

*N*early everyone can surf the web anytime and anywhere from a desktop computer, a tablet PC, or even a tiny mobile device such as a smartphone. So, you're probably not surprised that your BlackBerry has a web browser of its own.

In this chapter, we show you how to use BlackBerry Browser. We give you shortcuts and timesaving tips, including the coolest ways to make pages load quickly, as well as a complete neat freak's guide to managing your bookmarks.

And because your network service provider may also have its own custom browser for you to use, we compare these proprietary browsers with the default BlackBerry Browser so that you can decide which of them best suits your needs.

Kicking Up Browser

BlackBerry Browser comes loaded on your smartphone and accesses the web by using a cellphone connection. Browser may have a different name, depending on how the service provider customizes it. Sometimes, Browser is named BlackBerry Browser; Internet Browser; Hotspot Browser; or, most likely, just Browser. We use Browser in this book for simplicity.

Browser has multiple personalities:

✓ **One that's connected to your company's BlackBerry Enterprise Server:** *BlackBerry Enterprise Server* is a software application from RIM (Research in Motion) that companies can use to control and manage BlackBerry devices. The software also allows your device to see your company's network and connect to your company's databases.

If you're a corporate BlackBerry user, your company administrator may turn off or not install browsers except for the one that connects through the company's BlackBerry Enterprise Server.

✓ **One that goes directly to your service provider's network:** The network service provider's brand-name browser.

✓ **One that uses a Wi-Fi connection:** A browser that accesses the Internet through a Wi-Fi connection and retrieves page content without having to go through BlackBerry Enterprise Server or BlackBerry Internet Service. Therefore, no web page you view goes through extra processing (such as compressing, or encrypting content and images) before Browser retrieves it. This lack of processing gives you a fast web-browsing experience.

The following sections get you started using Browser. After you get your feet wet, we promise that you'll be champing at the bit to find out more!

Getting to Browser

Browser is a main application on your device, and its Globe icon appears on the All panel of the Home screen, as shown in Figure 12-1. Open Browser by scrolling to this icon and then pressing the trackpad.

Figure 12-1: Open Browser from the All panel of the Home screen.

You can launch Browser from any application that distinguishes a web address. For example, from Contacts, you can open Browser by opening the link in the Web Page field. If you get an e-mail that contains a web address, just scroll to that link. The link is highlighted, and you can open the page by pressing the trackpad and selecting Yes from the pop-up confirmation message that appears, as shown in Figure 12-2.

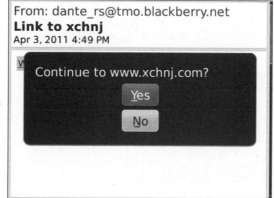

Figure 12-2:
Open
Browser
from
Messages.

When you access Browser from another application, you don't have to close that application to jump to Browser. Just press the Alt key (to the left of the Z key) and the Escape key at the same time to open a pop-up screen that contains application icons, like the ones in Figure 12-3. Use your trackpad to highlight the Browser icon, and then press the trackpad to launch Browser.

Figure 12-3:
Press
Alt+Escape
to open a
screen that
contains a
Browser
icon.

By default, accessing Browser by selecting a web address or a web link within another application opens the web page associated with that address. (In Figure 12-2, we're opening Browser from a link within the Messages application.)

Opening Browser by selecting its icon on the All panel of the Home screen displays a start page screen similar to Figure 12-4, which lists the latest websites you've visited. The page also shows a Bookmarks link. You can find out more about adding bookmarks in the "Bookmarking Your Favorite Sites" section, later in this chapter. Also, you can reconfigure how the start page screen and bookmarks appear, as explained in the "Exercising Options and Optimization Techniques" section, later in this chapter.

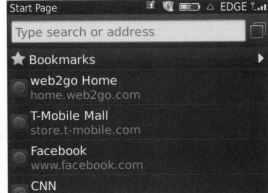

Figure 12-4: Browser's default start page screen.

Hitting the (air) waves

After you locate Browser, you're ready to surf the web. Follow these steps:

1. **From the All panel of the BlackBerry Home screen, press the Menu key twice, and then select the Browser application.**

   Unless you've changed the configuration, BlackBerry displays a default start page screen when you open Browser (refer to Figure 12-4).

2. **Type a web address in the field at the top of the screen, as shown in Figure 12-5.**

3. **Press the trackpad to load the page.**

   While the page is loading, you can see its progress at the bottom of the screen.

Figure 12-5:
Easily open
a web page
in Browser.

When you see a phone number or an e-mail address on a web page, you can scroll to that information to highlight it. Then, press the trackpad to initiate a phone call or open a new e-mail message, respectively.

Navigating web pages

You can easily navigate to a web page by using Browser. Hyperlinks appear highlighted onscreen. To jump to a page that a particular hyperlink connects to, scroll to the highlighted link and press the trackpad.

If your BlackBerry has a keypad, here are a few shortcuts that you can use while navigating a web page:

- **A:** Bookmark the page you're on.
- **B:** Go to the bottom of the page.
- **D:** Show recent downloads.
- **F:** Find text on the current page. A Find field appears, in which you can enter search criteria.
- **G:** Go to the start page.
- **I:** Zoom in.
- **K:** Display the Bookmarks screen.
- **O:** Zoom out.

- **P:** Display page properties.
- **R:** Refresh the page.
- **S:** Display the Options screen.
- **T:** Go to the top of the page.
- **W:** Select a different tab.
- **Y:** Display the History screen.
- **Space:** Move down one full display page at a time.
- **Shift+Space:** Move up one full display page at a time.
- **Escape:** If a page is loading, stop loading that page. If a page isn't loading, go back to the previous page (if there is one).
- **Alt+Escape:** Open another application without closing Browser.

Don't forget the Browser menu (which you can access by pressing the Menu key). It has some useful shortcuts, as shown in Figure 12-6.

Figure 12-6:
The
Browser
menu gives
you a lot of
options.

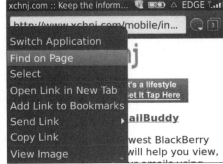 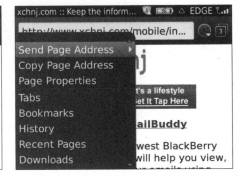

Here are the Browser menu options:

- **Switch Application:** Allows you to open other applications without closing Browser. This is the same as pressing Alt+Escape.
- **Find on Page:** Locates and highlights text within the current page. When you select this option, a Find field appears in which you can enter the text you want to find. After the initial search, a Find Next on Page is added to the Browser menu, allowing you to find the next matching text.
- **Copy:** Appears if you have highlighted text. Selecting Copy copies the highlighted text into memory so that you can paste that text somewhere else, such as in MemoPad.

✔ **Cancel Selection:** Appears if you have highlighted text. Selecting Cancel Selection removes the highlights.

✔ **Select:** Appears only if you have the trackpad pointer placed on text. Use this feature to highlight text onscreen so that you can copy it.

✔ **View Image:** Appears only if you highlight an image. Selecting View Image displays the image alone on the screen.

✔ **Save Image:** Appears only if you highlight an image, allowing you to save the image in the BlackBerry's built-in memory or to a microSD card.

✔ **Send Image Link:** Allows you to share a web link to the currently highlighted image via Email, Text Message, PIN, Messenger Contact, or Group Message, or through installed social networking apps.

✔ **Copy Image Link:** Copies the web link to the image into memory and allows you to paste it in other apps.

✔ **Zoom:** Zooms in and out. After selecting this option, slide the trackpad up to zoom in and down to zoom out. Press the trackpad to cancel zooming.

✔ **Back:** Appears only if you've navigated to more than one web page. If you select the Back option, you go back to the preceding page you viewed.

Also, you can go back to the preceding page by pressing the Escape key if no page is currently loading.

✔ **Forward:** Appears only if you've gone back at least one web page. The Forward option progresses one page at a time.

✔ **Stop:** Appears only if you're in the middle of requesting a page. Use Stop to cancel the request. This option is the same as pressing the Escape key while a page is loading.

✔ **Refresh:** Updates the current page. This option is helpful when you're viewing a page that contains data that changes frequently (such as stock quotes).

✔ **Home:** The shortcut to your home page. The default home page can vary from carrier to carrier, but to change it, press the Menu key, and then select Options from the menu that appears. In the Browser Options screen that appears, change the Home Page Address field.

✔ **Go To:** Opens the default start page. In the text field on this screen, enter the web address of the page you want to load, and then press the trackpad. When you enter addresses, they appear in the History portion of the screen so that you don't have to retype them. To find out how to clear this list, see the "Exercising Options and Optimization Techniques" section, later in this chapter.

- ✔ **Add to Bookmarks:** Allows you to bookmark the page you're currently on. See the section "Bookmarking Your Favorite Sites," later in this chapter, for more on how to create and manage bookmarks.

- ✔ **Add to Home Screen:** Creates a shortcut to this page in the Home screen.

- ✔ **Send Page Address:** Allows you to share this page's address through e-mail, text message, PIN message, BlackBerry Messenger, or one of the installed social networking apps. See the following section for more details.

- ✔ **Copy Page Address:** Copies the current page's address into memory, so you can paste the address to other apps.

- ✔ **Page Properties:** Shows the properties of the current page.

- ✔ **Tabs:** Open the Tabs screen, which displays all the current tabs. Tabs allow you to have multiple pages open at the same time.

- ✔ **Bookmarks:** Displays the Bookmarks screen, which lists the web pages you've bookmarked. See the section "Bookmarking Your Favorite Sites," later in this chapter, for the complete scoop on Bookmarks.

- ✔ **History:** Displays a list of the web pages you've visited and allows you to jump back quickly to them. The list is grouped by date.

- ✔ **Downloads:** Opens the Downloads screen, which lists files you've recently downloaded.

- ✔ **Options:** Opens the Browser Options screen, where you can change certain Browser settings. See the section "Exercising Options and Optimization Techniques," later in this chapter, to find out about these settings.

- ✔ **Help:** Like all BlackBerry applications, Browser always offers this option, which displays a quick guide.

When you try to open a web page, indicators that show the progress of your request appear at the bottom of the screen. The left side of Figure 12-7 shows Browser requesting a page; the right side of the figure shows that you've reached the page, which is still loading.

Your connection type appears on the upper-right side of the screen. Figure 12-7 shows 3G, for third generation wireless network. Likewise, you see WiFi if your BlackBerry is connected on a Wi-Fi network.

If you lose patience waiting for a page to load and want to browse somewhere else, press the Escape key to stop the page from loading.

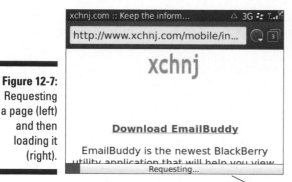 

Figure 12-7:
Requesting
a page (left)
and then
loading it
(right).

Progress indicators

Saving and sharing a web page address

Entering a web address when you want to view a page can get tedious.
Fortunately, you can return to a page without typing the same address. While
you're viewing a web page, simply press the Menu key to display the Browser
menu, shown in Figure 12-8, and then select Copy Page Address to copy that
page's address.

You can save and share a web page address in a couple of ways, using
options in the Browser menu:

Figure 12-8:
Use the
Browser
menu to
copy a
web page
address.

> ✓ **Send Page Address:** Presents a screen so that you can choose whether to send the address by e-mail, text message, PIN, or SMS. You can also send the address to a Messenger contact or through one of the social networking apps installed on your BlackBerry.
>
> ✓ **Copy Page Address:** Saves the page's address to your BlackBerry Clipboard and allows you to paste it somewhere else.

If you press a letter key while a menu is displayed, you select the first menu item that starts with that letter. Pressing the same letter again selects the next menu item that starts with that letter.

Saving web images

You can save images in BMP, GIF, JPEG, or PNG format from a web page. Your BlackBerry stores any saved image in the Pictures application, where you can view it later. To save an image, just highlight the image, and then select Save Image from the menu that appears.

Bookmarking Your Favorite Sites

You don't have to memorize all the addresses of your favorite sites. Instead, use BlackBerry Browser to keep a list of sites you want to revisit. In other words, make a bookmark so that you can come back to a site quickly.

Adding and visiting a bookmark

Add a new bookmark by following these steps:

1. **From the All panel of the BlackBerry Home screen, press the Menu key twice, and then select the Browser application.**

   The Browser application appears.

2. **Press the Menu key, and then select Go To from the menu that appears.**

3. **On the start page that appears, enter the web address to which you want to navigate, and then press the trackpad.**

   Browser loads the page.

4. **Press the Menu key, and then select Add to Bookmarks from the Browser menu that appears.**

5. **(Optional) In the Add to Bookmarks pop-up screen that appears, enter a title for the bookmark in the Title field.**

   The title of the bookmark defaults to the website title and, in most cases, you probably want to use that title as the name. But you always have the option to change this name.

6. **In the Add to Bookmarks pop-up screen, navigate to the folder where you want to save the bookmark.**

   You can see the pop-up screen in Figure 12-9. The default saved-bookmark folder is BlackBerry Bookmarks, but you can save the bookmark in any folder you create. To see how to create a bookmark folder, head to the section "Adding a bookmark subfolder," later in this chapter.

7. **Scroll to the bottom of the pop-up screen and Select Add.**

Follow these steps to open a bookmarked page:

1. **In Browser, press the Menu key, and then select Bookmarks from the menu that appears.**

   The Bookmarks screen appears, displaying all the pages you've bookmarked.

2. **Select the bookmark for the page you want to visit.**

   The page loads and appears on your BlackBerry.

Figure 12-9: Name the bookmark and specify where to store it.

Organizing your bookmarks

Over time, you'll increase your number of bookmarks. And when you have a lot of bookmarks, you may find trying to find the name of a certain site on a tiny screen tough. As a handy work-around, you can organize your bookmarks into folders. For example, you can group related sites in individual folders, and each folder can have one or more other folders inside it (subfolders). Having a folder hierarchy narrows your bookmark search and allows you to easily find the bookmark for a particular site.

For example, your sites might fall into the following categories:

- ✔ Reference
  - *New York Times*
  - Yahoo!
- ✔ Technology Reference
  - *TechCrunch*
  - *Wired*
- ✔ Fun
  - Flickr
  - *The Onion*
- ✔ Shopping
  - Etsy
  - Gaiam

Adding a bookmark subfolder

You can add subfolders only to folders that already appear on the Bookmarks page, which means that you can't create your own root folder. You can add your first subfolder in the web2go or BlackBerry Bookmarks folder.

Suppose that you want to add a Reference subfolder within your BlackBerry Bookmarks folder. Follow these quick and easy steps:

1. **In Browser, press the Menu key, and then select Bookmarks from the menu that appears.**

   The Bookmarks screen appears.

2. **On the Bookmarks screen, highlight BlackBerry Bookmarks.**

   The BlackBerry Bookmarks folder is called the parent of the new subfolder. In our example, we add the Reference subfolder to the BlackBerry Bookmarks folder.

3. **Press the Menu key, and then select Add Subfolder from the menu that appears, as shown in Figure 12-10.**

   A pop-up screen appears, where you can enter the name of the folder. (We're using Reference.)

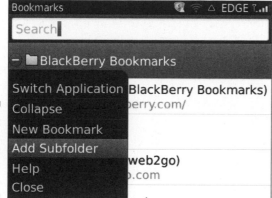

Figure 12-10:
The BlackBerry Bookmarks menu.

4. **Type the folder name in the text field, and then select OK.**

   The subfolder you created now appears on the Bookmarks screen (as shown in Figure 12-11), bearing a folder icon.

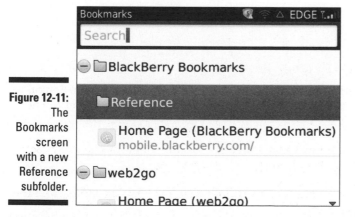

Figure 12-11:
The Bookmarks screen with a new Reference subfolder.

Renaming a bookmark folder

Although you can't rename the root bookmark folders, BlackBerry Bookmarks and web2go, the folders you create in them are fair game. Renaming a bookmark folder that you created is as easy as editing a bookmark. Follow these steps:

1. **In Browser, press the Menu key, and then select Bookmarks from the menu that appears.**

   The Bookmarks screen appears.

2. **On the Bookmarks screen, highlight the name of the folder that you want to change.**

3. **Press the Menu key, and then select Rename Folder from the menu that appears.**

   A pop-up screen appears, showing the folder name preselected within a text field.

4. **Type the name of the folder in the text field.**

5. **Select OK to save your changes.**

Moving a bookmark

If you feel like you've placed a bookmark in the wrong folder, move that bookmark where it belongs. Follow these steps:

1. **In Browser, press the Menu key, and then select Bookmarks from the menu that appears.**

   The Bookmarks screen appears.

2. **In the Bookmarks screen, highlight the bookmark, press the Menu key, and then select Move Bookmark from the menu that appears.**

3. **Use the trackpad to move to the location in the list where you want the bookmark to appear.**

4. **After you find the right location, press the trackpad.**

   Your bookmark is in its new home.

Cleaning up your bookmarks

Maybe you like a site but eventually stop visiting it. Or maybe a site disappears, and every time you select the bookmark, you see a 404 Not Found error. It's time to do a little spring cleaning. From the Bookmarks screen, highlight the name of the bookmark that you want to delete. Press the Menu key, and then select Delete Bookmark from the menu that appears. It's that easy.

You can — repeat, *can* — clean up bookmarks wholesale by deleting a folder. A word to the wise, though: All contents of that folder are deleted, so purge with caution.

Exercising Options and Optimization Techniques

Sure, Browser works out of the box, but folks have their own tastes, right? Look to Browser Options for attributes and features that you can customize.

In Browser, press the Menu key, and then select Options from the menu that appears. The Browser Options screen opens, as shown in Figure 12-12. This screen is divided into three sections: General, Web Content, and Privacy & Security.

Figure 12-12: The first two pages of the Browser Options screen.

Starting from the General section of the Browser Options screen, you can amend the following customization items (shown in Figure 12-12):

- **Startup Page:** Specify a starting page to load when you open Browser. You can choose from the default start page, which is the preloaded page that lists the web sites you've previously visited, or the home page, which is a web page you can specify in the Home Page field.

- **Home Page:** Enter the address of the page you want to make your home page, which you can access from the Browser menu.

- **Use Current:** Assigns the current web page you're browsing as your default home page.

✔ **Default Search:** Choose Browser's default search engine from the pop-up menu, which includes Google, Yahoo!, Live Search, Wikipedia, and Dictionary.com.

✔ **Enable Keyboard Shortcuts:** Keep this field selected if you want the keyboard shortcuts active.

✔ **Prompt Before:** You can have BlackBerry Browser give you a second chance before you do the following:

• *Closing Browser on Escape:* A confirmation screen appears before you exit BlackBerry Browser.

• *Closing Tabs on Exit:* A confirmation screen appears, notifying you that exiting Browser will close tabs you have open.

• *Switch to Carrier Network for Streaming Media:* A confirmation screen appears, prompting you to switch to Carrier Network when you stream media. Carrier Network is the wireless carrier's Internet network. This prompt shows up only if you're using the network carrier wireless signal and aren't using a Wi-Fi hotspot. Using your carrier's Internet network could mean additional bandwidth cost if you don't have an unlimited data plan.

Some network carriers may charge you a stiff fee after you go beyond your data plan's bandwidth. Be sure to check the terms of your data plan to avoid having to pay a ridiculous monthly bill for simply watching YouTube videos on your BlackBerry.

In the Web Content section of the Browser Options screen (the beginning of which is shown on the right of Figure 12-12), you can adjust the following settings:

✔ **Load Images:** Controls whether your BlackBerry displays websites' images. This setting is checked by default, which means Browser loads and displays images.

✔ **Enable JavaScript:** Many websites use the JavaScript scripting language to create dynamic web pages. A web page might not behave normally if you turn off this option. It's on by default.

✔ **Block Popups:** Most ad pages are launched as JavaScript pop-ups, so having this check box selected (which is the default) minimizes these ads. Be aware, though, that some important pages are also displayed as JavaScript pop-ups.

✔ **Enable Embedded Media:** Select this option to support media such as scalable vector graphics (SVG). Think of SVG as Adobe Flash for mobile devices such as the BlackBerry. SVG can include a still image or an animated one.

✔ **Default Font Size:** When a web page doesn't specify the text font size, Browser uses the one you specify in this option. The smaller the size, the harder it is to read, but the more text can fit onscreen.

✔ **Default Text Encoding:** Text encoding defines the encoding standards used for a transmitted web page. These standards ensure that a web browser can display characters properly. In most cases, the encoding is specified within the web page itself, so any browser knows how to decode the message. In cases where a web page's author doesn't specify the text encoding standards, BlackBerry uses the encoding specified in this field. Don't worry about this field unless you're viewing a web page that has a special encoding — we recommend you leave the default value (Windows-1250) because otherwise, some web pages may not be legible or may not even appear.

✔ **Auto-Detect Text Encoding:** When a web page doesn't specify text encoding, Browser tries to detect the most likely encoding used for that web page. Keep the default (Windows-1250) selected because this encoding also covers other sets of popular encoding standards and therefore encompasses a much wider set of characters, including characters used in European languages.

In the Privacy & Security section of the Browser Options screen, you can control the following settings:

✔ **Accept Cookies:** Most websites use *cookies* (pieces of text that a website creates and places in your BlackBerry's memory to remember something about you, such as your username). In many instances, not allowing cookies can greatly impair a web page from behaving properly, thus degrading your web-browsing experience. So, keep this option selected, which is the default, unless you don't want companies tracking your activities on the web and are willing to deal with browsing broken pages.

Caching your web experience

At any given time, your BlackBerry uses a few cache mechanisms. A *cache* (pronounced "cash") temporarily stores information used by Browser so that the next time the information is needed, Browser doesn't have to go back to the source website. The cache can speed up displays when you want to view the web page again, and you can access a cached site, even when you suddenly don't have any network coverage. A BlackBerry's cache may contain these bits of information:

✔ When you visit a site that uses cookies, Browser caches those cookies.

✔ When a website *pushes* (sends) web pages to your BlackBerry device. An icon appears on the Home screen, which you can select to quickly view the page. After the web page is delivered to your BlackBerry, it becomes available, even if you leave the coverage area.

✔ The addresses of the pages you've visited (meaning the latest 20 sites in your history list).

✓ **Enable Geolocation:** Allows websites to know your location by using the built-in GPS of your BlackBerry. If a web page is trying to get your location for the first time, a prompt appears in which you need to grant permission before a website can access your location information.

✓ **Geolocation Permissions:** Displays a screen that shows all the websites you've granted permission to know your location.

✓ **Clear Browsing Data:** By selecting Clear Now at the bottom of the Browser Options screen, a pop-up progress screen momentarily appears, disappearing as soon as Browser finishes clearing the cache. What Browser information storage areas you can clear by selecting Clear Now depends on the following options (which you can set towards the bottom of the Browser Options screen):

- *Passwords:* All website passwords that your BlackBerry has cached. Selected by default.

- *History:* The list of sites you've visited by using Browser. You may want to clear the History if you don't want other people to know which websites you visit on your BlackBerry, in case someone gets hold of your device. This setting is selected by default.

- *Cookies:* Any cookies stored on your BlackBerry. Cookies contain information that a website needs to remember about you, such as your user ID and password. Unchecked by default.

- *Cache:* All existing cookies used by web pages. Unchecked by default.

- *Pushed Content:* Any content that was pushed to your BlackBerry from Push Services subscriptions. Push Services was popular during the early years of the BlackBerry, when network carriers didn't have broadband-like speed offerings. Some companies provided services to push data into your BlackBerry regularly. The most common ones are news-related web pages. Links to these pushed web pages appear in the Home screen, which you can open through Browser. You may want to clear this option to free memory on your BlackBerry. Unchecked by default.

The Clear Browsing Data option at the bottom of the Browser Options screen, as shown in Figure 12-13, allows you to manually clear your cache. Select Clear Now to clear the selected cache information.

Speeding up browsing

On a wireless network, many factors can affect the speed with which web pages load. If you find that browsing the web is extremely slow, you can make your pages load faster in exchange for not using a few features. Here are some of the speed-enhancing work-arounds you can use:

✔ **Don't display images.** You can achieve a big performance improvement by turning off image display. Press the Menu key in Browser, select Browser Options from the menu that appears, scroll to Load Images in the Web Content section of the Browser Options screen that appears, and then press the trackpad to uncheck the field.

✔ **Check your BlackBerry memory.** When your BlackBerry's running low on free memory, its performance degrades. The BlackBerry low-memory manager calls each application every now and then, telling each one to free resources.

  Hint #1: Don't leave many e-mail messages unread. When the low-memory manager kicks in, Messages tries to delete old messages, but it can't delete unread messages.

  Hint #2: Purge the BlackBerry event log to free needed space. Enter the letters **LGLG**

while holding down the Alt key. An event log opens, displaying entries that may not make sense to you (they consist mostly of cryptic codes). Although technical-minded folks trying to figure out what's going on in your BlackBerry might find these codes helpful, you don't need the codes. You can clear the event log to free memory.

✔ **Turn off other features.** If you're interested mostly in viewing content, consider turning off features that pertain to processing the content, such as Enable JavaScript. Also, select Block Popups so that Browser doesn't have to download the page that displays the pop-ups. To turn off other Browser features, navigate to Browser Options by pressing the Menu key and selecting Options (see the section "Exercising Options and Optimization Techniques," in this chapter).

Warning: We don't advise having features turned off while you perform an important task, such as online banking. Depending on what features you turn off, you may not be able to perform certain actions on the page. For example, the Submit button might not work — and you definitely want to be able to submit that bank deposit information.

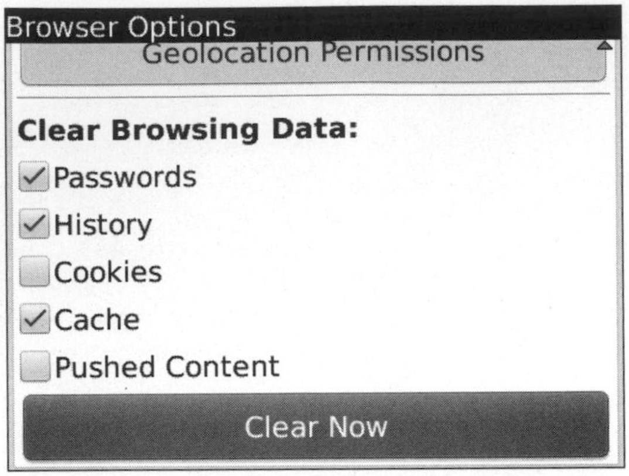

Browser Options
Geolocation Permissions

Clear Browsing Data:

☑ Passwords

☑ History

☐ Cookies

☑ Cache

☐ Pushed Content

Clear Now

Figure 12-13:
The Cache
Operations
screen.

Installing Applications from the Web

You can download and install applications on your BlackBerry via Browser if the application has a link that lets you download and install the files. (See Chapter 20 for other installation options.) You can easily download and install apps that include links. Follow these steps:

1. **From the All panel of the BlackBerry Home screen, press the Menu key twice, and then select the Browser application.**

2. **From the Browser screen, press the Menu key, and then select Go To from the menu that appears.**

3. **In the start page that appears, type a web address in the field at the top of the screen.**

4. **Press the trackpad to load the page.**

   A simple prompt that looks like the screen shown in Figure 12-14 appears. The screen displays what you're about to download. In the case of Figure 12-14, we're downloading SendMeLater (from www. xchnj.com), an application that lets you send form e-mails.

5. **Select Load.**

   The download starts, and a progress screen appears.

   As long as you stay within network coverage while the download is progressing, your BlackBerry can finish the download *and* install the application for you. If the download and installation finishes without any problems, you see the screen shown in Figure 12-15.

Figure 12-14:
A typical page that lets you download an application on your BlackBerry.

Figure 12-15:
The download and installation were completed.

Like with a computer, the download might or might not work for a variety of reasons. Sometimes the application

✔ Requires you to install software that the application needs

✔ Works only on a certain version of the BlackBerry OS

You may be able to avoid these issues, depending on the sophistication of the site that publishes the link. Most reputable sources have resolved these issues, and you can successfully download and install their apps in a snap.

Installing applications from a source that isn't reputable can cause your BlackBerry to become unstable. Before you download an application from the web, be sure to read reviews about that particular app. Most of the time, other people who tried the software provide reviews or feedback.

BlackBerry App World isn't the only place to find app reviews — be sure to check BlackBerry enthusiasts' websites, too. The top websites include CrackBerry.com, BlackBerry Cool (www.blackberrycool.com), BerryReview.com, and IntoMobile (www.intomobile.com).

If you have a company-issued device, your BlackBerry Enterprise Server administrator can disable the feature in your BlackBerry to download and install an application. If you have problems downloading and installing an application, check your company policy or contact the BlackBerry support person in your company.

If you download an application that turns out to be a dud, uninstall it. See Chapter 20 for more on uninstalling an application from your BlackBerry.

Browser's Behavior in Business

Getting a device from your employer has both a good side and an ugly side:

- ✔ **Good:** Your company foots the bill.
- ✔ **Ugly:** Your company foots the bill.

Because your company pays, it dictates what you can and can't do with your BlackBerry, especially with respect to browsing the web.

Two scenarios come into play when it comes to using your BlackBerry Browser in business:

- ✔ **Browser is running under your company's BlackBerry Enterprise Server.** In this setup, your BlackBerry Browser is connecting to the Internet by using your company's Internet connection. It's like using your desktop machine at work.
- ✔ **Browser is connected through a network service provider.** Most of the time, this kind of Browser has the company's name.

In most cases, your device fits into only one scenario — for example, when your Browser is connected by your company's BlackBerry Enterprise Server. Some lucky folks may have both. Whichever scenario you're in, the following sections describe the major differences between the two situations and explain what you can expect.

Using Browser on your company's BlackBerry Enterprise Server

In an enterprise setup, your BlackBerry Browser (named simply BlackBerry Browser) is connected through your company's BlackBerry Enterprise Server, which is located inside your company's intranet. This setup allows the company to better manage the privileges you have and the functions you can use on your device.

The company uses the existing Internet infrastructure, including the company's firewall. Because you're within the company's network, the boundaries that your network administrator set up on your account apply to your BlackBerry, as well. For example, when you browse the web, your BlackBerry doesn't display any websites that your company's server blocks.

The good thing, though, is that you can browse the company's intranet, meaning that all the company web pages you have access to when you use your company's computer are available also on your BlackBerry.

 Know (and respect) your company's web-browsing policy. Most companies keep logs of sites you view on your BlackBerry Browser and might even have software to monitor usage. Also, your company might not allow downloading from the web.

Using your network provider's browser

Any new device that comes from a network service provider can come with its own, branded web browser. It's the same BlackBerry Browser, but the behavior might differ in the following ways:

- ✔ **The name is different.** For example, T-Zones for T-Mobile.

- ✔ **The default home page usually points to the provider's website.** You may want to keep this site as your home page because, most of the time, the network provider's website is full of links that you may not find on BlackBerry Browser.

- ✔ **You can browse more sites.** Your company's policy doesn't limit the sites you can access.

Part IV
Applications and Media on Your BlackBerry

The 5th Wave   By Rich Tennant

"Hold on, Barbara. I'm sure App World has a BlackBerry application for just such a situation."

In this part . . .

In this part, we explain how to navigate your way by using GPS on your BlackBerry, as well as how to use your BlackBerry as a still and video camera. You can get the scoop on entertaining yourself and having fun through BlackBerry's multimedia capabilities. And, finally, we help you figure out how to manage your media files.

Chapter 13

Getting Around with Your BlackBerry GPS

A few years back, when some of the North American network carriers introduced GPS on their versions of the BlackBerry, we were quite impressed . . . until we tried it. The response time was slow, and it wasn't accurate. On top of that, the network carriers charged users an arm and a leg for this inferior service. As it turns out, those GPS functions were implemented by using the network — that is, GPS wasn't embedded in the BlackBerry. How low-tech!

Today, most BlackBerry smartphones come with built-in GPS, which makes finding yourself easy. In this chapter, we show you how to use your BlackBerry's built-in GPS and discuss the best GPS applications that you can use on your BlackBerry, two of which are free!

Putting Safety First

Some GPS features are useful while you're driving a car. However, even if you use your BlackBerry GPS while driving, we *strongly* suggest that you *don't* adjust it while you're driving because risk of an accident increases when you're not paying attention to the road.

Before you start using BlackBerry GPS in your car, you need a BlackBerry car holder — preferably a car kit that includes a car charger. You can buy a car kit on the Internet; just search for *BlackBerry car kit*. Or go to one of the following websites:

You're being watched!

RIM opted to enable GPS by default on all devices shipped for the past few years purely to collect GPS info from all users. Why, you ask? Because RIM bought Dash, a company that developed GPS-related tech to gather GPS information from as many users as possible so that it can provide directions that take road conditions and traffic patterns into consideration when it routes users around problem areas. Because RIM enables GPS by default, all users are providing their location info (including speed) to RIM, and RIM feeds that info into a central database. But your BlackBerry incurs data charges to pass data back to RIM, you compromise battery life by leaving the GPS receiver operating 24/7, and you even put personal privacy at risk because RIM can locate any user who has GPS enabled without that user's knowledge or approval.

To prevent RIM from collecting your location data, follow these steps:

1. **On the Home screen, press the Menu key twice, and then select Options Application.**

   The Options screen appears.

2. **Select Device, and then select Location Settings Options.**

   The Location Settings screen opens.

3. **On the Location Settings screen, select Disable from the Location Data Setting pop-up menu.**

4. **Press the Menu key, and then select Save from the menu that appears.**

✔ BlackBerry Authentic Accessories (www.shopblackberry.com)

✔ ShopCrackBerry.com (http://shop.crackberry.com)

What Your BlackBerry Needs for GPS

For GPS to work on your BlackBerry, it needs navigation maps, which it usually downloads in little pieces, as required. And because these maps are downloaded, you must subscribe to a data plan and have a radio signal to obtain them.

The more you use your GPS while you move about, the more data (map pieces) your BlackBerry downloads. If you don't subscribe to an unlimited data plan from your network carrier, you'll incur charges if you go over your data limit.

In summary, for your BlackBerry GPS to work, you need

- **A data plan from your network carrier:** We recommend an unlimited data plan.

- **To be in an area where you have a radio signal:** You need a signal to be able to download the maps.

Your GPS Application Choices

The GPS applications that you can use on your BlackBerry are

- **BlackBerry Maps** (comes with your BlackBerry): Free

- **Google Maps for Mobile** (www.google.com/mobile/maps): Free

- **Garmin Mobile** (www.garmin.com/mobile/mobilext): $99 one-time fee

- **TeleNav GPS Navigator** (www.telenav.com/products/tn): $9.99 per month

The icons for Google Maps for Mobile and BlackBerry Maps are shown in Figure 13-1.

Figure 13-1:
BlackBerry
GPS
applications.

BlackBerry Maps

Your BlackBerry probably comes with the BlackBerry Maps application loaded (refer to Figure 13-1).

If you have a BlackBerry with AT&T as your network carrier, you might not have BlackBerry Maps installed out of the box. You can download it from your BlackBerry at `http://mobile.blackberry.com`. (Also, the following sections discuss alternatives to BlackBerry Maps that still take advantage of your BlackBerry GPS.)

With or without GPS (built-in or external), you can use BlackBerry Maps to do the following (see Figure 13-2):

- ✔ Find a location by typing an address or by using Contacts.
- ✔ Get point-to-point directions.
- ✔ E-mail or SMS a location to colleagues and friends.
- ✔ Turn GPS on or off.
- ✔ Zoom in and out of the map.

Of course, with GPS turned on, you can track where you are and follow point-to-point directions, as shown in Figure 13-2.

Figure 13-2:
BlackBerry
Maps on a
BlackBerry
with GPS
turned on.

Google Maps for Mobile

Google Maps for Mobile is the app version of the Google Maps website (http://maps.google.com). It has most of the features of the online version, including satellite imaging and traffic information. Best of all, it's free.

Like BlackBerry Maps, you can use Google Maps for Mobile even without GPS. With Google Maps on your BlackBerry, you can search for businesses and landmarks; it's like having the ultimate 411 (with a map) at the tip of your fingers.

Because Google Maps for Mobile doesn't come with your BlackBerry, you need to download it. To do so, use your BlackBerry to go to www.google.com/gmm and select the Install Now button. After the program downloads, its icon appears on your Home screen (refer to Figure 13-1).

After installation, the Google Maps for Mobile icon appears on your Home screen. Select the icon, and then press the Menu key to display the menu shown in Figure 13-3.

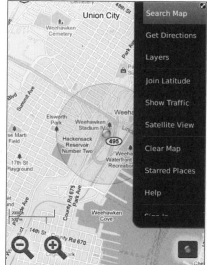

Figure 13-3: The Google Maps for Mobile menu.

From the menu, you can do the following:

- ✔ Find businesses and landmarks, including phone numbers, address information, and web addresses.
- ✔ Find and map exact addresses.
- ✔ Get step-by-step directions from Point A to Point B.
- ✔ View a satellite image of the current map (see Figure 13-4).
- ✔ Get traffic information for major highways.

Figure 13-4: Google Maps for Mobile can display a satellite photo.

With Google's MyLocation feature turned on, you can see your current location as a blue blinking dot.

Here are some keyboard shortcuts for Google Maps for Mobile:

- ✔ **Zoom in:** I key
- ✔ **Zoom out:** O key
- ✔ **Go to the current location:** 0 (zero) key

You need a radio signal to download maps to your BlackBerry. Additionally, we recommend that you have an unlimited data plan if you frequently use the GPS feature on your BlackBerry because downloading maps can use up a limited data plan quickly.

TeleNav GPS Navigator

TeleNav GPS Navigator is a full-featured GPS solution. It's intended as a GPS device replacement, which means the folks at TeleNav want you to use your BlackBerry in the car. TeleNav's feature list is extensive. From 3D maps to a real-time compass to finding Wi-Fi hotspots, the list goes on and on. It even lets you input the address by speaking it, rather than typing, and it responds by speaking the directions to you. Figure 13-5 shows the main menu for TeleNav. (***Note:*** Some versions of TeleNav have network branding; for example, Figure 13-5 shows an AT&T version. TeleNav has similar functionalities, regardless of network branding.)

Figure 13-5: The AT&T-branded version of the TeleNav main screen.

The extensive features come at a price. Depending on your network carrier, TeleNav costs about $10 per month. TeleNav does offer a 30-day free trial. Visit www.telenav.com/products/tn for more information. After the product is downloaded, its icon appears on your screen.

Garmin Mobile

Like TeleNav, Garmin offers a full-featured GPS solution. Garmin charges a one-time fee of $99, which is good for the life of the device. The features of Garmin Mobile are very similar to its GPS counterpart. If you've ever owned a Garmin GPS, you'll be familiar with the Garmin Mobile user interface. Figure 13-6 shows the main menu for Garmin Mobile.

Figure 13-6:
Garmin
Mobile's
main
screen.

We like the simplicity of Garmin's user interface and its one-time cost.

To find out more, visit www.garmin.com/mobile/mobilext.

Chapter 14

Taking Great Pictures and Capturing Videos

....

....

*O*h, shoot, you forgot your camera. Don't worry! Your BlackBerry is there when you need to capture the unbelievable: Grandma doing a handstand, Grandpa doing a cartwheel, or your roommate doing her laundry. And, if pictures aren't enough, you can record your unbelievable scene in full motion.

Before you try taking pictures, read this chapter so that you know what to expect and how to get the best shot. We walk you through the easy steps for capturing that funny pose and tell you how to store those photos and videos. Don't miss reading how to share the joy with your buddies, too.

Just about every BlackBerry has a camera, but some companies have a no-camera policy. Yes, Research in Motion (RIM) makes versions of some of their models minus the camera. If you're holding that camera-less BlackBerry smartphone, you can skip this chapter.

Saying "Cheese"

Snapping shots with your BlackBerry couldn't be easier. Just turn on the Camera app, line up your shot, and snap away. Follow these general steps:

1. **Press the right convenience key (the bottom key on the right side of your BlackBerry) to open the Camera application.**

   Figure 14-1 shows the Camera screen on the BlackBerry Bold. Most network carriers set the right convenience key on the BlackBerry to bring up the Camera application. However, network carriers may change this setting. Therefore, if you don't see the Camera app when you press the right-side key, use the alternative to launching the Camera application: Select the Camera icon from the Home screen.

Figure 14-1:
The camera
screen,
ready to
take
pictures,
on the
BlackBerry
Bold.

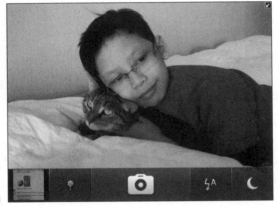

   Make sure that your finger isn't blocking the lens on the back of your device.

   The camera button on the right side of your BlackBerry is really a convenience key, which you can program to open your favorite application. By default, it's set to launch Camera. Chapter 3 shows how to change this setting.

2. **When you see the image onscreen, press the Camera key to take the picture.**

   You should hear a funky shutter-like sound. Neat and easy, isn't it?

Reading the screen indicators

When you open the Camera application, you see the screen shown in Figure 14-1. The top portion of this screen shows you the image you're about to capture. Immediately below the preview are selectable icons (starting from the left):

✔ **Image of the last picture you took:** Access Camera Pictures screen.

✔ **Red location dot:** Turn geotagging on or off.

✔ **Zigzagging arrow:** Turn flash on or off.

✔ **Crescent moon:** Display scene modes.

Choosing the picture size

Your BlackBerry can capture images with as much resolution as 2.0 megapixels (MP) to 5.0 MP, depending on the model. Saving images at this resolution requires considerable space. When you shoot photos, consider saving the images at a small size to save some space on your BlackBerry.

Get a big microSD card. A 32GB microSD card is inexpensive, and it holds thousands of pictures.

Here are the three sizes, in pixels, that you can choose:

✔ **Large:** 2048 x 1536 for 3MP and 2592 x 1944 for 5MP. The default setting.

Large uses the most memory of all the size options.

✔ **Medium:** 1024 x 768.

✔ **Small:** 640 x 480.

If you're just taking pictures of your friends' faces so that you can attach them to caller IDs, Small gets the job done.

Changing picture size is a snap. Follow these steps:

1. **Press the right convenience key to open the Camera application.**

2. **Press the Menu key, and then select Options from the menu that appears.**

   The Options screen appears.

3. **Highlight Image Size, press the trackpad, and then select the size you want from the menu that appears.**

4. **Press the Escape key, and then select Save from the confirmation screen that appears.**

   The picture size you chose is active.

Zooming and focusing

You need a steady hand to get a good focus while you take your shots. Although it's convenient to use one hand while taking pictures, most of the time, you get a blurry image if you do.

When you take pictures, hold your BlackBerry with both hands — one holding the smartphone steady and the other pressing the trackpad. If the right convenience key is set to Camera, you can press that key, rather than the trackpad. Holding the smartphone with both hands is even more important if you're zooming in.

Here's what you need to do to focus and zoom:

- ✓ **To focus:** Your camera has autofocus. Just hold it steady.
- ✓ **To zoom in:** Slide up on the trackpad.
- ✓ **To zoom out:** Slide down on the trackpad.

While zooming, a vertical zoom indicator appears on the right side of the screen. The white fill on the bar goes up and down, depending on the direction you scroll, to indicate the amount of zoom.

When you zoom, your thumb is already on the trackpad. What a convenient way to take the picture — just press.

We don't recommend using the zoom. Digital zoom (which is what your camera has) gives poor results because its software degrades the quality of the picture. The higher the zoom factor, the more pixelated the picture becomes. To get a clearer picture, get closer to the object.

Setting the flash

Most BlackBerry models come with a flash, indicated by the second icon from the right on the Camera screen. The default is Automatic, which shows a lightning bolt with the letter *A*. Automatic means that the camera detects the amount of light you have at the moment you capture the image. If you're taking the picture in a dark environment, the flash fires; otherwise, it doesn't.

If your BlackBerry has flash, you can set it to On, Off, or Automatic. The default setting is Automatic. When set to Off, the lightning bolt is encircled with a diagonal line running over it, similar to what you see on No Smoking signs. To cycle through the settings, scroll to highlight the flash indicator and then press the trackpad.

Setting the scene mode

In photography, the quality of the picture you take always depends on the amount of light you have on the subject. You need to find the optimum amount of light to make the best picture. Not enough light can create a dark image; too much light can result in overexposure. Many factors affect the amount of light hitting the camera sensor. (For folks who want to know more about this photography thing, we suggest you pick up *Photography For Dummies, 2nd Edition,* by Russell Hart.)

Fortunately, you don't have to be a photography geek to snap a good photo. BlackBerry has several settings designed for everyday camera use that can help you get the best photograph possible. Each scene mode has certain predefined settings. To display the scene modes (shown in Figure 14-2), select the bottom-right icon on the Camera screen. You can choose from any of the following modes:

- **Auto:** The default. Your camera determines what settings to apply.

- **Face Detection:** Best for taking pictures of a group of people. The camera detects faces and puts them in focus.

- **Portrait:** The settings of this scene mode accurately reproduce skin tones. Use this scene mode when you're capturing people's portraits.

- **Sports:** Designed to get a good image of quick-moving objects.

- **Landscape:** Allows you to have a much bigger area of focus, giving sharp details on a large subject, such as a mountain range.

- **Party:** Ideal for capturing people in an indoor environment that doesn't have much light.

- **Close-Up:** Captures an image of an object that's very close to the camera.

- **Snow:** For taking pictures with snow as the background. This scene mode compensates for the whiteness around you by adjusting the brightness to accurately reproduce colors.

- **Beach:** Accurately reproduces scenes that combine sea, sand, and sky.

- **Night:** Captures nighttime outdoor scenes that have low light.

- **Text:** Takes an image of a document that has a white background (paper).

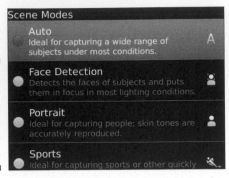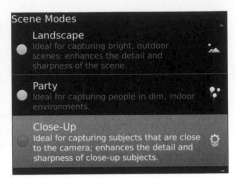

Figure 14-2: Choose your scene mode in the Scene Modes screen.

Geotagging

Because your BlackBerry has GPS capability, it can easily determine your location based on longitude and latitude. BlackBerry can also look up the city you're currently in and store the city information in the filename on the pictures that you take from your camera. So, you don't have to wonder where you took that crazy pose. Adding geographic information to photos is called *geotagging*.

Your BlackBerry has geotagging enabled by default. Select its icon (second from the left on the bottom of the Camera screen) to display the Geotagging Options screen, shown in Figure 14-3, which allows you to show or hide the location overlay or turn off geotagging completely.

Figure 14-3: Specify whether you want to overlay location information in your photos.

Working with Pictures

After you take a bunch of pictures, you probably want to see them. And maybe delete the unflattering ones. Or perhaps organize them. No problem — the following sections tell you how to deal with your BlackBerry photos.

Viewing pictures

If you take a picture, you want to see it, right? When you capture an image, it appears on your BlackBerry screen right then and there, as shown in Figure 14-4. You can select the camera icon to go back to the Camera screen so that you can take more pictures. Or select the red X icon to delete the current picture. If you don't do anything, after about three seconds, your photo disappears, and you go back to the Camera screen, which is ready to take more pictures.

Figure 14-4: The Camera screen after taking a picture.

From the Camera screen, you can easily get to your pictures by selecting the bottom-left icon. The last picture you took appears on the screen, and a number that indicates the ordinal position of the picture appears momentarily, as shown in Figure 14-5. You can browse through your pictures by sliding the trackpad left to right (or right to left).

Camera Pictures
1 of 180

Figure 14-5:
Look at the
pictures
you've taken
with your
BlackBerry.

All the pictures you take with your Camera are saved in a folder in your BlackBerry. The default folder location depends on whether you have a microSD card:

✔ **Device Memory:** `/Device Memory/home/user/pictures`

✔ **Media Card:** `/Media Card/BlackBerry/pictures`

If you have a microSD card on your BlackBerry, the pictures taken from your camera always go to Media Card. The format of the filename is based on the city (if you have geotagging on), the current date, and a certain number. The filename format looks like this: `<City>-<yyyymmdd>-<counter>`.`jpg`. So, if you take the 12th picture on April 20, 2012 in New York City, you end up with `New York-20120420-00012.jpg`.

If you're browsing through your picture folders, view a picture by highlighting it and then pressing the trackpad.

Creating a slide show

To see your pictures in a slide show, follow these steps:

1. **Press the right convenience key to open the Camera application.**

2. **From the Camera screen, press the Menu key, and then select View Pictures from the menu that appears.**

    The Camera Pictures screen shows up, displaying your camera pictures.

3. **Press the Menu key, and then select View Slide Show from the menu that appears.**

    Voilà! Your BlackBerry displays your pictures one at a time at a regular time interval. Each picture also is zoomed in and out while it's displayed during the slide show.

The default interval between each picture in a slide show is two seconds; if you aren't happy with this interval, change it in the Options screen. (Press the Menu key, and then select Options from the menu that appears to get to the Options screen.)

Trashing pictures

If you don't like an image that you captured, you can delete it. Follow these steps:

1. **Press the right convenience key to open the Camera application.**

2. **From the Camera screen, press the Menu key, and then select View Pictures from the menu that appears.**

   The Camera Pictures screen appears, displaying your camera pictures.

3. **Highlight the picture that you want to trash.**

4. **Press the Menu key, and then select Delete from the menu that appears.**

   Alternatively, press the Del key.

   A confirmation screen appears.

5. **Select Delete on the confirmation screen.**

You can also delete an image right after you take the picture; just select the red X icon when you view the photo (refer to Figure 14-4).

Listing filenames versus thumbnails

When you open a folder packed with pictures, your BlackBerry automatically shows *thumbnails,* which are small previews of your pictures.

A preview is nice, but what if you want to search for a picture by filename? Follow these steps to change the thumbnails to filenames:

1. **Press the right convenience key to open the Camera application.**

2. **From the Camera screen, press the Menu key, and then select View Pictures from the menu that appears.**

   The Camera Pictures screen appears, displaying your camera pictures.

3. **Press the Menu key, and then select View List from the menu that appears.**

   That's exactly what you get: a list of all the pictures in the folder. The View List option also displays the file size, which can give you a clue about what settings you used to take the picture. For example, a Large-size photo produces a much bigger file compared to a Small-size photo.

Checking picture properties

If you're curious about the amount of memory your picture is using or want to know at what time you took a photo, you can find out. To see a photo's properties, follow these steps:

1. **Press the right convenience key to open the Camera application.**

2. **From the Camera screen, press the Menu key, and then select View Pictures from the menu that appears.**

   The Camera Pictures screen shows up, displaying your camera pictures.

3. **Highlight the picture whose properties you want to see.**

4. **Press the Menu key, and then select Properties from the menu that appears.**

   A screen similar to Figure 14-6 appears, displaying the file's location in your BlackBerry, the file's size, and its last modification.

 Scroll down the Picture Properties screen to find the Hidden check box field. If you select the Hidden check box, you hide the file when you navigate through your picture list. After you hide a file, you can see it in your BlackBerry again only by using Explore. Check out Chapter 15 for details about Explore.

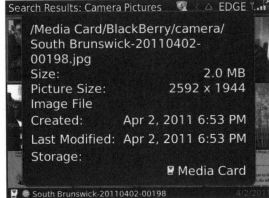

Figure 14-6: Your picture's properties.

Search Results: Camera Pictures ◌ ⊗ △ EDGE 📶
/Media Card/BlackBerry/camera/
South Brunswick-20110402-00198.jpg
Size: 2.0 MB
Picture Size: 2592 x 1944
Image File
Created: Apr 2, 2011 6:53 PM
Last Modified: Apr 2, 2011 6:53 PM
Storage:
                                 🗎 Media Card
🗎 ◎ South Brunswick-20110402-00198   4/2/2011

Renaming a picture file

BlackBerry automatically names a file when you capture a picture. However, the name of the picture is generic, something like *City-CurrentDate-Number*. Not very descriptive.

If you can, make it a habit to rename a photo as soon as you capture it. Using a name such as Dean Blows Out Birthday Candles is much more helpful than New Brunswick-20111014-00029.

You can easily rename a photo file by following these steps:

1. **Press the right convenience key to open the Camera application.**

2. **In the Camera screen, press the Menu key, and then select View Pictures from the menu that appears.**

   The Camera Pictures screen appears, displaying your camera pictures.

3. **Select the picture.**

4. **Press the Menu key, and then select Rename from the menu that appears.**

   A Rename screen appears, as shown in Figure 14-7.

5. **Enter the name that you want to give this picture, and then select Save.**

   You return to Camera Pictures screen, which displays your renamed picture.

Figure 14-7:
Rename
your pic-
ture in the
Rename
screen.

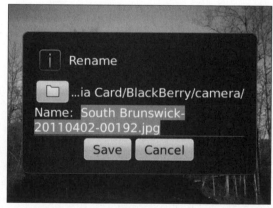

Sharing your pictures

Where's the joy in taking great pictures if you're the only one seeing them? Your BlackBerry has several options for sharing your bundle of joy. Follow these steps to send a photo to friends:

1. **Press the right convenience key to open the Camera application.**

2. **From the Camera screen, press the Menu key, and then select View Pictures from the menu that appears.**

   The Camera Pictures screen shows up, displaying your camera pictures.

3. **Highlight a picture that you want to share.**

4. **Press the Menu key, and then select Send from the menu that appears.**

   A submenu appears, allowing you to choose how you want to share the picture.

5. **Select one of the choices that appears in the submenu.**

   Here are your options:

   - *Email:* Selecting this option takes you directly to the Message screen so that you can compose an e-mail, with the selected picture as an attachment.

   - *Text Message:* Similar to Email, this option opens a Compose Text Message screen, with the selected picture as an attachment. Selecting Text Message first displays Contacts, where you select the person with the phone number you want to receive the text message. Also, when you send a photo by text message, the BlackBerry sends a tiny version of the picture, rather than the original size you see on your BlackBerry.

   - *Twitter:* Upload this picture to Twitter and post it as a status on your home page.

   - *Messenger Contact:* This option is available if you have BlackBerry Messenger installed. This function is similar to Text Message, but it displays only those contacts you have in BlackBerry Messenger. It uses BlackBerry Messenger to send a tiny version of the picture file.

   - *Group:* This option is available if you're a member of a group on BlackBerry Messenger. This function is similar to Messenger Contact, but it displays only your BlackBerry Messenger groups.

   - *Facebook:* This option is available only if you have Facebook installed on your BlackBerry. Selecting it uploads this picture to your Facebook Profile page.

   - *Bluetooth:* Send the picture to any Bluetooth-capable device.

You might see other ways to send a picture file if you have other Instant Messaging (IM) clients installed. For example, if you have Google Talk installed, you see the Google Talk option, which lets you send the picture in a Google Talk IM.

Setting a picture as Caller ID

Wouldn't it be nice if, when your girlfriend calls, you could see her beautiful face? You can. Start by taking a photo of her by using your BlackBerry. Then, follow these steps:

1. **From the Media panel of the Home screen, select Pictures.**

   The Pictures screen appears.

2. **Navigate to the location of the photo.**

3. **Highlight the photo that you want to appear when the person calls.**

4. **Press the Menu key, and then select Assign to Contact from the menu that appears.**

   The photo appears onscreen, with a superimposed, portrait-size cropping rectangle. Inside the rectangle is a clear view of the photo; outside the rectangle, the photo is blurry. The clear view represents the portion of the photo that you want to show. You can move the trackpad to move the rectangle to make sure that your cropping captures the face.

5. **Crop the photo by pressing the trackpad and then selecting Crop and Save from the menu that appears.**

   The Contacts screen appears.

6. **Select the contact you want this picture to represent.**

   A message that indicates a picture is set for that contact appears. You're done.

   You can also add a photo to your contacts through the Contacts application (refer to Chapter 4).

Setting a Home screen image

Suppose you have a stunning picture that you want to use as the background image for your BlackBerry. Follow these steps to set the image:

1. **From the Media panel of the Home screen, select Pictures.**

   The Pictures screen appears.

2. **Navigate to the location of the picture you want to use.**

3. **Highlight the picture.**

4. **Press the Menu key, and then select Set as Wallpaper from the menu that appears.**

Say Action: Capturing Video

Your BlackBerry camera application can do more than take still photos. You can also use it to shoot videos.

Follow these quick and easy steps to use Video Camera mode:

1. **Open the Camera application.**

2. **Press the Menu key, and then select Video Camera from the menu that appears, as shown in Figure 14-8.**

   The screen appears like a viewfinder on a typical digital video camera.

3. **Select the Record button to start recording.**

Figure 14-8: Switch your BlackBerry's Camera to Video Camera mode.

The onscreen controls are all context-related. When you launch the video camera, you see only the Record button that has the big white dot at the bottom of the screen (shown on the left of Figure 14-9). When you use the trackpad to select the Record button, the video camera starts taking video, and the only available control is a Pause button (shown on the right of Figure 14-9).

Figure 14-9: BlackBerry as a digital video camera.

The indicators on your screen, from left to right, are as follows:

- ✔ **Storage type:** Should always indicate a media card because you can record video only if you have a microSD card in your BlackBerry.

- ✔ **Available Storage:** The more blue you see on the horizontal measure bar, the more free space you have for saving videos to the media card.

- ✔ **Record/Pause:** A circle indicates the video camera is ready for recording (as shown on the left of Figure 14-9), and two vertical short lines show that the camera is actively recording (as shown on the right of Figure 14-9), so you can select the indicator to pause recording.

- ✔ **Video Light:** Shows up only if your BlackBerry has a flash. A circle around the lightning icon, similar to what you see in Figure 14-9, indicates that Video Light is Off, which is the default setting.

  The following section shows how to enable Video Light.

- ✔ **Recorded Time:** Tells you how long, in minutes and seconds, you've been recording.

You can press the Escape key to stop recording and save the captured video, or press the trackpad to pause recording. When you pause the recording, the screen updates to show the rest of the controls, as you can see in Figure 14-10.

Figure 14-10: The video camera controls.

The controls are the familiar buttons you see on a typical video recorder/ player. From left to right, they are

- **Record:** Continue recording.

- **Stop:** End the recording.

- **Play:** Play the video you just recorded.

- **Send:** Share your video recording. When you select this menu item, a sub-menu appears, listing the options to send the video by using Bluetooth, as a text message or e-mail, by uploading it to YouTube, or to a BlackBerry Messenger contact. When you make a selection from this submenu, an appropriate screen appears. For example, if you select BlackBerry Messenger, a Select a Contact screen appears, where you can select from the list of Messenger contacts to whom you want to send this video.

- **Rename:** A Rename screen appears, where you can enter the new name for this video file.

- **Delete:** Get rid of the video file of the recording.

Customizing the Video Camera

Your BlackBerry has a few settings that you can tweak to change the behavior of the video camera. And, like with every other BlackBerry application, to see what you can customize, don't look anywhere else but the application's Options screen — in this case, the Video Camera Options screen.

Follow these steps to get to the Video Camera Options screen:

1. **Open the Camera application.**

2. **Press the Menu key, and then select Video Camera from the menu that appears (refer to Figure 14-8).**

   A video camera screen appears.

3. **Press the Menu key, and then select Options from the menu that appears.**

   The Video Camera Options screen appears, as shown in Figure 14-11.

The available options are easy to digest, but in case you need a little help, here's what you can tweak:

- **Video Light:** In case it's a little dim, you can turn on the video camera's lights. This option is available only if your BlackBerry has a flash. Video Light is the flash that you use when taking still pictures, only it stays lit when you change the setting to On (the default is Off) and then use the video camera. While on the Video Camera screen, you can toggle this setting on or off simply by pressing the Space key.

Video Camera Options

Features

Video Light

Image Stabilization:

Scene Mode: Auto ▾

Video Format   Normal (640 x 480) ▾

Set Convenience Keys

Storage

Folder

Figure 14-11: Customize your video camera in the Video Camera Options screen.

Dropped something in a dark alley? This video light is a good alternative to a flashlight when you need one.

Using Video Light is a drain on your battery.

✓ **Image Stabilization:** When selected, this setting minimizes shakiness on the video.

✓ **Scene Mode:** Similar to the still camera, the video camera offers a few predefined groups of camera settings. You can select Auto (the default), which lets BlackBerry decide the appropriate mode, or you can set it to Portrait, Landscape, Close-Up, or Beach. (We discuss these options for still photos in the section "Setting the scene mode," earlier in this chapter.)

✓ **Video Format:** This option specifies the screen resolution size. The default is Normal, which is set at the maximum size of your BlackBerry screen. In most 6.0 models and above, Normal appears at 640 x 480 pixels.

If you're planning to send your video to friends through MMS, you can choose MMS mode, which has the smaller size of 176 x 144 pixels.

✓ **Set Convenience Keys:** Allows you choose the applications that you want to launch when you press the left and right convenience keys.

✓ **Folder:** Use this option to change the default location in which your BlackBerry saves the video file.

Chapter 15

Satisfying All Your Senses with the Media Player

In This Chapter

▶ Accessing all kinds of media on your BlackBerry

▶ Recording video and sound

▶ Sorting through your media files

▶ Customizing Media

*I*f one word describes today's phone market trends, it's *convergence,* which means having a phone that does multiple things. Your BlackBerry is among the participants in this convergence race. In addition to sending and receiving e-mail, and being a phone, a camera, and a PDA, the BlackBerry is an excellent portable media player.

In this small package, you can

✔ Listen to music

✔ Record and watch video clips

✔ Sample ringtones

✔ Snap and view pictures

These capabilities are bundled into a panel that has a name you can recognize easily, even after sipping a couple of pints of strong ale — Media.

Accessing Media

To access the Media apps, from the Home screen, simply slide the trackpad to the right until you see the Media panel. While you slide the trackpad, the Home screen scrolls through its panels. The Media panel looks like the screen in Figure 15-1.

Figure 15-1: Explore Media in your BlackBerry's Media panel.

Media is a collection of the following media applications:

- ✔ Music
- ✔ Videos
- ✔ Pictures
- ✔ Ring Tones
- ✔ Podcasts
- ✔ Video Camera
- ✔ Voice Notes Recorder
- ✔ Voice Notes

When you're in the Media panel, each application is represented by an icon, as shown in Figure 15-1. You can probably easily figure out what media application each one of these icons represents.

These apps can *cooperate,* meaning you can access one of them from the other. For example

- ✔ The videos you capture in the Video Camera app appear in Videos. You can even launch the Video Camera from the Videos app.
- ✔ You can launch Voice Notes Recorder from Voice Notes and play recorded notes within Voice Notes.

Letting the Music Play

Unlike a jukebox, you don't need to cough up any coins to play music on your BlackBerry. Just select the Music application from Media panel (refer to Figure 15-1). The Music app's icon looks like an image of musical notes. The Music screen appears, listing several potential views of your music collection, as shown in Figure 15-2:

- ✔ **All Songs:** Displays all your music files in alphabetical order.
- ✔ **Artists:** Lists your music files by artist — so you can play your John Mayer songs in one go.
- ✔ **Albums:** Displays your music collection one album at a time.
- ✔ **Genres:** If you prefer not to mingle your country with your cutting-edge techno, navigate through this view.
- ✔ **Playlists:** Organize and play songs the way you prefer — create the perfect mix tape!
- ✔ **Sample Songs:** Go here when you're dying to check the player but haven't yet put your collection into the BlackBerry.
- ✔ **Shuffle Songs:** Life is all about variety, and when you're tired of the song order in your playlist, select this option to mix it up.

Figure 15-2: Choose how to view your music collection.

After you choose a view, select one of the songs to start playing it. After BlackBerry starts playing a song, it plays the rest of the music listed in the view you selected. The standard interface shown in Figure 15-3 doesn't require much explanation.

Figure 15-3:
BlackBerry's
music
player.

The two small icons at the top-left and top-right of the music player indicate whether you have the Repeat or Shuffle options turned on, respectively. You can toggle the features on and off by clicking the icons:

✓ **Repeat:** This icon, which looks like a looping arrow, appears in the top-left corner of the music player. If you want the songs to play again after the last song in the list plays, just click this icon. The icon changes, displaying a number one (1) inside the loop image. To disable repeat, click the icon again.

✓ **Shuffle:** Tired of hearing the same sequence of songs played? Click the Shuffle icon, which resembles two crossing arrows, located in the top-right corner of the music player. The arrows brighten a little bit, and your BlackBerry plays the songs from the current group you're listening to randomly.

You can't fast-forward or rewind, but you can position where in the song BlackBerry is playing by dragging the progress slider. Select the progress slider, and then slide the trackpad to change the slider's position. Press the trackpad, and the music starts playing from that position.

The earpiece-and-microphone combo that comes with your BlackBerry is designed for one ear only, which can become an issue when you're in a noisy place, such as on a train, because you can't block the ambient noise. To improve your experience, you can buy a *stereo* (two-ear) headset. A Bluetooth headset is a good option.

Some BlackBerry models (such as the BlackBerry Curve) come with built-in Media keys on the top of the device. Starting from the left (with the front of the BlackBerry facing you), they are

- ✔ **Backward:** The standard symbol of two arrows pointing to the left. You can press this key to go back to the previous song or movie in your playlist.

- ✔ **Play/Pause:** The standard symbol of one arrow key pointing to the right beside two vertical lines. Pressing this middle key displays the Media panel of the Home screen when you're anywhere other than the Media panel. If a list of songs or videos appears on the BlackBerry, pressing this key plays the currently highlighted media file. If a media file is playing, pressing this key pauses the file.

- ✔ **Forward:** The standard symbol of two arrows pointing to the right. Press this key to go to the next media file.

Creating a playlist

Sure, you have favorites in your song library. Having a playlist would be nice, right? On your BlackBerry, you can create two types of playlists:

- ✔ **Standard:** A bare-bones playlist in which you manually add the music you want.

- ✔ **Automatic:** You can specify a combination of songs that your BlackBerry assembles by Artists, Albums, Genres, or any combination thereof.

If you listen to a song and happen to like it, want to add it to your playlist? No problem. While you're playing the song, simply press the Menu key, and then select Add to Playlist from the menu that appears. Then, in the screen that appears, select the playlist to which you want to add that song.

Standard playlists

To create a standard playlist, follow these steps:

1. **In the Media panel of the Home screen, select Music.**

   The Music screen appears.

2. **On the Music screen, select Playlists.**

   The Playlists screen appears.

3. **Select New Playlist.**

   A pop-up screen appears, asking whether you want to create a standard or automatic playlist.

4. **Select Standard Playlist.**

   Another pop-up screen appears, asking you to name the playlist.

5. **In the text field of the pop-up screen, enter the name of the playlist, and then select the OK button.**

   A screen appears, bearing the name of the playlist you just entered.

6. **On your playlist screen, click Add Songs.**

   Your music library listing appears.

7. **Scroll to the library's music list and select a song that you want to add to your playlist.**

   You return to your playlist screen, with the selected song added to your playlist.

   Repeat Steps 6 and 7 to select and add each additional song that you want.

8. **When you finish adding songs, press the Escape key, and then select Save from the confirmation screen that appears.**

   The section "Playing from your playlist," later in this chapter, explains how to get your new playlist going.

Automatic playlists

To create an automatic playlist, follow these steps:

1. **In the Media panel of the Home screen, select Music.**

   The Music screen appears.

2. **From the Music screen, select Playlists.**

   The Playlists screen appears.

3. **Select New Playlist.**

   A pop-up screen appears, asking whether you want to create a standard or automatic playlist.

4. **Select Automatic Playlist.**

   Another pop-up screen appears, asking for the name of the playlist.

5. **In the text field of the pop-up screen, enter the name of the playlist, and then click the OK button.**

   A screen appears, bearing the name of the playlist you just entered. This screen is divided into three sections that list songs by artists, by albums, and by genres.

6. **Select the + (plus sign) to the right of the Music Type criteria, and then select one of the combinations in the list that appears.**

   You can choose Songs by These Artists, Songs in These Albums, Songs of These Genres, or a combination of any of the three options. If you choose Songs by These Artists, a list of artists appears; if you choose Songs in These Albums, a list of albums appears; and if you choose Songs of These Genres, a list of genres appears.

7. **Select the artist, album, or genre you want, depending on what you selected in Step 6.**

   Each artist, album, or genre can include one or more songs. All the songs in the collection you select are added to your playlist.

   You can repeat Steps 6 and 7 to add more values to your criteria.

8. **After you add all the criteria you want in the Automatic Playlist, press the Escape key, and then select Save from the confirmation screen that appears.**

   You're finished! To play your newly constructed playlist, check out the following section.

Playing from your playlist

Playing your playlist is a no-brainer. Just follow these steps:

1. **Open the Music screen by selecting Music in the Media panel of the Home screen.**

2. **From the Music screen, select Playlists.**

3. **Select the playlist that you want to start playing.**

   A playlist screen appears.

4. **Directly below the header of the playlist screen, click Play.**

Now Showing

Videos take a lot of storage space. To make sure that you don't affect important applications by using most of the built-in storage space on your BlackBerry for videos, your device can record a video only if you have a microSD card.

Playing or recording a video is similar to playing music. If you have a microSD card on your BlackBerry, follow these steps:

1. **From the Media panel of the Home screen, select Videos.**

   The screen displays the Video Camera icon, and a list of video files appears at the bottom, as you can see in Figure 15-4. If you want to watch a video, skip to Step 6.

2. **To start video recording, select Video Camera.**

   The video camera screen appears, displaying an image of what's in front of the camera.

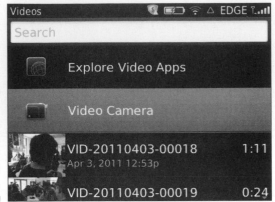

Figure 15-4: Record your home video by selecting Video Camera.

3. **Press the trackpad to start recording.**

Don't wait for "Cut!" You can pause the camera by pressing the trackpad. The familiar video and audio controls appear on the screen. From left to right, they are Continue Recording, Stop, and Play. The other buttons are Rename (for renaming the file), Delete, and Send via Email or Text Message.

4. **Select the Stop button when you're ready to wrap up your home video.**

The video camera screen reappears, ready to take another video.

5. **Press the Escape key to go back to the Videos screen, where the video file you just saved appears.**

6. **Select the file to play it onscreen.**

To record a video from the Video Camera app directly, follow these steps:

1. **Select Video Camera from the Media panel of the Home screen.**

The video camera screen appears, ready to record a video.

2. **Press the trackpad to start recording.**

3. **Press the Escape key to wrap up your home video.**

You can access the Video Camera through the Camera application, too. In fact, Video Camera and Camera were one application in older BlackBerry models. Check out Chapter 14 for more about the Video Camera, including how to customize its behavior.

Looking Over Your Pictures

Even in older BlackBerries, you can use Pictures to view and zoom into images. Follow these steps:

1. **From the Media panel, select the Pictures app, which has an icon that looks like two mountains and a sun.**

2. **Select one of the listed collections (refer to Figure 15-5) to navigate to your pictures.**

    You can choose among the following collections:

    • *All Pictures:* Displays pictures filed in device memory and on the microSD card.

    • *Picture Folders:* Displays only pictures filed in the current location of images captured by the Camera app. The default folder is the picture folder on the microSD card.

    • *Sample Pictures:* Displays sample pictures that come with your smartphone.

3. **Scroll to find the picture you want to view.**

4. **Select the file.**

    Pretty easy, right? At this point, your photo appears on the screen.

5. **To zoom in the photo, press the trackpad.**

    The picture zooms in. You can press the trackpad again to increase the degree of zoom.

6. **Press the Escape key to zoom out.**

Check out Sample Pictures. Your BlackBerry comes with a collection of pictures that you can use as the Home screen background. You can even assign a cartoon to a contact as a Caller ID until you get a chance to take a picture of that person. (We describe how to take a picture with your BlackBerry in Chapter 14.)

When you're in Pictures and navigating in a folder, you can view those pictures in a number of ways:

Figure 15-5:
Navigate to
your
pictures.

- ✔ **Thumbnails:** This default view allows you to quickly see many pictures at the same time before deciding which one to open.

- ✔ **Slide show:** Want to view all the pictures in full size, one at a time? Run a slide show. Press the Menu key, and then select View Slide Show from the menu that appears.

- ✔ **Manual scrolling:** A convenient way to view pictures is to open a picture by selecting it from the Pictures screen, and then pressing the trackpad sideways. Scrolling right transitions to the next picture in the folder you're viewing, and you see a smooth sideways movement of the picture on the screen. Scrolling left transitions in the opposite direction until the preceding picture appears onscreen.

Becoming Lord of the Ringtones

Nothing beats hearing a loud funky ringtone while you're sleeping on a bus or a train. You can wake other passengers, too, whether you want to use the Top 40, old-fashioned digital beats, or something you recorded.

To hear ringtones that come with your BlackBerry, follow these steps:

1. **From the Media panel of the Home screen, select the Ring Tones app (the icon with an image of a phone and a musical note).**

   The Ring Tones screen appears, featuring two options: All Ring Tones and My Ring Tones.

2. **Select All Ring Tones.**

   All the ringtones on your BlackBerry appear, including the preloaded ones, as shown in Figure 15-6.

Ring Tones	🔋 📶 △ EDGE ▼.ₐₗₗ
Search	
3 Beeps	0:01
3 Bells	0:03
Action	0:01
Adventurous	0:02
AIM_BuddyAlert	0:01
AIM_ReceiveIM	0:01
AIM_SystemMessage	0:01

Figure 15-6: You may stumble on a catchy ringtone on the Ring Tones screen.

3. **Select the ringtone whose preview you want to hear.**

   While a ringtone plays, you can select the right arrow to go to the next tone; select the left arrow to go the previous one.

4. **Select a ringtone that you want to use.**

5. **Press the Menu key, and then select Set as Ring Tone from the menu that appears.**

   A pop-up screen appears, allowing you to choose the profile to which this ringtone applies. (Check out Chapter 3 for a quick refresher on profiles.)

6. **Select an option from the pop-up screen.**

   You can choose from All Profiles, Normal Profile Only, or Cancel.

If you're familiar with any audio-editing software, you can make your own ringtones. Save the file and copy it to your BlackBerry. (See Chapter 16 to find details on how to copy files from your computer to your BlackBerry.) The Internet has a plethora of ringtones, and many are free. The only possible harm from downloading one is being annoyed by how it sounds. The default home page on BlackBerry Browser (http://mobile.blackberry.com) includes links to sources of ringtones — just select Fun and Pages.

Listening to Podcasts

Podcasting started with audio files syndicated through the web. Nowadays, people publish episodes of their podcasts in video format, as well. And you can subscribe to — and watch or listen to — them via your BlackBerry. The Podcasts application appears in the Media panel of the Home screen, to the right of the Ring Tones app. Its icon looks like a person's upper body with two circles around the head.

Subscribing to a podcast

When you first launch the Podcasts app, you aren't subscribed to any podcasts yet. But you can locate and subscribe to a podcast in three easy ways:

- ✔ **Featured Channels:** When you launch the app, a Podcasts screen like the one on the left of Figure 15-7 appears. Select Explore Podcasts to open a Featured Channels screen (similar to the screen on the right of Figure 15-7). This screen offers a carousel of channels that Research in Motion (RIM) features. The channels update on a daily basis. Simply select a channel to open a screen that describes the channel and features a Subscribe button.

- ✔ **Top Episodes:** A list of the most-subscribed podcast episodes. An *episode* is simply one of the podcasts published by a certain channel. A podcast channel is like a TV show, and a podcast episode is like an episode of that TV show. You can look at what podcast episodes are popular to help you decide what channel you want to subscribe to. To get to the Top Episodes, select Explore Podcasts, and then, in the Featured Channels screen that appears, select the bottom-left image of an award cup. The Top Episodes screen appears. Select an episode to open a screen that describes the channel and features a Subscribe button.

- ✔ **Entering the web address:** If you know the web address of the podcast channel to which you want to subscribe, you can directly enter it in your BlackBerry. Follow these steps:

  1. *On the Podcasts screen, press the Menu key, and then select Add Podcast Channel from the menu that appears.*

     The Add Podcast Channel screen appears (see Figure 15-8).

Figure 15-7:
The main screen of Podcasts (left) and the Featured Channels screen (right).

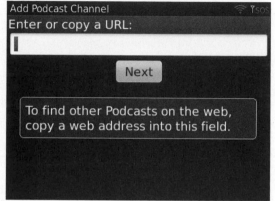

Figure 15-8:
Enter a
podcast's
web
address to
subscribe.

2. *Enter the web address in the Enter or Copy a URL text field, and then select Next.*

The Podcasts app tries to locate the podcast at that web address. If it finds the podcast, it automatically subscribes you. Otherwise, you get a message telling you that it can't find the site.

Playing a podcast

After you successfully subscribe to podcasts, the Podcasts app regularly downloads the latest episodes of those podcasts. When you launch the app, you can see the new episodes available for playback conveniently listed on the Podcasts screen. To play an episode, simply select it in this list.

Using the BlackBerry Voice Recorder

A feature-packed smartphone like your BlackBerry *should* come with a voice recorder, and it does. In the Media panel of the Home screen, you can find Voice Notes Recorder, a neat recording application.

Recording your voice

You can record your billion-dollar ideas without having to type every detail — just follow these steps:

1. **Select Voice Notes Recorder (the icon that shows a little microphone beside waves) from the Media panel of the Home screen.**

   The Voice Notes Recorder application launches, sporting the simple and clean screen shown in Figure 15-9.

2. **When you're ready to record, press the trackpad.**

   Your BlackBerry's microphone is designed to be close to your mouth.

   You can pause any time you want by pressing the trackpad. Familiar video/audio controls appear. From left to right, they are Continue Recording, Stop, and Play. Other buttons include Rename (for renaming the file), Delete, and Send via Email or Text Message.

3. **Press the trackpad, and then select Stop from the video/audio controls that appear at the bottom of the screen to wrap up the recording.**

   Your recording is saved, and the Voice Notes Recorder screen reappears, ready to make another recording. Check the next section to find out how to play your voice notes.

4. **When you're done recording, press the Escape key to close the Voice Notes Recorder.**

Figure 15-9: Record your voice by using your BlackBerry.

Playing your voice notes

After you record your billion-dollar idea, you can play it back easily by following these steps:

1. **From the Media panel of the Home screen, select Voice Notes.**

   The Voice Notes app launches, displaying a list of your voice notes.

2. **Select the voice recording that you need to hear.**

   A Voice Note player appears and starts playing the voice notes. The bottom of this screen features the familiar audio/video controls. From left to right, they're Previous Voice Note, Pause, Stop, and Next Voice Note.

You can access Voice Notes Recorder through Voice Notes, too. In fact, Voice Notes and Voice Notes Recorder were one application in older BlackBerry models. To record from Voice Notes, simply select Voice Notes Recorder, which appears near the top of the Voice Notes screen. Then, follow the steps in the preceding section, starting with Step 2.

Viewing and Controlling Media Files

The preceding sections show what types of files you can record or play on your BlackBerry. The following sections give you the lowdown on controlling those files when you're playing or viewing them.

Turning it up (or down)

Whether you're listening to music or watching a video, you can easily adjust the volume on your BlackBerry. Your BlackBerry comes with dedicated volume buttons on the upper-right side of the device. The top button turns up the volume; the bottom button turns down the volume. The onscreen volume slider reflects anything you do with the volume buttons.

Navigating the menu

Almost all Media applications have a common menu, with the exception of Pictures. The menu items are mostly self-explanatory, but the following sections highlight what each menu includes.

Navigating the Pictures menu

When you look at a picture on your BlackBerry, press the Menu key to open the Pictures menu, which includes the following items:

✔ **Copy:** Copies the highlighted image file to memory. Navigate to a folder where you want to copy the image, press the Menu key, and select Paste on the menu that appears to copy the file to that folder.

✔ **View on Map:** If a picture includes location information, select this option to display a map that shows the location where this photo was taken.

✔ **Rename:** A Rename pop-up screen appears, where you can rename the image file.

✔ **Properties:** Displays a screen that shows the location on your BlackBerry of the image file, the file's size, and the time it was last modified. You can also find on this screen a check box labeled Hidden. Selecting this check box makes this image file disappear from the list. After you hide an image file, you can unhide it only through Explore, which we discuss in the section "Using Explore," later in this chapter.

✔ **Delete:** Deletes the image file.

Navigating the Music, Videos, Ring Tones, and Voice Notes menus

Whether you're watching a video, playing music, sampling a ringtone, or listening to a voice note, you see the following options after you press the Menu key:

✔ **Media Home:** Displays the Media panel of the Home screen.

✔ **<Media App> Home:** This menu option depends on the Media application you're in. For example, if you're in the Music app, the menu item displays Music Home. If you select this menu item, the Home screen of the Media application you're in appears.

✔ **Activate Handset:** Mutes the device's speaker. Select this option if you want to use the earpiece. This menu item appears only if you've activated the speakerphone.

✔ **Activate Speakerphone:** Uses the device's speaker and mutes the earpiece. This menu item appears only if the handset is activated.

Using Explore

You can navigate to a media file in many ways, but Explore is probably the quickest way to find a file. It has some similarities to Windows Explorer, and it also has a search facility similar to Find in other BlackBerry applications, such as Contacts, MemoPad, and Tasks.

To launch Explore, in the Media panel of the Home screen, press the Menu key, and then select Explore from the menu that appears. The Explore screen (shown in Figure 15-10) opens, displaying the device root folders: Media Card and Device.

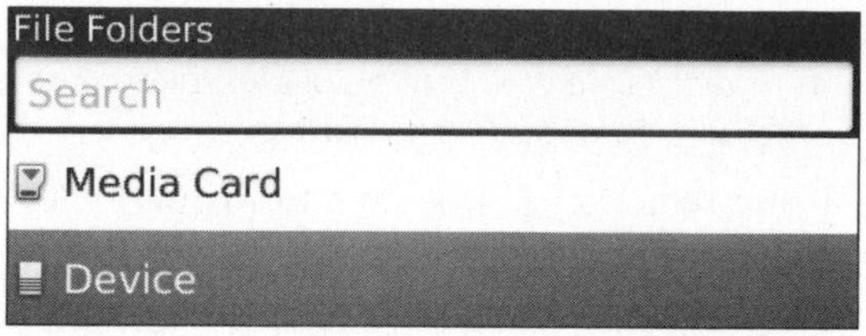

Figure 15-10:
Explore your
media files.

File Folders
Search
Media Card
Device

Folders are in a tree hierarchy. You can get into the *child folders* (subfolders) by selecting them from the parent folder, starting from either the Media Card or Device folder. For example, you can find the Camera folder (the folder where your BlackBerry stores images taken from its camera) in the BlackBerry folder, which is in the Media Card folder. So, to navigate your way to the Camera folder, you have to select the following folders in succession: Media Card, then BlackBerry, and then Camera.

If you've set a picture's property to Hidden through the image file's Properties screen (see the section "Navigating the Pictures menu," earlier in this chapter), Explore is the only place in your BlackBerry through which you can locate the file again. Follow these steps:

1. **Navigate to the folder where your picture file is located.**

   If you don't know exactly where the picture file is located, you may have to search through different folders until you find the file.

2. **Press the Menu key, and then select Show Hidden from the menu that appears.**

   If you hid the file in this folder, the filename appears in the list of files.

The default location for pictures taken by your BlackBerry's Camera is either `/Device Memory/home/user/pictures`, or `/Media Card/BlackBerry/pictures` if your BlackBerry have a microSD card.

Customizing the Media Apps

Like with the rest of your BlackBerry applications, you can customize some parts of the applications through the Options screen, which you can access from the Media panel of the Home screen. In the Media panel, press the Menu key, and then select Media Options from the menu that appears. The screen looks like the one shown in Figure 15-11.

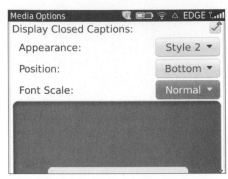

Starting at the top of the Media Options screen, in the General section, you can finesse the following options:

- ✓ **Built-in Media Storage Limit:** The maximum amount of device memory Media can use. This limit ensures that important applications, such as Messages and Phone, don't experience problems because of lack of memory, even if you're a heavy media user.

  Leave the default value of 32MB so that the Media applications don't use memory that your BlackBerry needs for essential applications, such as Phone.

- ✓ **Close Media Player When Inactive:** The default is 45 Min., but you can set this option to Off or 5, 10, 20, or 30 minutes. This option can save battery life if you get distracted and leave your BlackBerry on a table playing your favorite video.

- ✓ **Set Convenience Keys:** Change the settings for the right and left convenience keys, which are shortcut keys to an application:

  - The right convenience key defaults to launching the Camera app.
  - The left convenience key defaults to launching Voice Dialing.

In the Media Options screen's Playback section, you can customize the following options:

- ✓ **Headset Music EQ:** The equalizer setting, which is Off by default. If you want to have a different audio setting, you have several options: Bass Boost, Bass Lower, Dance, Hip Hop, Jazz, Lounge, Loud, R&B, Rock, Treble Boost, Treble Lower, and Vocal Boost.

- ✓ **Audio Boost:** Allows you to increase the volume beyond the normal level. The default setting is Off. If you set it to On, it gives you fair warning by displaying a pop-up screen about possible ear discomfort when you're using headphones.

✓ **Turn Off Auto Backlighting:** Your BlackBerry includes a backlight feature, which provides additional screen lighting. The backlight turns on when you move the smartphone from shade to direct sunlight. If you find backlighting bothersome — for example, when you're watching a movie — you can toggle it off here.

Turn off backlighting when you need to conserve battery juice because it uses a significant amount of battery power.

✓ **Display Closed Captions:** This option applies only to videos that support closed captions. By default, this option's check box is selected. You can also tweak the following settings related to closed captions:

- *Appearance:* Changes how Media closed captions look. You can choose Style 1 or Style 2 (the default). Style 1 has a blue caption on a black background, and Style 2 uses a black caption on a gray background.

- *Position:* The location of the closed captions on the screen. You can choose Top Left, Top, Top Right, Bottom Right, Bottom (the default), or Bottom Left.

- *Font Scale:* Choose the size of the font that you want to appear in closed captions during playback — Largest, Larger, Large, Normal (the default), Small, Smaller, or Smallest.

The display that reads For Your Viewing Pleasure below the Display Closed Captions options illustrates the style, fonts, and where the closed captions will appear during playback with the current settings you've chosen for Appearance, Position and Font Scale.

Toward the bottom of the Media Options screen, in the Pictures section, you can change the Pictures application in the following ways:

✓ **Slide Show Interval:** When you're viewing your files in a slide show, a picture appears for this many seconds before moving to the next picture.

✓ **Reserved Pictures Memory:** This setting makes sure your BlackBerry always has device memory reserved for the Pictures application. The default setting is 0, or no reserved memory. We recommend leaving the default value because we don't see any difference in the Pictures application when we change this setting.

Chapter 16

Managing Media Files

- -

- -

*T*he ways that you can get your hands on media continue to evolve. Ten years ago, who would have thought that you could buy music from a tiny card or from an all-you-can-download monthly subscription? Someday, you'll wake up with a technology that doesn't require you to constantly copy media files to your handheld music player. But for now, enjoying music while on the move means managing those files.

The Media app on your BlackBerry is a great music player, but without music files, it's as useless as a guitar without strings. In this chapter, we show you how to move your music library from your computer to your BlackBerry. And to satisfy your quest for mobile media satisfaction, this chapter gives you good information on ways to manage your media files.

Using Your BlackBerry as a Flash Drive for a PC

The most common way to manipulate media files into and out of your BlackBerry is to attach it to a PC and use Windows Explorer. Just follow these steps:

1. **Connect your BlackBerry to your PC, using the USB cable that came with your BlackBerry.**

   Only folders and files stored on the microSD card are visible to your PC. Make sure to have the microSD card in your BlackBerry *before* you connect your BlackBerry to the PC.

   When connected, the BlackBerry screen displays a prompt.

2. **On the BlackBerry screen, select USB Drive.**

   This option makes your BlackBerry behave as a flash drive.

3. **Type your BlackBerry's password into the Password field that appears on your BlackBerry.**

   The device is now ready to behave like an ordinary flash drive. On your PC, the Removable Disk dialog box appears.

4. **In your PC's Removable Disk dialog box, click Open Folder to View Files, and then click OK.**

   The Windows Explorer screen appears.

5. **Manipulate your media files.**

   You can do anything you typically do with a normal Windows folder, such as drag and drop, copy, and delete files.

6. **When you're finished, click the X icon in the right corner of the screen to close Windows Explorer, and then unplug your BlackBerry.**

Using Your BlackBerry as a Flash Drive for the Mac

You can attach your BlackBerry to a Mac and make that BlackBerry appear as a flash drive, but only the microSD card is visible to your Mac. Follow these steps to use your BlackBerry as a flash drive on a Mac:

1. **Connect your BlackBerry to your Mac, using the USB cable that came with your BlackBerry.**

   When connected, the BlackBerry screen displays a prompt.

2. **On the BlackBerry screen, select USB Drive.**

   This option makes the BlackBerry behave as a flash drive.

3. **Type your BlackBerry's password into the Password field that appears on your BlackBerry.**

   On your Mac, a BlackBerry folder appears on the desktop screen.

4. **On your Mac, double-click the BlackBerry folder.**

   The Finder screen appears.

5. **Manipulate your media files.**

   You can do anything you typically do with a normal folder under the Finder screen, such as drag and drop, copy, and delete files.

6. **When you're finished, right-click the BlackBerry folder on the Mac's desktop, and then select Eject from the pop-up menu that appears.**

   The BlackBerry folder in the desktop disappears.

7. **Unplug your BlackBerry.**

Using Media Sync

BlackBerry Desktop Software's Media Sync program is your key to managing files between your BlackBerry and Windows PC. If you maintain a media library on your desktop machine at home, most likely, you're using iTunes or Windows Media Player. Fortunately, Media Sync supports both programs.

If BlackBerry Desktop Software isn't installed on your PC, see Chapter 17 for details on downloading and installing the latest version for free.

Setting the music source

You can use BlackBerry Desktop Software with either iTunes or Windows Media Player to locate media files that you want to sync to your BlackBerry. Simply follow these quick and easy steps to configure BlackBerry Desktop Software to the music source of your choice:

1. **Connect your BlackBerry to your PC.**

2. **On your PC, choose Start➪All Programs➪BlackBerry➪Desktop Software.**

   The BlackBerry Desktop Software screen appears.

3. **Click the Device menu and then click Device Options.**

   The Device Options dialog box appears.

4. **Click the Media tab.**

   The screen shown in Figure 16-1 appears.

5. **From the Music Source drop-down list, select iTunes or Windows Media Player.**

   Select whichever program you use on your PC.

6. **Click OK.**

After you set the music source, BlackBerry Desktop Software is smart enough to figure out the location of the music files stored by the application, as we explain in the following section.

Device Options

| General | Enterprise Email | Media | Backup |

Wi-Fi music sync

☐ Sync music between my device and my computer within my
home Wi-Fi network

Tell me more about Wi-Fi music sync
Troubleshoot my Wi-Fi connections

Media on My Computer

Music source: Windows Media Player ▾

Imported media from your device is saved to folders on your computer. You
can select different import folders for each media type.

Pictures: My Pictures\BlackBerry   Change folder...
Videos: My Videos\BlackBerry   Change folder...

Media on My Device

Store media on: Media card (2 GB) ▾

Delete all media from this location: Delete all media...

Keep this amount of space free on my media card:

0 GB ───────┤   2 GB
                    192 MB

OK   Cancel

Figure 16-1:
Set your
music
source
application
in the
Device
Options
Media tab.

Synchronizing music files

After you set your music source to iTunes or Windows Media Player (see
the preceding section), you can easily get your music library into your
BlackBerry. Simply use BlackBerry Desktop Software to select music files
by following these steps:

1. **Connect your BlackBerry to your PC.**

2. **On your PC, choose Start➪All Programs➪BlackBerry➪Desktop Software.**

   The BlackBerry Desktop Software screen appears.

3. **Click the Music link (in the Media Sync section).**

   A screen similar to Figure 16-2 appears, displaying your music library.

4. **Select All Music or select music by artists, playlists, and genres.**

   When you make a selection, the bottom portion of the screen displays
   the amount of storage remaining on the microSD card.

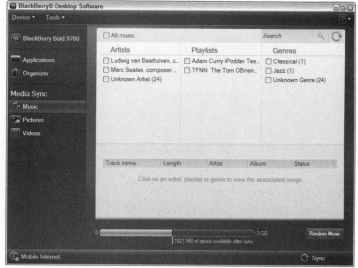

Figure 16-2:
Choose
music files
that you
want to
transfer
to your
BlackBerry.

Get a big-capacity microSD card. A 16GB microSD costs about $30 from Amazon.com and can hold thousands of music files.

5. **Click the Sync button located in the lower-right of the BlackBerry Desktop Software window.**

   Synchronization kicks in and includes your music selections.

Synchronizing picture files

You can copy your PC's folders that contain picture files to your BlackBerry. By the same token, you can also import pictures from your BlackBerry to your PC.

To set the folder location on your PC and select picture folders that you want to copy to your BlackBerry, follow these steps:

1. **Connect your BlackBerry to your PC.**

2. **On your PC, choose Start⇨All Programs⇨BlackBerry⇨Desktop Software.**

   The BlackBerry Desktop Software screen appears.

3. **Click the Pictures link (in the Media Sync section).**

   A screen similar to Figure 16-3 appears, displaying the Device Pictures tab, which shows you all the pictures on your BlackBerry. The other tab, Computer Pictures, displays the pictures on your computer.

Figure 16-3:
View images and choose where you want to import them.

4. **Select a folder on your PC to which you want to import your BlackBerry pictures.**

   To select a folder, follow these steps:

   a. *Click the Change Import Folder button.*

   A Browse for Folder dialog box appears, listing an outline of the Windows folders.

   b. *Navigate to the folder, and then click OK.*

   The Browse for Folder dialog box closes, and the Device Pictures tab now displays the folder name in the Picture Import Folder field.

5. **Select picture folders that you want to copy to your BlackBerry.**

   Follow these steps:

   a. *Click the Computer Pictures tab.*

   The screen shown in Figure 16-4 appears, displaying all the picture folders you previously copied to your BlackBerry. The My Pictures folder on your desktop is initially listed here by default.

   b. *Click the Add Folder button.*

   The Browse for Folder dialog box appears, listing an outline of the Windows folders.

   c. *Navigate to the folder that you want to add, and then click OK.*

   You return to the Computer Pictures tab (refer to Figure 16-4), with the selected picture folder added to the list. You can opt to not include this folder later by removing the check mark to the left of the folder's name in the Computer Pictures tab.

6. **Click the Sync button located on the lower-right of the BlackBerry Desktop Software window.**

Synchronization kicks in and includes your picture selections.

Synchronizing video files

You synchronize and configure videos in the same way that you do pictures. You can copy PC folders that contain video files to your BlackBerry, and you can import pictures stored on your BlackBerry to your PC.

To set the import folder location in your PC and select video folders to copy to your BlackBerry, follow these steps:

1. **Connect your BlackBerry to your PC.**

2. **On your PC, choose Start⟿All Programs⟿BlackBerry⟿Desktop Software.**

The BlackBerry Desktop Software screen appears.

3. **Click the Videos link (in the Media Sync section).**

The screen shown in Figure 16-5 appears, with the Device Videos tab displaying the videos on your BlackBerry.

4. **Select a folder on your PC to which you want to import videos from your BlackBerry.**

Select a folder by following these steps:

Figure 16-5:
View Device videos and choose where you want to import them.

a. *Click the Change Import Folder button.*

The Browse for Folder dialog box appears, listing an outline of the Windows folders.

b. *Navigate to the folder, and then click OK.*

The Browse for Folder dialog box closes, and the Device Videos tab now displays the folder name in the Video Import Folder field.

5. Select video folders that you want to copy to your BlackBerry.

Follow these steps:

a. *Click the Computer Videos tab.*

BlackBerry Desktop Software appears, displaying the video folders you've selected to copy to your BlackBerry.

b. *Click the Add Folder button.*

The Browse for Folder dialog box appears, listing an outline of the Windows folders.

c. *Navigate to the folder that you want to add, and then click OK.*

You return to the Computer Videos tab, and the selected video folder is added to the list. You can opt to not include this folder later by removing the check mark to the left of the folder's name in the Computer Videos tab.

Synchronizing media manually

With the effort you put into selecting media files (discussed in the preceding sections), it's time to get those files into your BlackBerry by following these steps:

1. **Connect your BlackBerry to your PC.**

2. **On your PC, choose Start➪All Programs➪BlackBerry➪Desktop Software.**

   The BlackBerry Desktop Software screen appears.

3. **Click Device, and then select Sync by Type from the menu that appears.**

   A submenu listing Media and Organizer appears.

4. **On the submenu, click Media.**

   The synchronization starts, and a progress screen appears. When synchronization is finished, a Summary screen displays a Complete message.

5. **Click the Close button to close the Summary screen.**

Synchronizing media automatically

After you configure Media Sync with the media files you want to sync, you don't have to navigate back to the BlackBerry Desktop Software screens and manually run media synchronization. The best way to keep your BlackBerry updated is to set BlackBerry Desktop Software to automatically sync your media files whenever you connect your BlackBerry to your PC. Set it up by following these steps:

1. **Connect your BlackBerry to your PC.**

2. **On your PC, choose Start➪All Programs➪BlackBerry➪Desktop Software.**

   The BlackBerry Desktop Software screen appears.

3. **Click Device, and then select Device Options from the drop-down list that appears.**

   The Device Options dialog box appears.

4. **In the Synchronize section of the Device Options dialog box, select the Media Files check box.**

5. **Click the OK button to close the Device Options dialog box.**

   BlackBerry Desktop Software saves your changes, and the next time you connect your BlackBerry to your PC, the BlackBerry Desktop Software automatically runs and starts synchronizing media files.

Part V
Working with BlackBerry Desktop Software

The 5th Wave   By Rich Tennant

TECH SOLUTIONS

Try unplugging it and then plugging it back in.

What kind of money did you use?

We should see the can right down here.

Bobby! What do you know about a Buthel VP 500 vending machine?!

Cola

OPEN

In this part . . .

Here, you can discover essential information about some behind-the-scenes, yet integral, processes. Read all about BlackBerry Desktop Software for Windows and for Mac, which you can direct to monitor and control database synchronization. You also can find how to back up your data and discover the many ways of installing third-party applications and upgrading your BlackBerry's operating system.

Chapter 17

Installing BlackBerry Desktop Software

In This Chapter

▶ Hooking up your BlackBerry to your PC

▶ Making your BlackBerry Mac-compatible

Your BlackBerry by itself is a standalone product, which means you can enjoy the benefits of having a smartphone by just having the BlackBerry. However, if you maintain personal information such as an address book or a calendar on your computer, it makes sense to synchronize this information with your BlackBerry. To do this synchronization business, you need software from Research in Motion (RIM) called BlackBerry Desktop Software (for a PC or the Mac). The program includes these main features:

✔ **BlackBerry Application Installation:** Installs BlackBerry applications and updates the BlackBerry operating system (OS).

✔ **Backup and Restore:** Backs up your BlackBerry data and settings. Check out Chapter 19 for details.

✔ **Synchronize Organizer Data:** Synchronizes BlackBerry Organizer data with your computer.

✔ **Media Sync:** Uploads media files to your BlackBerry from your computer and vice versa. See Chapter 16 for the scoop.

✔ **Switching Device:** Helps you transfer data from your existing BlackBerry to a new BlackBerry.

The BlackBerry Desktop Software program for PCs is loaded on the CD that comes with your BlackBerry, but download the latest version from BlackBerry's website to keep your software up to date.

In this chapter, we introduce the program for Windows and the Mac, show you where and how to download the version you need, and then provide instructions for how to install each. And you can find out how to back up data automatically from an old BlackBerry onto your new BlackBerry.

Most companies have strict policies about what software an employee can install on his or her computer, and the company's tech support often must install that software. This chapter applies to those who have a personal BlackBerry.

Using BlackBerry Desktop Software for Windows

BlackBerry Desktop Software for Windows has been around for many years, and RIM updates it regularly. To make sure that you benefit from new features of the software, keep your copy updated.

Downloading

You can find and download BlackBerry Desktop Software from RIM's website. Follow these easy steps:

1. **On your PC, open Internet Explorer.**

2. **In Internet Explorer's address bar, type** http://us.blackberry.com/apps-software/desktop.

   If RIM has changed the download location, this address doesn't get you to the download page. Your best bet is to enter *BlackBerry Desktop Software for Windows download* in a search engine such as Google. The top search results should lead you to the download page.

3. **On the BlackBerry Desktop Software download page, click Download for PC, and then click Download on the web page that appears.**

   A prompt appears, asking whether you want to run or save the file.

4. **Click Save.**

   A standard Windows Save As dialog box appears, where you can select the folder location where you want to place the installation file.

5. **Change the folder location of the installation file, if you want, and then click Save.**

   Take note of the location and the name of the installation file in the Save As dialog box.

   A progress dialog box appears. The installation file is large, so downloading should take a few minutes. After the file is downloaded, a confirmation dialog box appears.

6. **Click the OK button to close the confirmation dialog box.**

   You now have an installation file on your PC.

Installing

After you download the installation file for BlackBerry Desktop Software, as described in the preceding section, you need to install the software, which is easy but requires a little patience. The process takes 15 to 20 minutes.

To install BlackBerry Desktop Software, follow these steps:

1. **On your PC, double-click the BlackBerry Desktop Software installation file.**

   An Open File — Security Warning dialog box appears.

2. **Click Run.**

   A Winzip Self-Extractor window appears and, after the installation program is extracted and loaded (which happens quickly), the Choose a Setup Language window appears.

3. **From the drop-down list, select the language that you want BlackBerry Desktop Software to use, and then click OK.**

   An installation welcome window appears.

4. **Click Next.**

   The window displays the option to choose your country location.

5. **Select your location from the Country drop-down list, and then click Next.**

   A long license agreement appears. You have to accept this agreement before you can proceed.

6. **Select the I Accept the Terms in the License Agreement option to confirm, and then click Next.**

   The window that appears allows you to choose the destination folder and whether you want BlackBerry Desktop Software available for all users of your computer. We suggest you keep the default settings because you can much more easily find any software if it's in a standard location.

7. **Click Next.**

   A dialog box similar to Figure 17-1 appears, with the check box to create a shortcut on your desktop already selected. We suggest that you keep the default and create a shortcut so that you can launch the software quickly.

8. **Click Install.**

   The actual installation starts, and the progress window shown in Figure 17-2 appears.

Figure 17-1:
Create a shortcut on your desktop for BlackBerry Desktop Software.

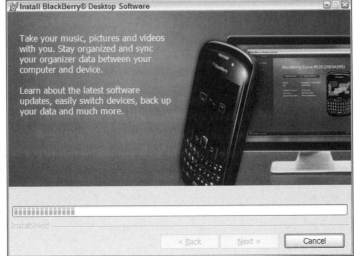

Figure 17-2:
You can watch the progress of the installation.

9. **When the Installation Completed message appears, click Finish.**

   A dialog box appears telling you that some configurations take effect only after you restart the machine, and it prompts you to restart now or later.

   Before you click the Yes button to restart your machine, make sure you don't have any unsaved files from other programs open. You don't want to lose the changes you made to those files, right? Close other programs manually before restarting your computer.

10. **Click Yes.**

   Your machine restarts, and BlackBerry Desktop Software is fully installed.

Launching

If you don't change the default settings during the installation, a shortcut to launch BlackBerry Desktop Software appears on your Windows desktop or in the Start menu. Launch the program by double-clicking the shortcut or by choosing Start➪All Programs➪BlackBerry➪BlackBerry Desktop Software. A window similar to the one in Figure 17-3 appears.

Figure 17-3: BlackBerry Desktop Software in Windows.

On the left side of the window are the following main links:

- ✔ BlackBerry (shows information of the connected BlackBerry)
- ✔ Applications (see Chapter 20)
- ✔ Organizer (see Chapter 18)
- ✔ Media Sync (see Chapter 16)

Connecting to your BlackBerry

After BlackBerry Desktop Software is running, it tries to find a BlackBerry (your BlackBerry) on the type of connection specified. The default connection is USB, so you don't need to configure anything.

Follow these steps to connect your BlackBerry to BlackBerry Desktop Software:

1. **Use the USB cable to plug your BlackBerry into your PC.**

   Keep your device on.

2. **Launch BlackBerry Desktop Software.**

   BlackBerry Desktop Software tries to find a BlackBerry on the computer through a USB connection.

3. **If your device has a password, enter your password at the prompt.**

   If your BlackBerry doesn't have a password, you don't see the prompt. After you enter the password (or if you don't have to), a summary of your BlackBerry appears (refer to Figure 17-3).

If you're connecting your BlackBerry to the BlackBerry Desktop Software for the first time, the program displays the prompts shown in Figure 17-4.

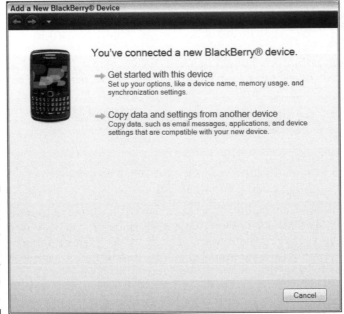

Figure 17-4:
Set up your
BlackBerry
with
BlackBerry
Desktop
Software.

These prompts allow you to

- Set up Organizer data synchronization options and customize the information about your device.
- Transfer data from your older BlackBerry to your new BlackBerry.

You can perform either task at any time. You don't have to do them now. See Chapter 18 for details on setting up Organizer data synchronization options. You can find out how to transfer data from your old BlackBerry in the following section.

Switching to a new BlackBerry

You may think that switching from an older BlackBerry to your new BlackBerry will be a painstaking task because you need to manually copy all the data that you want from your old BlackBerry smartphone and transfer it to your new BlackBerry. However, BlackBerry Desktop Software has a Device Switch Wizard that helps you with this process. Just follow these steps:

1. **Launch BlackBerry Desktop Software by double-clicking the shortcut on your computer's desktop.**

   Alternatively, you can choose Start➪All Programs➪BlackBerry➪ BlackBerry Desktop Software.

2. **Click Device, and then select Device Switch from the drop-down list that appears.**

   The Desktop Software dialog box appears, displaying the Device Switch Wizard and asking you to connect your current device, as shown in Figure 17-5. (The current device means your older BlackBerry.)

3. **Select the BlackBerry that appears in the window.**

   The dialog box shown in Figure 17-6 appears, where you can choose what to copy to your new BlackBerry.

4. **Deselect the appropriate check box if you don't want to include device data or third-party applications.**

   If you want to back up all the data, leave the screen untouched. *Device data* consists of your contacts, calendar, call history, e-mail, configuration information, and a lot more. *Third-party applications* are the programs you installed — the ones that didn't come with the device originally.

5. **Click Next.**

   A status dialog box appears, showing the progress of the backup. When the backup is finished, the dialog box prompts you to connect your new BlackBerry.

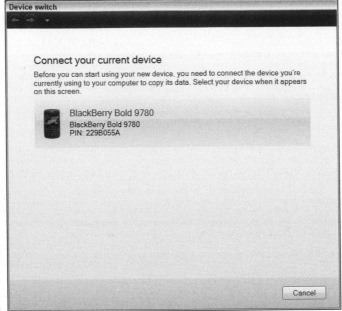

Figure 17-5:
The Device
Switch
Wizard
helps you
back up
your data.

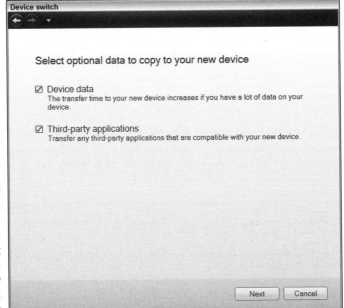

Figure 17-6:
Decide
what data
you want
to copy to
your new
BlackBerry.

6. **Disconnect your old BlackBerry and connect your new BlackBerry to your PC by using the USB cable, and then click Next (see Figure 17-7).**

   In the Device Switch dialog box, a long license agreement appears. You have to accept this agreement before you can proceed.

7. **Select the check box on the Device Switch dialog box to accept the license agreement, and then click Next.**

8. **Confirm that the connected device is your new BlackBerry by clicking it in the dialog box.**

   The data transfer kicks off.

9. **When the Success dialog box appears, click the Close button.**

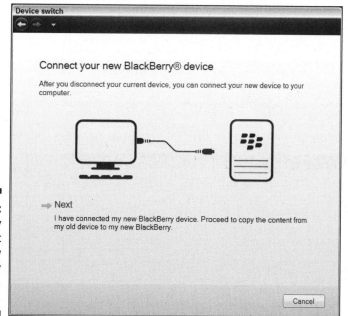

Figure 17-7: You're ready to connect your new BlackBerry for data transfer.

Using BlackBerry Desktop Software for the Mac

To perform data synchronization and data backup between a Mac and your BlackBerry, you use BlackBerry Desktop Software for the Mac. The program doesn't come with your BlackBerry packaging. No worries — you can download an installation program from RIM's website.

Downloading

Downloading BlackBerry Desktop Software for the Mac is as easy as following these steps:

1. **On your Mac, open Safari.**

2. **In the Safari address bar, type** http://us.blackberry.com/apps-software/ desktop/desktop_mac.jsp, **and then press Enter.**

   If RIM has changed the download location, this address doesn't get you to the download page. Your best bet is to enter *BlackBerry Desktop Software for Mac download* in a search engine such as Google. The top search results should lead you to the download page.

3. **On the download page, click Download.**

   A progress dialog box appears while the installation file downloads. The process takes a few minutes.

   When the file is downloaded, a window opens on your Mac, displaying two icons: `BlackBerry Desktop Software.mpkg` and BlackBerry Desktop Software Uninstaller. The file that ends with `.mpkg` is the installation file.

Installing

After you download BlackBerry Desktop Software (see the preceding section), you need to install it. Follow these steps:

1. **Double-click `BlackBerry Desktop Software.mpkg`.**

   A dialog box appears, displaying a standard Mac warning message that tells you you're about to run the installation of a program.

2. **Click Continue.**

   An installation welcome screen appears.

3. **Click Continue.**

   Another prompt appears, this time asking you to agree to the license agreement.

4. **Click Agree.**

   A dialog box appears where you can choose the location of the installation. The default is your Mac's hard drive.

5. **Navigate to a different drive location if you want to install the program somewhere other than your Mac's hard drive.**

6. **Click Continue.**

   You're prompted for your Mac password.

7. **Enter your Mac password, and then click OK.**

   A long license agreement appears.

8. **Accept this license by selecting the check box, and then click Continue Installation.**

   The installation kicks in. This process may take a few minutes.

   When the installation is complete, you're asked to restart your Mac. Before you proceed, save any unsaved files and close any programs manually.

9. **Click Restart.**

Launching

After installation, BlackBerry Desktop Software may not be on the Mac's dock (the bottom bar on Mac OS 10.5 or later that contains application icons) or the Mac's desktop. If that's the case, follow these steps:

1. **Find BlackBerry Desktop Software.**

   Finding the program depends on which Mac OS you have:

   - *Mac OS 10.5 or later:* Click the Finder application (the leftmost icon) on your Mac's dock. In the Search text box of the Finder screen (in the top-right corner), type **BlackBerry Desktop**, and then press Enter.

   - *Mac OS before 10.5:* Press ⌘+F to launch the Find utility. In the Find text box of the Find screen, type **BlackBerry Desktop**, and then press Enter.

2. **Connect your BlackBerry to your Mac by using the USB cable that came with your BlackBerry.**

3. **In the Finder or Find screen (depending on your OS), click BlackBerry Desktop Software.**

   The window shown in Figure 17-8 appears, displaying the BlackBerry connected to your Mac.

Figure 17-8:
The main
screen of
BlackBerry
Desktop
Software.

Your newly installed BlackBerry Desktop Software is ready. Start enjoying your desktop media library on your BlackBerry (see Chapter 15) and check out Chapter 18 if you want to update your BlackBerry with your desktop's organizer data.

Switching to a new BlackBerry

With the help of BlackBerry Desktop Software, you can easily transition from an older BlackBerry to your new BlackBerry through your Mac, and you can avoid the painstaking process of manual backup-and-restore of your older settings. Follow these steps:

1. **Connect your old BlackBerry to your Mac by using the USB cable that came with that BlackBerry.**

2. **Launch BlackBerry Desktop Software (as described in the preceding section).**

3. **Click Device, and then select Switch Device from the drop-down list that appears.**

   The Switch Device dialog box appears, as shown in Figure 17-9, offering you the options to update the software on the new device, as well as copy third-party apps from the older device that are still supported on the new device. We suggest you leave both options checked so that your new BlackBerry is updated with the latest OS and you can get your previous third-party apps installed.

4. **If, for some reason, you don't want to update the OS or copy any third-party apps from the older device, deselect the check box for the content that you don't want BlackBerry Desktop Software to copy to your new device.**

5. **Click Start.**

   A screen appears, giving you instructions about how to set up your new BlackBerry so that it starts receiving e-mails from your e-mail accounts.

Figure 17-9: Choose what to update on your new device.

6. **Click Continue.**

   The Switch Device Wizard starts backing up data, and a status dialog box appears, showing the progress of the backup. When the backup is finished, the dialog box prompts you to connect your new BlackBerry, as shown in Figure 17-10.

7. **Disconnect your old BlackBerry and connect your new BlackBerry to your Mac by using the BlackBerry's USB cable, and then click OK.**

   A long license agreement appears. You have to accept this agreement before you can proceed.

8. **Select the check box to accept the license agreement, and then click OK.**

   The BlackBerry Desktop Software screen displays a list of connected BlackBerry devices. In this case, you should see only one BlackBerry connected, which is your new BlackBerry.

9. **Confirm that the connected device is your new BlackBerry by clicking the name.**

   The data transfer kicks off.

10. **When the Success dialog box appears, click the Close button.**

Figure 17-10:
Connect
your new
BlackBerry
to your Mac
for data
transfer.

Chapter 18

Synchronizing Organizer Data

In This Chapter

▶ Synchronizing your BlackBerry's data with a Windows PC

▶ Synchronizing data between your BlackBerry and your Mac

*W*hat better way to keep your BlackBerry updated than to synchronize it with your computer application's data? You can use BlackBerry Desktop Software to synchronize your Organizer data (notes, appointments, contacts, and tasks) and to upload and download media files between your computer and your smartphone.

In this chapter, you can explore how to manually and automatically synchronize your BlackBerry with your computer. You can find tips about which options you may want to use. (In Chapter 17, we give you the nitty-gritty about BlackBerry Desktop Software on a PC and the Mac.)

If you're using a corporate BlackBerry that's running under BlackBerry Enterprise Server, you can skip this chapter. BlackBerry smartphones running under BlackBerry Enterprise Server (BES) synchronize automatically.

Synchronizing Your BlackBerry with a Windows PC

Organizer data synchronization on a PC has two parts: configuring how and what to synchronize, and actually running the sync. We describe both parts in detail in the following sections.

Configuring Organizer data synchronization

With BlackBerry Desktop Software (for the PC), you do the configuration in the Organizer window and run the sync by clicking Sync All or Sync by Type in the Device menu.

To configure Organizer synchronization, click the Configure Settings button (refer to Figure 18-1). When you do, the dialog box shown in Figure 18-2 appears. This dialog box is the entry point for the entire synchronization configuration for Organizer applications. The names on the dialog box correspond to BlackBerry applications, except for Address Book, which the BlackBerry calls Contacts. Selecting an application allows you to pair the Organizer handheld application with a computer application (most likely Outlook).

You can synchronize the following types of application data with your BlackBerry:

- **Calendar:** The appointments and events stored in your favorite Organizer app
- **MemoPad:** Notes or text you've stored in your Organizer app
- **Address Book:** Contact information, which syncs to BlackBerry's Contacts app
- **Tasks:** Your to-do list

Follow these steps to set up your device's synchronization:

1. **Connect your BlackBerry to your PC by using the BlackBerry's USB cable.**

2. **Double-click the BlackBerry Desktop Software desktop icon.**

   Alternatively, you can choose Start➪All Programs➪BlackBerry➪BlackBerry Desktop Software.

   The BlackBerry Desktop Software window appears, displaying the device description.

3. **Click the Organizer link, on the left side of the window.**

   The window shown in Figure 18-1 appears.

4. **Click the Configure Settings button.**

   The Select Device Application dialog box, shown in Figure 18-2, appears.

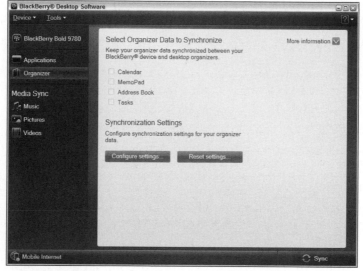

Figure 18-1:
The
BlackBerry
Desktop
Software
Organizer
window.

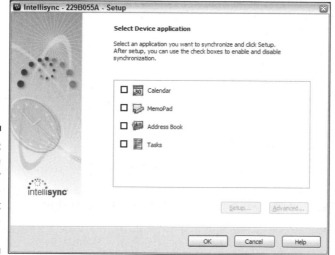

Figure 18-2:
Select the
Organizer
applica-
tions that
you want to
sync.

5. **Select the check box next to the application data type (Calendar, MemoPad, Address Book, or Tasks) that you want to synchronize.**

   For this example, we selected the Calendar application data type.

6. **Click the Setup button.**

   The dialog box displays information about the application — in our example, Calendar Setup — as shown in Figure 18-3.

7. **From the Available Desktop Applications list, select an Organizer application from which to retrieve application data, and then click Next.**

   BlackBerry Desktop Software pulls your selected application data from the application you select.

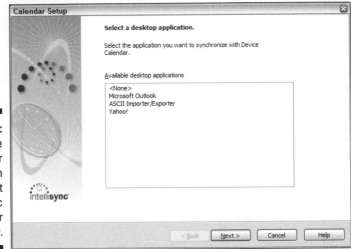

Figure 18-3:
Choose the computer application you want to sync with your BlackBerry.

8. **In the Synchronize Options dialog box that appears, select which direction you want the synchronization to follow (see Figure 18-4).**

   Synchronization Options provides three synchronization options:

   • *Two Way Sync:* Synchronizes changes in both your BlackBerry and in your computer application.

   • *One Way Sync from Device:* Synchronizes only the changes made to your BlackBerry. Changes to your computer application aren't reflected in your BlackBerry.

   • *One Way Sync to Device:* Synchronizes changes made in your computer application with your BlackBerry. Any changes made in your BlackBerry aren't reflected in your computer application.

9. **Click Next.**

   The options that you selected in Step 5 for the Organizer application appear in the dialog box. Figure 18-5 shows the Microsoft Outlook Options.

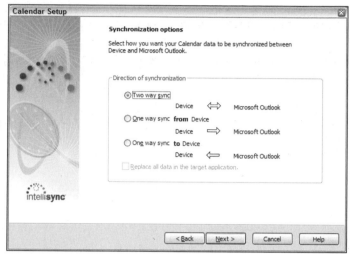

Figure 18-4:
Decide
which
direction
synchro-
nization
follows.

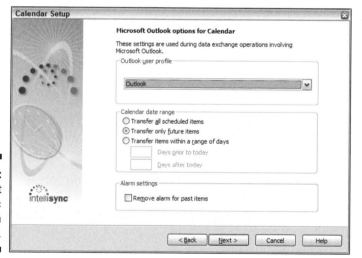

Figure 18-5:
Select
specific
application
settings.

10. **If you selected Outlook, select a user profile from the Outlook User Profile drop-down list.**

For synchronization to Microsoft Outlook, make sure that you choose the correct user profile, especially if you have multiple user profiles in your computer. Choosing the wrong one may put the wrong data into your BlackBerry.

11. **In the Calendar Date Range section, select a radio button to limit the calendar data you want synchronized.**

    For this example, we selected Transfer Only Future Items.

    You can control the amount of data that's reconciled or synchronized in a given application. For example, in Figure 18-5, you can specify whether to Transfer All Scheduled Items, Transfer Only Future Items, or Transfer Items within a Range of Days.

12. **(Optional) Select the Remove Alarm for Past Items check box if you don't want to keep the alarm setting for events that have already occurred.**

13. **Click Next to open the Calendar Setup Finish dialog box, and then click Finish.**

    You've completed the configuration of the Calendar synchronization you selected.

Mapping fields for synchronization

For all four Organizer applications, BlackBerry Desktop Software is intelligent enough to know which information — such as names, phone numbers, and addresses in Contacts — corresponds to information in Outlook. A specific bit of information, or *attribute,* is contained in a field. For instance, the value of a Home Phone Number field in Contacts needs to be mapped to the corresponding field in Outlook so that information is transferred correctly.

But not all fields on the computer side exist on the BlackBerry (and vice versa). For example, a Profession field doesn't exist in BlackBerry Contacts but is available in Exchange (Outlook) Address Book. In some instances, BlackBerry Desktop Software provides an alternative field and lets you decide whether to map it.

If you ever need to change the default mapping, you can. (The interface is the same for all Organizer applications, but we use Contacts in the following steps.) To map and un-map fields in Organizer, follow these steps:

1. **In the BlackBerry Desktop Software window, click the Organizer link.**

2. **Click the Configure Settings button.**

    The Select Device Application dialog box appears (refer to Figure 18-2).

3. **Select the Address Book check box.**

    The Advanced button is enabled.

4. **Click the Advanced button.**

    The Advanced dialog box appears, as shown in Figure 18-6.

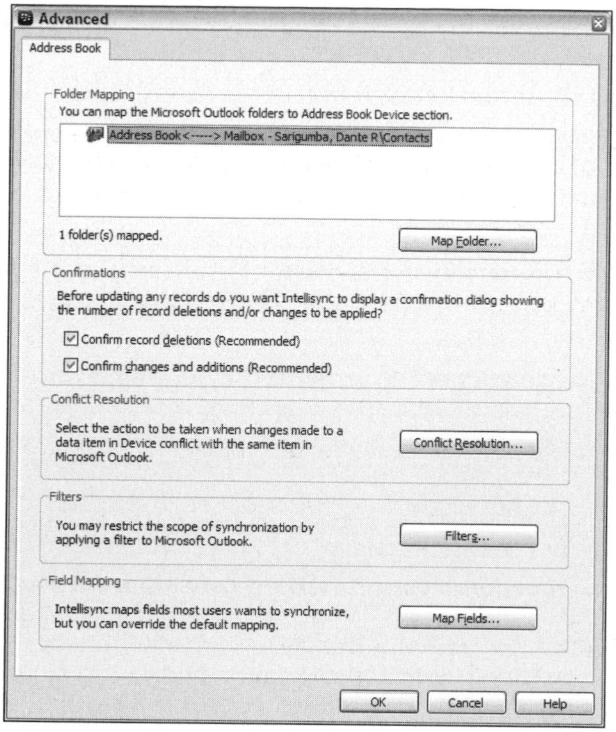

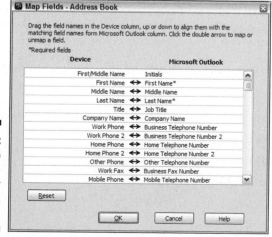

Figure 18-6:
The
Advanced
dialog box
for Address
Book.

5. Click the Map Fields button.

The Map Fields dialog box for the Address Book/Contacts application
appears, as shown in Figure 18-7.

Figure 18-7:
The Map
Fields dia-
log box for
Address
Book.

   6. **To map or un-map, click the arrow icons.**

   The arrow appears when you click an unmapped field and disappears when you click a mapped field.

   If you aren't careful, you can inadvertently deselect a mapping (such as Job Title) and suddenly have your titles out of sync. Double-check your mapping before you click OK. If you think you made a mistake, click Cancel to save yourself from having to restore settings.

   7. **Click OK to save your changes.**

Confirming record changes

Face facts: Doing a desktop synchronization isn't an interesting task, and few people perform it regularly. By default, BlackBerry Desktop Software prompts you for any changes it's trying to make (or perhaps undo) on either side of the fence. You can turn this feature on and off. You use the Advanced dialog box to set up whether you want a confirmation dialog box to appear when you make record changes to your Organizer data. Just follow these steps:

   1. **In the BlackBerry Desktop Software window, click the Organizer link.**

   The Organizer window appears.

   2. **Click the Configure Settings button.**

   The Select Device Application dialog box appears (refer to Figure 18-2).

   3. **Select the check box for the Organizer application for which you want a confirmation screen to appear.**

   For our example, we selected Address Book.

   4. **Click the Advanced button.**

   The Advanced dialog box appears, as shown in Figure 18-6. The Confirmations section gives you two options:

   • Confirm Record Deletions (Recommended)

   • Confirm Changes and Additions (Recommended)

   By default, both options are selected, so a prompt appears when you try to make any of these changes.

   5. **Deselect the check boxes next to the types of changes for which you don't want to receive a confirmation prompt.**

   Regardless of whether you select the Confirm Record Deletions (Recommended) option, BlackBerry Desktop Software displays a prompt if it detects that it's about to delete *all* records.

Resolving update conflicts

BlackBerry Desktop Software needs to know how you want to handle any conflicts between your BlackBerry and your computer application. A conflict normally happens when the same record is updated on your BlackBerry and also in Outlook. Suppose that you change Jane Doe's mobile number on both your BlackBerry and Outlook on your PC. Follow these steps to instruct BlackBerry Desktop Software how to handle conflicts:

1. **In the BlackBerry Desktop Software window, click the Organizer link.**

   The Organizer window opens.

2. **Click the Configure Settings button.**

   The Select Device Application dialog box appears (refer to Figure 18-2).

3. **Select the check box next to the application for which you want to specify how to handle record conflicts.**

   In our example, we selected Address Book.

4. **Click the Advanced button.**

   The Advanced dialog box appears (refer to Figure 18-6). This window has five sections, including Conflict Resolution.

5. **Click the Conflict Resolution button.**

   The Conflict Resolution dialog box, shown for Address Book in Figure 18-8, appears. You can tell BlackBerry Desktop Software to handle conflicts in the following ways:

   - *Add All Conflicting Items:* When a conflict happens, adds a new record to the BlackBerry for the changes on the computer and add a new record to the computer for the changes on the BlackBerry.

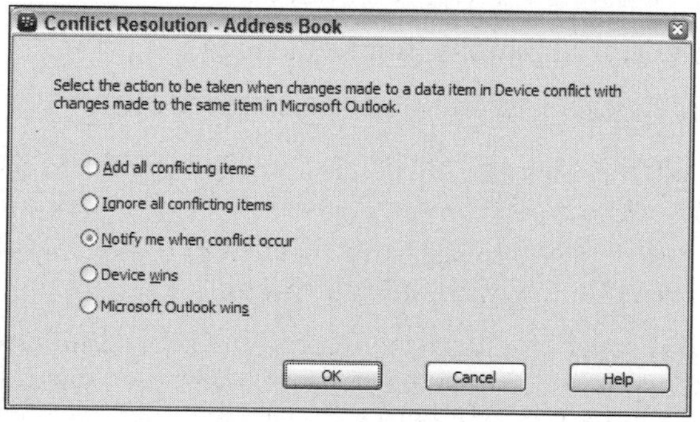

Figure 18-8:
Manage sync conflicts in the Conflict Resolution dialog box.

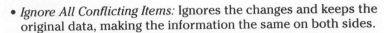

- *Ignore All Conflicting Items:* Ignores the changes and keeps the original data, making the information the same on both sides.

- *Notify Me When Conflict Occur:* This option is the safest because it prompts you at any conflict, giving you control over how BlackBerry Desktop Software deals with it. BlackBerry Desktop Software displays the details of the conflict and lets you resolve it.

- *Device Wins:* This option tells BlackBerry Desktop Software to disregard the changes in the computer and use handheld changes every time it encounters a conflict.

- *Microsoft Outlook Wins:* If you aren't using MS Outlook, this option is based on your application. This option tells BlackBerry Desktop Software to always discard changes on the smartphone and use the computer application's change when it encounters a conflict.

We don't recommend selecting either the Device Wins or Microsoft Outlook Wins option because you probably don't make the update that you want to keep on the same side every time.

6. **Select the radio button for the option you want, and then click OK to save the settings.**

Ready, set, synchronize!

Are you ready to synchronize? In the preceding sections, we show you ways to define synchronization filters and rules for your Organizer data. Now, it's time to be brave and synchronize. You can do so in one of two ways:

- **Manually:** In the BlackBerry Desktop Software window, select Device, and then select Sync All or Sync by Type from the menu that appears.

- **Automatically:** Select Automatically in the Device Options screen to synchronize organizer data every time you connect your device.

Using on-demand synchronization

On-demand synchronization is a feature in BlackBerry Desktop Software that lets you run synchronization manually. Remember that even if you set up automatic synchronization, actual synchronization doesn't happen right away. So, if you make updates to your appointments in Outlook while your BlackBerry is connected to your PC, this feature lets you be sure that your updates make it to your BlackBerry before you head out the door.

Follow these steps to manually synchronize with BlackBerry Desktop Software:

1. **In the BlackBerry Desktop Software window, click Organizer.**

   The Organizer window appears (refer to Figure 18-1).

2. **Select the check boxes for the data that you want to synchronize.**

   BlackBerry Desktop Software stores this setting and uses it for both manual and automatic synchronization.

3. **Click the Sync button located at the bottom of the window.**

   The synchronization starts, and a dialog box showing its progress appears. If you've set BlackBerry Desktop Software to have you confirm record additions, changes, or deletions (see the section "Confirming record changes," earlier in this chapter) and BlackBerry Desktop Software encounters such a record change, a dialog box similar to Figure 18-9 appears, prompting you to confirm the changes.

4. **If a Confirm Edits dialog box appears, click the appropriate button to Accept or Reject the change.**

   If you want to see the details of the change before you make a decision, you can click the Details button.

5. **If a conflict-related dialog box appears, select which record you want to keep from the two options — Record from BlackBerry or Record from the Computer — and then select Continue.**

   When the sync finishes, the progress dialog box disappears.

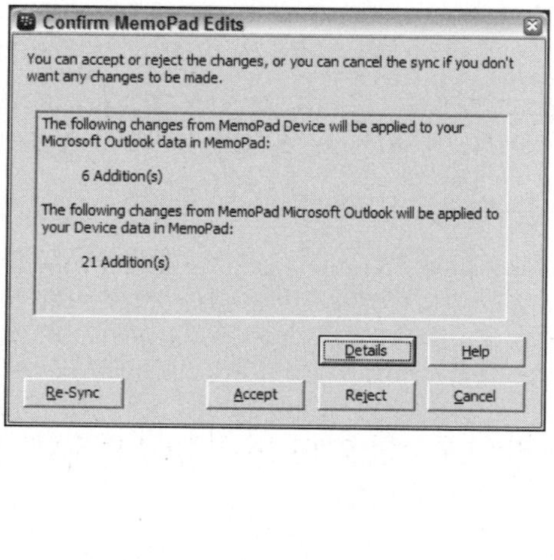

Figure 18-9:
Confirm record changes in the Confirm Edits dialog box.

Confirm MemoPad Edits

You can accept or reject the changes, or you can cancel the sync if you don't want any changes to be made.

The following changes from MemoPad Device will be applied to your Microsoft Outlook data in MemoPad:

6 Addition(s)

The following changes from MemoPad Microsoft Outlook will be applied to your Device data in MemoPad:

21 Addition(s)

Details   Help

Re-Sync   Accept   Reject   Cancel

If you turned on automatic synchronization (see the following section), the items you select in Step 2 automatically sync every time you connect your BlackBerry to your PC.

Synchronizing automatically

How many times do you think you'll want to reconfigure your Organizer synchronization setup? Rarely, right? After you configure it, you're done. And if you're like us, the reason you open BlackBerry Desktop Software is to sync your Organizer data. So, it's annoying to have to open BlackBerry Desktop Software and go to the trouble of selecting Device and then Sync All from the menu that appears.

To make BlackBerry Desktop Software run automatically every time you connect your BlackBerry to your PC, simply make sure that you select the Organizer Data check box in the Device Options dialog box by following these steps:

1. **In the BlackBerry Desktop Software window, select Device, and then select Device Options from the menu that appears.**

   A window like the one shown in Figure 18-10 appears.

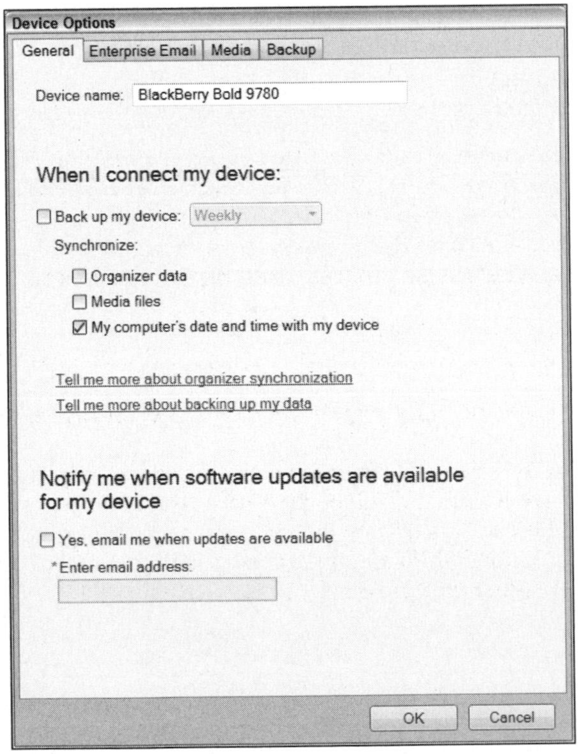

Device Options

| General | Enterprise Email | Media | Backup |

Device name: BlackBerry Bold 9780

When I connect my device:

☐ Back up my device: Weekly ▾

Synchronize:

☐ Organizer data
☑ Media files
☑ My computer's date and time with my device

Tell me more about organizer synchronization
Tell me more about backing up my data

Notify me when software updates are available for my device

☐ Yes, email me when updates are available
*Enter email address:

[   ]

OK   Cancel

Figure 18-10:
Sync automatically when you connect your BlackBerry to your PC.

2. **Select the Organizer Data check box below Synchronize.**

   This option is in the When I Connect My Device section.

3. **Click OK.**

   That's it. Whenever you connect your BlackBerry to your PC, BlackBerry Desktop Software automatically runs a synchronization process.

You may be asking, "What items will auto-synchronization sync?" Good question. BlackBerry Desktop Software automatically syncs the items you configured it to sync (see the section "Configuring Organizer data synchronization," earlier in this chapter).

Synchronizing Your BlackBerry on the Mac

When talking about BlackBerry Desktop Software on your Mac, you probably want to know about synchronizing Organizer data and music files. In the following sections, we delve into the details about configuring the sync, doing a manual sync, and doing an automatic sync on the Mac.

Setting synchronization options

You'll probably need to set synchronization options only once. To begin, connect your BlackBerry to your Mac by using your BlackBerry's USB cable; the BlackBerry Desktop Software window shown in Figure 18-11 should appear. If you don't have BlackBerry Desktop Software installed on your Mac, you can find the details on where to get and how to install the software in Chapter 17.

Device Options

Click the Device Options button to open the dialog box shown in Figure 18-12.

If you sync your BlackBerry with other computers, or even if you have Google Sync for Calendars and Contacts, select the With Other Computers (Safer Sync) radio button below This Device Is Synchronized. This option disables the automatic sync option, which can create duplicate contacts on your BlackBerry and your other computers if you leave it enabled.

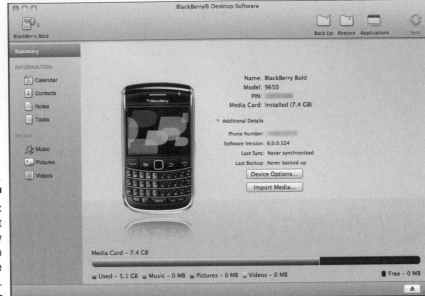

Figure 18-11:
The default
BlackBerry
Desktop
Software
window.

Figure 18-12:
Decide
whether you
want your
BlackBerry
to sync only
on this Mac.

Make sure that you select the With Other Computers (Safer Sync) option if you have sync software other than BlackBerry Desktop Software because each sync software has a different mechanism to update records on your BlackBerry. Record updates from any of these other sync software may appear as additions to BlackBerry Desktop Software, so it adds those updated records to the Mac's Organizer program.

However, if you sync your BlackBerry only with the Mac on which you're currently running the software, select the With This Computer Only radio button. After you select the appropriate radio button, click the OK button to return to the BlackBerry Desktop Software window.

The listing on the left (below the Summary heading) contains links for navigating to the option windows. We describe these options in the following sections.

Calendar and Tasks

Calendar and Tasks have very similar settings windows because most of the Tasks items have associated dates and are essentially tied to your Calendar.

Clicking the Calendar link on the BlackBerry Desktop Software window opens the window shown in Figure 18-13. Clicking Tasks opens the window shown in Figure 18-14.

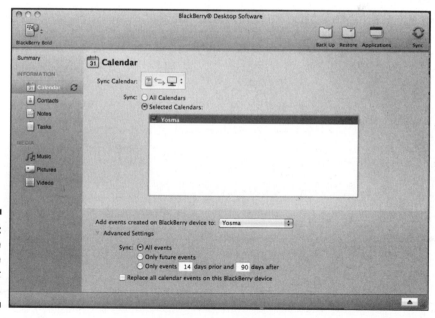

Figure 18-13: Configure how the Calendar syncs.

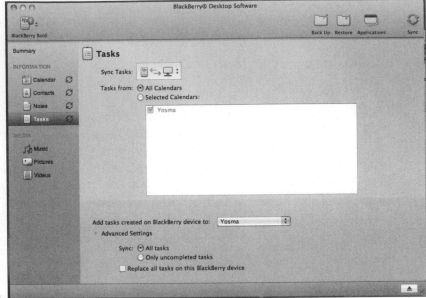

Figure 18-14:
Configure
the Tasks
sync.

You can configure how your appointments and tasks are synced with the following options:

✔ **Sync Calendar (or Sync Tasks):** Include Calendar or Tasks in the sync by clicking the box to the right of Sync and selecting Two Way (shown with two opposing arrows, as in Figure 18-13) from the drop-down list that appears; otherwise, select Do Not Sync (the default, showing an X, rather than the arrows).

To quickly verify that you set an app for Two Way sync, look for the Sync icon (two arrows forming a circle) next to the app's name on the left of the BlackBerry Desktop Software window (refer to Figure 18-13 for Calendar). This icon appears for Calendar, Contacts, Notes, Tasks, and Music.

✔ **Sync:** You need to worry about this section only if you have multiple calendar applications on your Mac. You can include all calendars or select one from the list. The BlackBerry Calendar app uses different colors to indicate which calendar an appointment belongs to.

✔ **Add Events Created on BlackBerry Device To:** The default Calendar on your BlackBerry doesn't tie directly to any Mac applications, and appointments you create in your BlackBerry aren't synced to any Mac applications. Selecting a particular Mac application from this drop-down list tells BlackBerry Desktop Software to sync those appointments or events to that application.

✓ **(Advanced Settings) Sync:** Use this setting to limit the number of appointments, events, or tasks to sync on your BlackBerry. After all, past events and tasks just occupy valuable space on your smartphone with no purpose but a record. By selecting the appropriate radio button, you can control which ones your BlackBerry carries.

For Calendar, select All Events (the default), Only Future Events, or Only Events *n* Days Prior and *n* Days After. The last option allows you to enter numbers that represent a range of dates relative to the current day. The default is 14 days in the past and 90 days in the future. For Tasks, select either All Tasks (the default) or Only Uncompleted Tasks.

✓ **(Advanced Settings) Replace All Calendar Events on This BlackBerry Device/Replace All Tasks on This BlackBerry Device:** Keep this check box deselected unless you want a fresh start, in which you copy to your BlackBerry appointments, events, or tasks from your Mac. Any appointments you have on your BlackBerry that are not on the Mac will be gone after the sync.

Contacts

Click the Contacts link on the BlackBerry Desktop Software window to display the window shown in Figure 18-15.

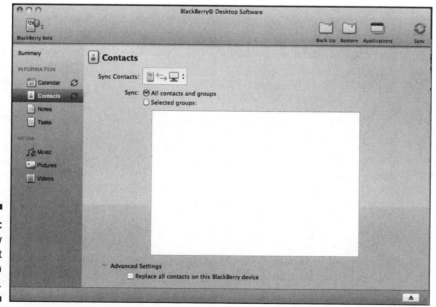

Figure 18-15:
Specify how you want Contacts to sync.

In this window, you can do the following:

- ✔ **Sync Contacts:** Click the box to the right of Contacts to open a drop-down list that allows you to select either Two Way (shown with two opposing arrows, as in Figure 18-14) or Do Not Sync (the default, which shows an X, rather than the arrows).

  You can quickly verify that you set an app for Two Way sync by locating the Sync icon (two arrows forming a circle) next to the app's name on the left of the BlackBerry Desktop Software window.

- ✔ **Sync:** Select the radio button for either All Contacts and Groups, or Selected Groups. If you select Selected Groups, you can specify in the list the groups to which you want to sync.

- ✔ **(Advanced Settings) Replace All Contacts on This BlackBerry Device:** Keep this check box deselected unless you want a fresh start, copying all contacts from your Mac to your smartphone. Any contacts that you have on your BlackBerry but not on your Mac disappear after the sync.

Notes

When you select Notes on the BlackBerry Desktop Software window, the window shown in Figure 18-16 appears. In this window, you can configure the syncing of Notes or MemoPad items on your BlackBerry:

- ✔ **Sync Notes:** Specify whether you want Notes included in the sync by clicking the image to the right of Sync Notes. From the drop-down list that appears, select either Two Way (two opposing arrows, as shown in Figure 18-16) or Do Not Sync (the default, which shows an X).

  When you set an app for Two Way sync, a Sync icon (two arrows forming a circle) appears next to the app's name on the left of the BlackBerry Desktop Software window.

- ✔ **Sync Account:** If you have multiple note-keeping programs on your Mac, this setting allows you to choose with which one you want to sync your BlackBerry. The default is Apple Mail Notes.

- ✔ **(Advanced Settings) Replace All Notes on This BlackBerry Device:** If you select this option, the Mac notes are copied to your BlackBerry, replacing all the notes you have on your BlackBerry. Keep this check box deselected unless you want a fresh start, copying to your BlackBerry all notes from your Mac. Any notes you have on your BlackBerry that aren't on the Mac disappear after the sync.

Music

You can easily sync your iTunes playlists to the BlackBerry by clicking Music in the BlackBerry Desktop Software window. The window shown in Figure 18-17 appears.

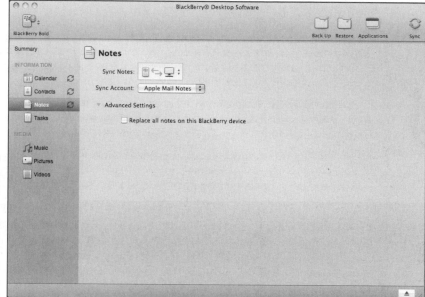

Figure 18-16:
Tell
BlackBerry
Desktop
Software
how you
want to
sync Notes.

Figure 18-17:
Configure
how iTunes
music syncs
with your
BlackBerry.

You can specify the following options:

- **Sync Music:** Decide whether to include Music in the sync. Just below this check box, the Sync All Music and Include Videos check boxes appear. If you have a big music library in iTunes and your microSD card can't hold them all, pick and choose from the different categories listed.

  On the left of the BlackBerry Desktop Software window, the Sync icon (two arrows forming a circle) appears next to Music if you set Two Way sync.

- **Fill with Random Music:** If you want BlackBerry Desktop Software to fill the rest of your BlackBerry's microSD card with random songs from iTunes that you haven't already selected from the Artists, Playlists, or Genres categories, select this option. You can find the songs in the Random Music playlist in the Media Player of your BlackBerry (we talk about the Media Player in Chapter 15). If you want to leave room on your microSD card for other storage, such as pictures you take, leave the check box deselected (which is the default).

Some useful information in this window relates to the memory space of your BlackBerry, giving you some idea about how much memory your playlist is occupying and how much free space is left on your device.

Pictures

BlackBerry Desktop Software lets you sync your iPhoto albums to your BlackBerry through the Pictures window on the BlackBerry Desktop Software (shown in Figure 18-18).

If you select the Sync iPhoto Albums and Events check box, you can specify which pictures in iPhoto you want to sync. Just below this check box, you can select either of two other check boxes:

- **All Events:** If you select this check box, you take everything iPhoto has. We recommend that you leave this check box deselected so that you can pick and choose the events you want to put in your BlackBerry. iPhoto maintains the albums and events listed in Figure 18-18. Each one may contain multiple photos.

- **Include Videos from iPhoto:** iPhoto also stores videos. This setting allows you to copy those videos to your BlackBerry.

If you select the Optimize Pictures check box, at the bottom-right of the window, BlackBerry Desktop Software resizes the images before copying them into your BlackBerry so that those images are the optimal size for viewing on your BlackBerry and saving some storage space.

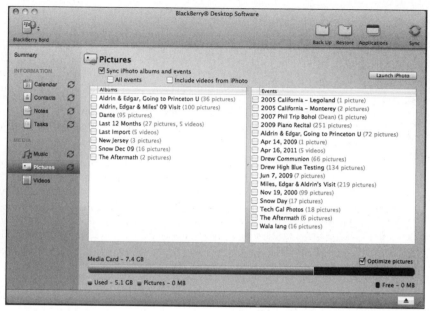

Figure 18-18:
Configure
how
Pictures
sync from
your Mac
to your
BlackBerry.

The bottom portion of the window shows useful information related to the memory still available on your BlackBerry's microSD card, so you have some idea of how much memory you can use for this sync.

Videos

You may want to copy your iTunes videos to your BlackBerry. Simply click Videos on the BlackBerry Desktop Software window to open the window shown in Figure 18-19.

If you select the Sync Specific Videos from iTunes check box, you can specify which videos to include in the sync. All the videos you have in iTunes appear in a list below this check box (see Figure 18-19). Simply select the check box to the left of the name of the video (or videos) you want include.

Like the other media-related sync windows, Music and Pictures (see the preceding sections), the bottom portion of the Video window shows useful information related to how much free memory your BlackBerry's microSD card contains.

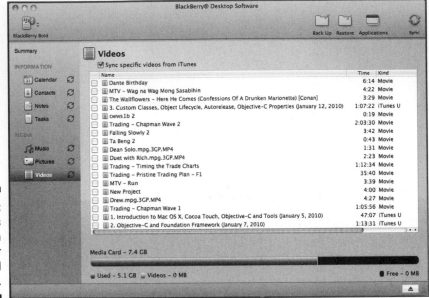

Figure 18-19:
Sync videos
between
your
Mac and
BlackBerry.

Deleting all music files on your BlackBerry

You might be wondering why we bother to include a section on deleting music files. What does deleting music files have to do with data synchronization? With BlackBerry Desktop Software, you have the option to sync your BlackBerry with iTunes playlists. You may want to start fresh and clear your BlackBerry of whatever music files it has because if music on your BlackBerry is a subset of what you have in iTunes, you end up with duplicate files.

To do a one-time deletion of all music files on your BlackBerry, follow these steps:

1. **Connect your BlackBerry to your Mac by using the USB cable that came with your BlackBerry.**

   The BlackBerry Desktop Software window appears.

2. **Click the Device Options button.**

   The Device Options screen appears. This screen has several tabs that you can access by clicking the appropriate icon.

3. **On the Device Options screen, click the Media icon.**

   The Media tab of the Device Options screen appears, featuring a Delete button and a short description explaining that if you click this button, you delete all music files on the BlackBerry.

4. **On the Media tab, click the Delete button.**

   A confirmation prompt appears, asking whether you really want to delete your music files on the device.

5. **Click OK.**

Syncing manually

After you choose the sync configuration you want (which we talk about in the "Setting synchronization options" section, earlier in this chapter), you're ready to sync.

To sync manually, click the green Sync button, which appears in the top-right corner of the BlackBerry Desktop Software window. If this is your first attempt at running the sync, the prompt shown in Figure 18-20 appears. BlackBerry Desktop Software needs to establish the latest copy of your data, and to do that, it needs to know how you want to proceed:

✔ **Merge Data:** Click this button if you want BlackBerry Desktop Software to merge the relevant data on your Mac with your BlackBerry data. Merging basically combines two sets of data without checking for duplicate content. If you click this button and have synced your Mac before by using a different type of software, such as PocketMac, you end up with duplicate content appearing on both your BlackBerry and Mac.

✔ **Replace Device Data:** Click this button if you want to transfer a fresh copy of data from your Mac to your BlackBerry. After the sync, your BlackBerry data is the same as what you have on your Mac.

Figure 18-20: Doing a manual sync for the first time.

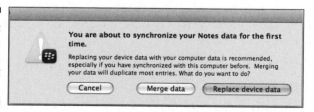

You are about to synchronize your Notes data for the first time.

Replacing your device data with your computer data is recommended, especially if you have synchronized with this computer before. Merging your data will duplicate most entries. What do you want to do?

Cancel | Merge data | Replace device data

Configuring an automatic sync

It's annoying to have to click the Sync button every time you want to sync. If you want the sync to occur automatically every time you connect your BlackBerry to your Mac, follow these steps:

1. **Connect your BlackBerry to your Mac by using your BlackBerry's USB cable.**

   The BlackBerry Desktop Software window appears.

2. **Click the Device Options button.**

   The Device Options screen appears, displaying the General tab.

3. **Select the Automatically Sync when Device Is Connected check box.**

4. **Click OK.**

   The next time you connect your BlackBerry to your Mac, the BlackBerry Desktop Software automatically runs and synchronization starts.

Chapter 19

Protecting Your Information

*I*magine that you left your BlackBerry smartphone in the back of a cab or on the train: You've lost your BlackBerry for good! Okay, not good. So, have you lost all your information forever? Not necessarily.

You don't need to worry about information security — assuming that you set up a security password on your BlackBerry (which we talk about in Chapter 3). But you *do* need to worry about how to get back all the information on your BlackBerry after you lose that BlackBerry. If you're like us and you store important information on your BlackBerry, this chapter is for you. Don't take lightly the need to protect vital information such as clients' and friends' contact information, notes from phone calls with clients — and, of course, those precious e-mail messages. Backing up this information is a reliable way to prevent losing it forever.

The Benefits of Backing Up

You can make sure your data is backed up properly in numerous ways. From BlackBerry Desktop Software (for either a PC or the Mac) to BlackBerry Enterprise Server, you can be sure you can find a way that works for you:

> ✓ **BlackBerry Desktop Software:** If you're part of a small business or purchased your own BlackBerry, then your best bet is the BlackBerry Desktop Software that came with your BlackBerry (or that you downloaded from BlackBerry's website). For installation instructions, please see Chapter 17.

The drawback of using BlackBerry Desktop Software is that you always need to connect your BlackBerry to a PC or Mac if you want to back up your information.

✔ **BlackBerry Enterprise Server:** If your employer handed you a BlackBerry and the BlackBerry is part of BlackBerry Enterprise Server (BES), you don't need to do anything because all your information is stored on the corporate BES server.

Backing Up Your BlackBerry

BlackBerry Desktop Software allows you to back up all the sensitive data on your BlackBerry, including contacts, e-mails, memos, to-do items, all personal preferences and options, and more. In the rest of this chapter, all the BlackBerry Desktop Software instructions assume that you have a PC platform. (The steps on the Mac platform are similar.)

You probably have your e-mails already stored in an account such as Gmail or Yahoo! Mail. But you can still back up e-mails, so when you switch to a replacement BlackBerry, all your emails are already in your BlackBerry inbox after you do a restore.

Creating a backup file

To back up information on your BlackBerry, follow these steps:

1. **Open BlackBerry Desktop Software on your PC by choosing Start⇨All Programs⇨BlackBerry⇨BlackBerry Desktop Software.**

   If you haven't already installed BlackBerry Desktop Software on your computer, see Chapter 17.

2. **Connect your BlackBerry to your PC by using the USB cable that came with your BlackBerry.**

   If everything is set up correctly, a dialog box on your PC asks you to type your BlackBerry security password. If you don't have a security password set up on your BlackBerry, then skip to Step 4.

3. **Type your password in the Password text box, and then click the OK button.**

   Your BlackBerry connects to your PC.

4. **Click the Backup Now button in the BlackBerry Desktop Software window.**

The Backup Options dialog box opens; see Figure 19-1. You're ready to back up data from your BlackBerry.

5. **Type the filename that you want to use for your backup in the File Name text box.**

6. **Specify a place to save your file in the Save Backup File To text box.**

   You can click the Change Folder button and navigate to the location you want.

7. **Click the Back Up button.**

   The backup process starts. A dialog box similar to Figure 19-2 appears. When finished, a new dialog box appears, indicating a successful backup.

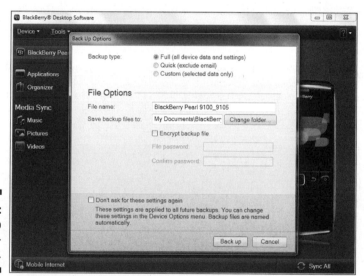

Figure 19-1: The Backup Options dialog box.

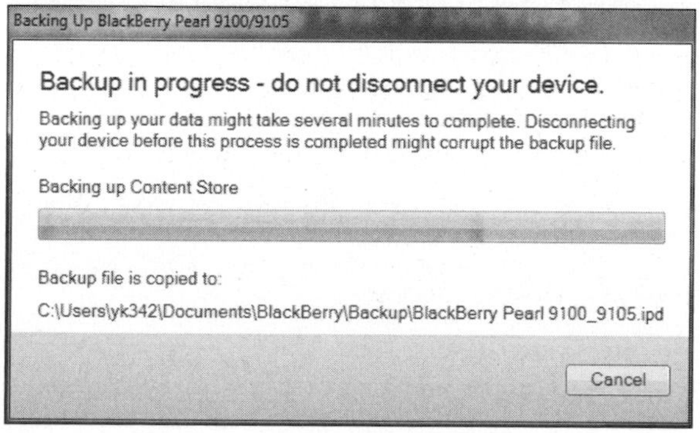

Figure 19-2: The Backing Up progress dialog box.

Setting up automatic backups

What's better than backing up your information once? Remembering to back up regularly! What's better than regularly backing up? You guessed it — having your computer and BlackBerry run backups automatically. After you schedule automated backups of your BlackBerry, you can really have peace of mind when it comes to preventing information loss.

To set up an auto-backup, follow these steps:

1. **Open BlackBerry Desktop Software on your PC.**

2. **Click Device, and then select Device Options from the drop-down list that appears.**

   The Device Options dialog box (shown in Figure 19-3) opens.

3. **Select the Backup My Device check box.**

   The Backup My Device drop-down list activates.

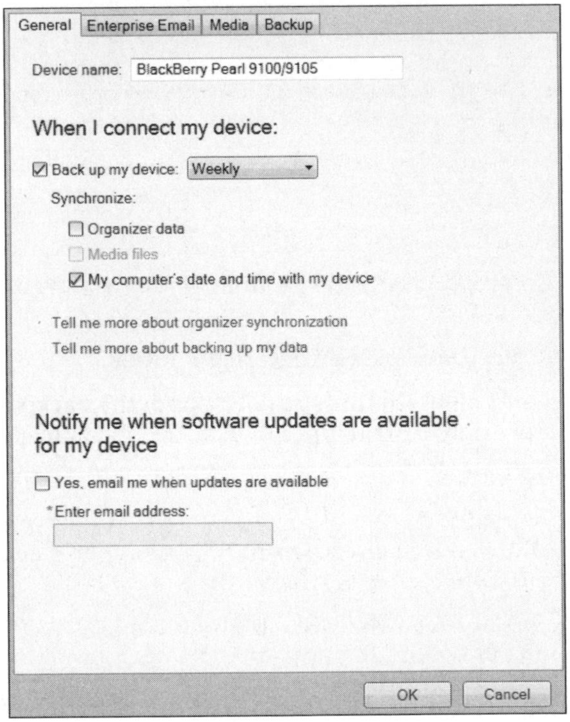

General | Enterprise Email | Media | Backup

Device name: BlackBerry Pearl 9100/9105

When I connect my device:

☑ Back up my device: Weekly ▼

Synchronize:
☐ Organizer data
☐ Media files
☑ My computer's date and time with my device

· Tell me more about organizer synchronization
Tell me more about backing up my data

Notify me when software updates are available for my device

☐ Yes, email me when updates are available
*Enter email address:

OK   Cancel

Figure 19-3:
Set auto-backups in the Options dialog box.

4. **Select how often you want to back up your Blackberry from the Backup My Device drop-down list.**

   Your options are Daily, Weekly, Bi-Weekly, and Monthly.

5. **Click the Okay button to confirm your settings.**

   From now on, every time you connect your BlackBerry to your PC or Mac, BlackBerry Desktop Software backs up your BlackBerry according to the schedule you set.

Restoring Your BlackBerry from Backup Information

We hope that you never have to read this section more than once because every time you perform a full restore from backup, it probably means that you've lost information that you hope to find from the backup you created on your computer.

The steps to fully restoring your backup information are simple:

1. **Open BlackBerry Desktop Software on your PC by choosing Start⇨All Programs⇨BlackBerry⇨BlackBerry Desktop Software.**

2. **Click Device, and then select Restore from the drop-down list that appears.**

   The Restore dialog box appears, as shown in Figure 19-4.

3. **From the table, select a backed up file from which you want to restore your BlackBerry.**

4. **Select the All Device Data and Settings radio button.**

   This option restores all the settings and data from the backed-up file. If you want to restore only certain types of data, see the following section.

5. **Click the Restore button.**

   A progress bar similar to Figure 19-5 appears, showing the progress of the full restore. When the progress bar disappears, your BlackBerry is now fully restored from the backup file.

   The full restore might take awhile to finish. Don't unplug your BlackBerry from your computer during this time!

6. **When the progress bar disappears, unplug your BlackBerry from the computer.**

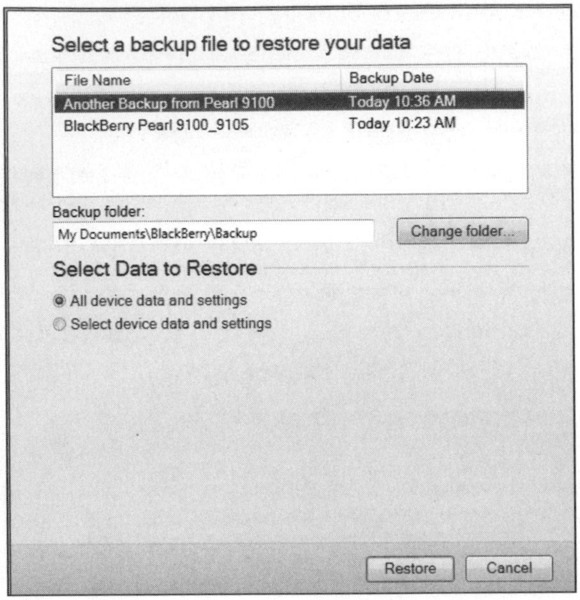

Figure 19-4:
The Restore
dialog box.

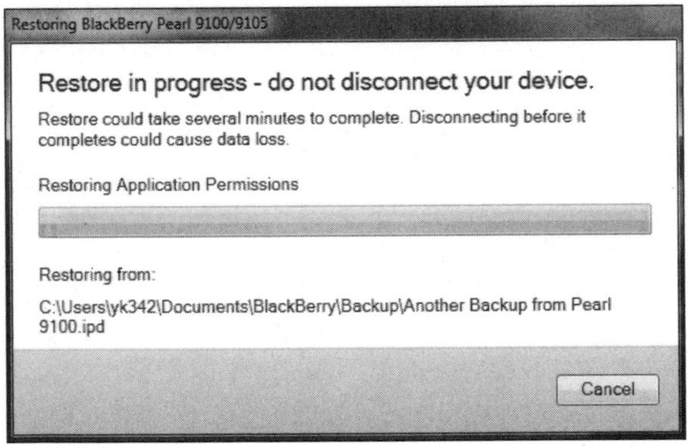

Figure 19-5:
A
BlackBerry
data restore
in progress.

Restoring only some of your backup data

You might not want a full restore in a particular situation; you might want to do only a selective restore. For example, say you don't want to override some of your new additions to Contacts. Rather, you want to restore only your e-mail messages.

To restore your BlackBerry the way you want, follow these steps:

1. **Open BlackBerry Desktop Software on your PC.**

2. **Click Device, and then select Restore from the drop-down list that appears.**

   The Restore dialog box appears, as shown in Figure 19-4.

3. **From the table, select a backed-up file from which you want to restore your BlackBerry.**

4. **Select the Select Device Data and Settings radio button.**

   A table of different data types appears, as shown in Figure 19-6.

5. **Select the check boxes for the data type(s) that you want to restore.**

   The different information categories, or databases, appear on the left side of the table.

6. **Click the Restore button.**

   A progress bar similar to Figure 19-5 appears, showing the progress of the selective restore. When the progress bar disappears, your BlackBerry has restored versions of the data types you selected in Step 5 from the backup file.

7. **When the progress bar disappears, unplug your BlackBerry from the computer.**

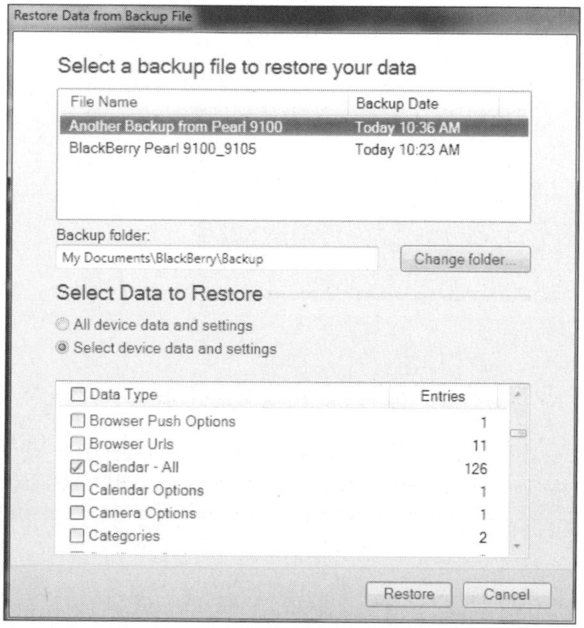

Figure 19-6: The Restore Data from Backup File dialog box.

Clearing some information from your BlackBerry

You can clear, or delete, information on your BlackBerry selectively by using BlackBerry Desktop Software. Suppose you want to clear only your phone logs from your BlackBerry. You can tediously select one phone log at a time and press Delete, and then repeat that process until you delete all your BlackBerry's phone logs. However, you can use a faster way: selective deleting. Just delete a database from the advanced Backup/Restore dialog box by using the Backup and Restore function of BlackBerry Desktop Software.

To selectively delete databases on your BlackBerry, follow these steps:

1. **Open BlackBerry Desktop Software on your PC.**

2. **Click Device in the top-left corner of the BlackBerry Desktop Software window, and then select the Delete Data option from the drop-down list that appears.**

   The Delete Device Data window appears, as shown in Figure 19-7.

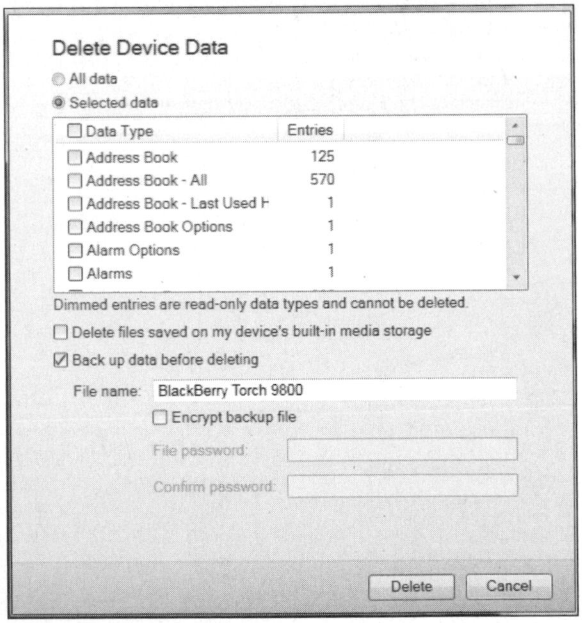

Figure 19-7:
The Delete
Device Data
window.

Delete Device Data

○ All data
◉ Selected data

☐ Data Type	Entries	
☐ Address Book	125	
☐ Address Book - All	570	
☐ Address Book - Last Used F	1	
☐ Address Book Options	1	
☐ Alarm Options	1	
☐ Alarms	1	

Dimmed entries are read-only data types and cannot be deleted.

☐ Delete files saved on my device's built-in media storage
☑ Back up data before deleting

File name: BlackBerry Torch 9800

☐ Encrypt backup file

File password:

Confirm password:

Delete   Cancel

3. **Select the database(s) you want to delete.**

   If you want to select more than one database, Ctrl-click each database.

4. **Click the Clear button on the right side of the dialog box.**

   A warning dialog box appears, asking you to confirm your deletion.

5. **Click OK.**

   A progress bar appears, showing the progress of the deletion. When the progress bar disappears, the information categories you selected are cleared from your BlackBerry.

Chapter 20

Finding and Installing Applications

T hink of your BlackBerry as a mini-laptop on which you can run preinstalled applications, as well as install new applications. You can even upgrade the operating system. (Yup, that's right — your BlackBerry has an OS.)

In this chapter, we introduce BlackBerry App World, which you can use to load applications (who'd have guessed?) onto your BlackBerry, as well as how to download BlackBerry apps from other online sources. And we talk about how you can upgrade the OS of your smartphone.

In Chapter 22, you can find some must-have applications that make your BlackBerry that much more amazing.

Using BlackBerry App World

Your BlackBerry comes with BlackBerry App World, an application store (or app store) that provides an organized listing of apps, both free and for purchase.

Navigating App World

To launch the App World store, simply select BlackBerry App World from your BlackBerry's Home screen. BlackBerry App World sports an icon similar to the one on the Menu key, but enclosed in a circle. After you launch App World, a progress screen appears, and, after the app is loaded, a Featured Items screen similar to Figure 20-1 appears.

Figure 20-1:
BlackBerry
App World
showcases
featured
applica-
tions.

If you don't have App World on your BlackBerry, you can download it from the Research in Motion (RIM) website at `http://us.blackberry.com/apps-software/appworld`.

The bottom of the screen in Figure 20-1 shows a few icons that you can use to navigate the store. From left to right, they are

✔ **Categories:** Apps are organized and showcased in a series of categories. Select this icon to open the Categories screen, where you can explore a certain type of app.

✔ **Top Free:** Find it here first. If you're lucky, the type of app you're looking for is offered free of charge. Select this icon to open the Top Free screen, where you can find the most popular free apps.

✔ **Top Paid:** Best-selling apps appear when you select this icon.

✔ **Search:** If you know the app that you're looking for, select this icon to open the Search screen. You can enter the name in the blank text field on the top of the Search screen and then press the trackpad to search the app in the store.

✔ **My World:** Select this icon to open the My World screen, where the apps you've downloaded from the store appear.

If you're sitting at a computer, you'll be glad to know that RIM created a web version of App World. Using your desktop Internet browser, you can visit the

site at `http://appworld.blackberry.com/webstore`. The site allows you to send an e-mail that includes a download link for the app that you're interested in to your device.

Installing an application by using App World

Find a free time-killing game at the store? You can install the app easily, and all the links you need to perform the installation probably appear on the screen when you select the app's name. Follow these steps to install an app:

1. **Select BlackBerry App World on your BlackBerry's Home screen.**

2. **Navigate to the application you want to install.**

3. **Select the application's icon.**

    A screen similar to Figure 20-2 appears (this example shows a Download button for the free app SmrtGuard Mobile Security).

Figure 20-2: Download an app.

4. **Select the Download button.**

    The My World screen appears. The app you're downloading and a progress bar appear at the top, as shown in Figure 20-3. When the download has finished, the installation kicks in. A prompt appears after the app is installed, as shown in Figure 20-4.

Figure 20-3:
The prog-
ress of the
download.

Figure 20-4:
The app is
successfully
installed.

Any app you download appears in the Downloads view on the Home screen.
To get to the Downloads view, follow these steps:

1. **From the BlackBerry Home screen, slide the trackpad to select the title of the panel.**

   For a quick refresher on panels, check out Chapter 2. The title of the panel is the text right above the application icons.

2. **Slide the trackpad sideways until you see the word Downloads in the title.**

You are now in the Downloads panel, which contains all the applications you downloaded.

3. **Click the trackpad to show the panel in full screen.**

   You can scroll vertically after you have the panel displayed in full screen so that you can see the rest of the application icons.

Finding and Installing Applications from Other App Stores

BlackBerry App World is not the only app store out there in BlackBerry Land. You also can check out the following pioneers. Why do you need additional app stores? So that you can shop for better prices, of course. These app stores have been around since even before BlackBerry App World appeared, and they have a decent collection of apps:

✔ **Handango (`www.handango.com`):** Handango is one of the oldest store-fronts that sell applications for mobile devices. It started selling apps through its website but eventually created an app store. Use BlackBerry Browser to download Handango's app store from it website.

✔ **CrackBerry.com AppVerse (`http://software.crackberry.com/appverse.asp`):** Partnering with MobiHand, CrackBerry.com also provides an app store where you can find great applications to download.

   Visit CrackBerry.com's app store, AppVerse, before you decide to buy an app (from AppVerse or anywhere else), for a couple of good reasons:

   • You may find daily promotions of up to a 50-percent discount.

   • They offer refunds. App World doesn't.

✔ **BlackBerry Application Center:** Software built by RIM, but the carrier has control over what applications show up in your BlackBerry's Application Center. Some of the big wireless carriers go through a rigorous process of testing an app before they list it in the store. Most carriers support the BlackBerry Application Center app, which is typically already installed on your BlackBerry, possibly under the brand name of your wireless carrier. If you don't find the app on your BlackBerry, your carrier most likely doesn't support it. To be sure, you can always contact your network carrier's customer support.

Finding and Installing Applications Directly from a Developer's Website

Most of the newly built applications are available in BlackBerry App World, but some of the free apps may not be listed there at all.

Publishing an app in BlackBerry App World (or any other app store, for that matter) requires effort from the developer. Most app developers who consider BlackBerry app development a hobby don't publish their apps anywhere but on their own websites.

To find useful applications, check out BlackBerry users' forums, such as CrackBerry.com and BlackBerryForums.com. You can get unsolicited feedback — both good and bad — from existing users about an app, which can help you make a decision about which app to try out.

If you find an app in the forums that isn't available in BlackBerry App World, simply do a Google search for the app name. You probably get results that include the app developer's website, where you can most likely install the app by using the BlackBerry Browser. Chapter 12 explains how to use Browser to install an app.

Upgrading the BlackBerry OS

The operating system (OS) used by BlackBerry has gone through a few revisions. The BlackBerry OS update comes from BlackBerry Handheld Software and is available on RIM's website at `http://us.blackberry.com/update`.

RIM historically changes its website addresses often. If the OS update link is broken, simply go to RIM's home page, where you always can find the Apps & Software link (which can lead you to the OS update page).

Upgrading the BlackBerry OS, Windows style

You don't need to have the BlackBerry Desktop Software to upgrade the OS of your BlackBerry. From any Windows computer, you can start the upgrade process by following these steps:

1. **Connect your BlackBerry to your PC by using the BlackBerry's USB cable.**

2. **On your PC, open Internet Explorer.**

3. **In Internet Explorer's address bar, type** http://us.blackberry.com/ update, **and then press Enter.**

   The Update Your BlackBerry page appears, which helps you figure out whether you need to download a new OS.

4. **On the Update Your BlackBerry page, click the Check for Updates button.**

   If your BlackBerry has an updated OS, a screen similar to Figure 20-5 appears, displaying the description of the latest OS for your device.

Figure 20-5:
Available
OS updates.

The OS appears only if you need an upgrade — meaning that your BlackBerry OS is out of date. If you still have the latest OS on your device, a message screen appears, telling you that no BlackBerry Device Software updates are available. If you receive this message, you can skip the rest of the steps.

5. **In the Update BlackBerry Device Software dialog box, click Get Update.**

   The Update Options dialog box appears, as shown in Figure 20-6, where you can decide whether you want to back up your BlackBerry device data before you upgrade your OS.

   We suggest that you back up your device data in case something goes wrong with the upgrade.

Figure 20-6:
Choose
whether
to back
up your
device data
before you
upgrade.

6. **Select the Back Up Device Data check box, and then click Install Update.**

   The BlackBerry OS upgrade starts, complete with a progress window that shows a series of steps and a progress bar. The entire process takes about ten minutes, depending on your PC model and the OS version to which you're upgrading.

   At times during the BlackBerry OS upgrade, your BlackBerry's display goes on and off. Don't worry; it's normal.

   When the progress window disappears, the OS upgrade is complete.

Upgrading the BlackBerry OS, Mac style

You upgrade your BlackBerry OS from your Mac by following these steps:

1. **Connect the BlackBerry to your Mac by using the BlackBerry's USB cable.**

2. **On your Mac, click BlackBerry Desktop Software on the Dock.**

   If you don't see the BlackBerry Desktop Software icon on the Dock, locate it by using the Finder, which appears at the left end of the Dock.

3. **In the BlackBerry Desktop Software window, click the Applications icon.**

   The Install/Remove Applications window appears, listing the applications installed on your BlackBerry and the ones available for installation.

4. Click the Check for Updates button, in the bottom-left of the window.

BlackBerry Desktop Software checks online for any new versions of the OS for your BlackBerry. If it finds one, it downloads that update and lists it on the Applications window.

5. Select the check box to the left of the OS in the list.

6. Click the Start button to start the upgrade.

A progress screen appears. Don't disconnect your BlackBerry during the upgrade. Your BlackBerry's screen turns on and off — don't worry; it's normal.

When the progress screen disappears, the OS upgrade is complete.

Part VI
The Part of Tens

In this part . . .

*I*f the earlier parts of this book are the cake and frosting, this part is the cherry on top. Delve into these two short but sweet chapters to find out how to accessorize your BlackBerry and extend your experience with a handful of must-have apps.

Chapter 21

Ten Great BlackBerry Accessories

*W*hen you purchase a BlackBerry, the box it comes in contains a few essentials: a battery, a charger, and a USB cable. If you're like us, though, you're not satisfied with just what's included in the box. In this chapter, we present the accessories that we think supplement your BlackBerry well, and we also tell you where to shop for them.

Cases for Protection and Style

If your BlackBerry didn't come with a case (most don't), you need to get one so that your BlackBerry doesn't get scratched or damaged. Cases from the following places can set you back anywhere from $15 to $35, which isn't too bad for looking hip. Check out CrackBerry.com (`http://shop.crack berry.com/blackberry-cases.htm`) and the official RIM online shop (`www.shopblackberry.com`).

BlackBerry Screen Protector

Rather than the protector cases described in the preceding section, you can try Invisible Shield for BlackBerry, which starts for about $15. You can get it at `www.zagg.com/invisibleshield`.

MicroSD Memory Card

If you want to store a lot of music, pictures, or simply files on your BlackBerry, you definitely need to get a microSD memory card. A microSD with the maximum memory capacity of 32GB costs about $55. If you don't need that much storage, you can get a microSD that has a memory capacity of 2GB for around $5. You can get a microSD card from almost any of the online shops (we get ours from Amazon.com because it offers free shipping).

If your laptop has an SD slot, make sure to buy a microSD card that comes with a card adapter. That way, you can use the same microSD card for your BlackBerry and your laptop. Two uses for the price of one. Nice!

Extra BlackBerry Battery

An extra battery for your BlackBerry comes in handy if you're a daily BlackBerry user. We recommend that you buy your battery only from Research in Motion (RIM), the maker of BlackBerry, and not from some other manufacturer, because a faulty battery can seriously damage your BlackBerry — maybe beyond repair.

You can buy a battery manufactured by RIM from the official RIM online shop (www.shopblackberry.com) or PocketBerry (http://store.pocket berry.com).

BlackBerry Car Charger

If you're always on the go, you'd better have a portable charger on hand. You can carry the charger that's included with your BlackBerry around town (and the world) because it has multiple adapters for different countries' electrical outlets. We recommend that you also get the BlackBerry Car Charger if you're a road warrior, which sets you back around $30. Get your car charger from the official RIM online shop (www.shopblackberry.com) because it comes direct from the source.

Make sure that the charger you buy works for your BlackBerry model before you make a purchase.

Bluetooth Hands-Free Headset

If you're a frequent phone user, we definitely recommend that you pick up a Bluetooth hands-free headset. Even though a wired hands-free headset comes with your BlackBerry, if you talk on a headset often, you can't beat the convenience of a Bluetooth headset. You can choose from plenty of Bluetooth headsets on the market.

When you choose a headset, consider a comfortable fit, the voice quality, and whether it has a rechargeable battery.

You probably need to spend anywhere from $50 to $150 for a quality wireless hands-free headset. The best place to get your Bluetooth headset is good ol' Amazon.com.

BlackBerry Presenter

If you think you need your laptop to give a PowerPoint presentation, you're in for a surprise. Yes, you can replace your laptop with your slim BlackBerry, paired with BlackBerry Presenter, when you need to give a PowerPoint presentation. Although Presenter sets you back $200, it can save you from needing to lug around a laptop if you want to impress your clients. Get it at http://store.shopblackberry.com.

External Speaker Phone

Although your BlackBerry may come with a speaker phone, sometimes the sound quality just isn't good enough for you to comprehend the phone conversation while you're in a car. Check out the wireless Bluetooth speaker phone by Motorola. It costs about $100, and you can get it from CrackBerry. com (http://shop.crackberry.com).

BlackBerry Car Mount

To complete your BlackBerry car experience, you need a place to mount your BlackBerry in your car. With so many road warriors out there, the competition for your wallet has grown. We recommend the Motorola MOTOROKR T505 or the BlackBerry Bluetooth Premium Visor; both are just under $90.

You can get them at Crackberry.com (`http://shop.crackberry.com/blackberry-car-kits-and-mounts.htm`).

BlackBerry Cleaner

After you have your BlackBerry for more than a day, it's no longer clean and shiny. Instead, it's covered with fingerprints and smudges. The solution: Monster ScreenClean Mini kit, which comes with a nonabrasive microfiber cloth. The ScreenClean Mini kit work wonders, not only on your BlackBerry, but also on all types of surfaces — LCDs, TVs, and iPods. You can get it at `www.monstercable.com`.

Chapter 22

Ten (or So) Must-Have BlackBerry Applications

The availability of BlackBerry software is growing at a dizzying rate. In this chapter, we introduce ten must-have applications that make your BlackBerry experience that much better.

We don't quote specific reviews. We made these choices based on our quest to find applications that people use: discussions with BlackBerry users, postings on message boards, and commentaries in the public domain. The applications that we talk about in this chapter are just the tip of the iceberg. Feel free to surf the Internet for that killer app because, by the time this book is published, people will have released a slew of new applications.

SmrtGuard, Your Smartphone Guardian

Have you wondered what would happen to your data — such as your sensitive e-mails, phone call histories, contacts, and appointments — if you lost your BlackBerry? It's scary to think of a stranger getting to know you through your e-mails and maybe even figuring out what you're going to do next. Fortunately, SmrtGuard allows you to

- ✔ **Locate and track your BlackBerry.** With no GPS signal required, you can track your BlackBerry's approximate location to determine whether you simply misplaced it or someone stole it.

- ✔ **Sound the audio ping.** If you simply misplaced your BlackBerry but can't find it by calling it because you muted it, don't worry. Just send an audio ping, and your BlackBerry emits a loud sound, regardless of your Profile setting. We wish our TV remote controls had this feature!

- ✔ **Self-destroy in five seconds.** Okay, perhaps not in five seconds, but you can decide when to destroy all your BlackBerry data. With SmrtGuard Remote Wipe, you can erase such data as e-mails, contacts, appointments, to-do lists, memos, phone logs, text messages, and even all the files on your microSD card. SmrtGuard also uninstalls all your third-party applications (such as Facebook and Gmail apps), as well as native Phone and Message applications. After a SmrtGuard Remote Wipe, your BlackBerry is rendered pretty much useless to others.

- ✔ **Back up data wirelessly.** Another must-have feature that SmrtGuard provides. If you self-destroyed your data and don't have a backup, the scheduled wireless backup of your PIM data comes in handy. From the SmrtGuard website (www.smrtguard.com), you can even see and browse through your backed-up data, as well as export it to a CSV file.

Always protect your BlackBerry by using a password. That way, if your BlackBerry gets into the wrong hands, it self-erases your data after ten unsuccessful password entries. However, this password-related erase doesn't delete the files on your microSD card, so you may want to use SmrtGuard for that reason alone.

With SmrtGuard by your side, you can concentrate on your business, instead of worrying about your BlackBerry data being stolen. You can get SmrtGuard for $3.99 a month, $22.99 for half a year, or $44.99 for a whole year's subscription. You can also use a free version of SmrtGuard, which gives you just tracking ability. Check out your options at www.smrtguard.com.

Tether

Subscribing to mobile broadband for your laptop is expensive. Tether provides an inexpensive solution for connecting to the Internet from your laptop by using your BlackBerry. You can check out the details at www.tether.com.

On the website, you can order the application for a one-time fee of $49.99. That's spare change as a one-time cost, considering that you can use it to get connectivity to your laptop through your BlackBerry. You also get a 30-day money-back guarantee.

VibAndRing

Don't like the fact that you can't get your BlackBerry to alert you the way you want? Do you need custom vibration when a phone call comes in?

Time to get your hands on VibAndRing. With this app, you can customize how many vibration bursts you get before your BlackBerry starts ringing and how long each vibration lasts.

To download a free trial or buy for $2.99, go to www.mobihand.com and search for *vibandring*.

Bloomberg for Mobile

Do you check your stocks constantly? Need to know how your portfolio is doing? Need a profit-and-loss view of your positions?

A simple black background and high contrasting text make it easy to read Bloomberg for Mobile's tons of Bloomberg content. Whether you need to track domestic stocks, foreign stocks, or even currencies, Bloomberg for Mobile has you covered.

To download a free version, go to App World (which you can download from http://us.blackberry.com/apps-software/appworld) and search for *Bloomberg*.

SmrtAlerts

Ever find yourself in the middle of browsing or composing an e-mail, and all of a sudden, a new e-mail finds its way to your inbox? Instead of stopping what you're doing and heading to the inbox, if you use SmrtAlerts, you can get a preview of the e-mail or SMS message that just arrived; you can then dismiss the preview, mark the message as read, go to your inbox, or delete the message — all from the alert pop-up window.

For a seven-day trial or to purchase it for $9.99, go to `www.smrtguard.com/smrtalerts.jsp`.

Google Talk Mobile and Yahoo! Messenger Mobile

If you use Google Talk or Yahoo! Messenger on your computer, both mobile versions are must-downloads for your BlackBerry so that you can keep up with your buddies, no matter where you are. To download, point your BlackBerry browser to

- **Google Talk for BlackBerry Smartphones:** `www.blackberry.com/googletalk`
- **Yahoo! Messenger for BlackBerry Smartphones:** `www.blackberry.com/yahoodownload`

WeatherEye

You can find numerous weather applications available, but we like the one from WeatherEye for its simplicity. You set up the location about which you want to know the weather, and WeatherEye displays an icon on your Home screen that indicates the current weather information, updated daily. This application is free; download it from `http://weyebb.pelmorex.com/blackberry`.

Nobex Radio Companion

FM radio on your BlackBerry? That's right. With Nobex, you can get streaming radio on your BlackBerry — either a free, ad-sponsored version or a paid version for $3.99 a month.

More than a hundred stations are available for streaming. Nobex works best if you have a 3G or EvDo network (the faster the network, the better your experience with Nobex). To find out more, go to `www.nobexrc.com`.

Online Personal Music Players

Two applications, Pandora and Slacker (both of which are free), stream CD-quality music right to your BlackBerry. After you download and sign up for Pandora, you just search for the music that you like to hear, and Pandora automatically feeds you similar songs. If you indicate to Pandora whether you like or dislike a particular song that it feeds you, future Pandora selections should be more to your liking. Download Pandora for BlackBerry at www.pandora.com/blackberry. To try Slacker (which is similar to Pandora), download it at www.slacker.com/everywhere/mobile/blackberry.

Neverfail

If you're a BlackBerry Enterprise Server (BES) administrator, this application can help you monitor your BlackBerry population.

With Neverfail, you will be the first to know about any problem that occurs in the BES infrastructure. Additionally, you can set up Neverfail so that your corporate BES has a hot-standby copy of the current production BES — in case the production BES fails, the hot-standby BES can take over in no time.

In short, your users can carry out business on their BlackBerry smartphones, no matter what.

Find out more at www.neverfailgroup.com.

B*Nator

ISEC7's B*Nator solution allows you, as the administrator, to fine-tune and monitor your corporate BlackBerry Enterprise Server (BES). With rich monitoring features, you can pinpoint the location of network bottlenecks and resolve the problem fast.

Additionally, B*Nator allows you to create extensive reports, which help your management team understand how their money is being spent on IT and BlackBerry infrastructure.

Check out www.isec7.com/products/managed-mobility/bnator for more information.

Index

• W •

• Y •

• Z •

Apple & Macs

iPad For Dummies
978-0-470-58027-1

iPhone For Dummies,
4th Edition
978-0-470-87870-5

MacBook For Dummies, 3rd
Edition
978-0-470-76918-8

Mac OS X Snow Leopard For
Dummies
978-0-470-43543-4

Business

Bookkeeping For Dummies
978-0-7645-9848-7

Job Interviews
For Dummies,
3rd Edition
978-0-470-17748-8

Resumes For Dummies,
5th Edition
978-0-470-08037-5

Starting an
Online Business
For Dummies,
6th Edition
978-0-470-60210-2

Stock Investing
For Dummies,
3rd Edition
978-0-470-40114-9

Successful
Time Management
For Dummies
978-0-470-29034-7

Computer Hardware

BlackBerry
For Dummies,
4th Edition
978-0-470-60700-8

Computers For Seniors
For Dummies,
2nd Edition
978-0-470-53483-0

PCs For Dummies,
Windows
7 Edition
978-0-470-46542-4

Laptops For Dummies,
4th Edition
978-0-470-57829-2

Cooking & Entertaining

Cooking Basics
For Dummies,
3rd Edition
978-0-7645-7206-7

Wine For Dummies,
4th Edition
978-0-470-04579-4

Diet & Nutrition

Dieting For Dummies,
2nd Edition
978-0-7645-4149-0

Nutrition For Dummies,
4th Edition
978-0-471-79868-2

Weight Training
For Dummies,
3rd Edition
978-0-471-76845-6

Digital Photography

Digital SLR Cameras &
Photography For Dummies,
3rd Edition
978-0-470-46606-3

Photoshop Elements 8
For Dummies
978-0-470-52967-6

Gardening

Gardening Basics
For Dummies
978-0-470-03749-2

Organic Gardening
For Dummies,
2nd Edition
978-0-470-43067-5

Green/Sustainable

Raising Chickens
For Dummies
978-0-470-46544-8

Green Cleaning
For Dummies
978-0-470-39106-8

Health

Diabetes For Dummies,
3rd Edition
978-0-470-27086-8

Food Allergies
For Dummies
978-0-470-09584-3

Living Gluten-Free
For Dummies,
2nd Edition
978-0-470-58589-4

Hobbies/General

Chess For Dummies,
2nd Edition
978-0-7645-8404-6

Drawing
Cartoons & Comics
For Dummies
978-0-470-42683-8

Knitting For Dummies,
2nd Edition
978-0-470-28747-7

Organizing
For Dummies
978-0-7645-5300-4

Su Doku For Dummies
978-0-470-01892-7

Home Improvement

Home Maintenance
For Dummies,
2nd Edition
978-0-470-43063-7

Home Theater
For Dummies,
3rd Edition
978-0-470-41189-6

Living the
Country Lifestyle
All-in-One
For Dummies
978-0-470-43061-3

Solar Power Your Home
For Dummies,
2nd Edition
978-0-470-59678-4

Internet

Blogging For Dummies,
3rd Edition
978-0-470-61996-4

eBay For Dummies,
6th Edition
978-0-470-49741-8

Facebook For Dummies,
3rd Edition
978-0-470-87804-0

Web Marketing
For Dummies,
2nd Edition
978-0-470-37181-7

WordPress
For Dummies,
3rd Edition
978-0-470-59274-8

Language & Foreign Language

French For Dummies
978-0-7645-5193-2

Italian Phrases
For Dummies
978-0-7645-7203-6

Spanish For Dummies,
2nd Edition
978-0-470-87855-2

Spanish
For Dummies,
Audio Set
978-0-470-09585-0

Math & Science

Algebra I
For Dummies,
2nd Edition
978-0-470-55964-2

Biology For Dummies,
2nd Edition
978-0-470-59875-7

Calculus For Dummies
978-0-7645-2498-1

Chemistry For Dummies
978-0-7645-5430-8

Microsoft Office

Excel 2010 For Dummies
978-0-470-48953-6

Office 2010 All-in-One
For Dummies
978-0-470-49748-7

Office 2010 For Dummies,
Book + DVD Bundle
978-0-470-62698-6

Word 2010 For Dummies
978-0-470-48772-3

Music

Guitar For Dummies,
2nd Edition
978-0-7645-9904-0

iPod & iTunes For
Dummies, 8th Edition
978-0-470-87871-2

Piano Exercises
For Dummies
978-0-470-38765-8

Parenting & Education

Parenting For Dummies,
2nd Edition
978-0-7645-5418-6

Type 1 Diabetes
For Dummies
978-0-470-17811-9

Pets

Cats For Dummies,
2nd Edition
978-0-7645-5275-5

Dog Training For Dummies,
3rd Edition
978-0-470-60029-0

Puppies For Dummies,
2nd Edition
978-0-470-03717-1

Religion & Inspiration

The Bible For Dummies
978-0-7645-5296-0

Catholicism For Dummies
978-0-7645-5391-2

Women in the Bible
For Dummies
978-0-7645-8475-6

Self-Help & Relationship

Anger Management
For Dummies
978-0-470-03715-7

Overcoming Anxiety
For Dummies,
2nd Edition
978-0-470-57441-6

Sports

Baseball
For Dummies,
3rd Edition
978-0-7645-7537-2

Basketball
For Dummies,
2nd Edition
978-0-7645-5248-9

Golf For Dummies,
3rd Edition
978-0-471-76871-5

Web Development

Web Design
All-in-One
For Dummies
978-0-470-41796-6

Web Sites
Do-It-Yourself
For Dummies,
2nd Edition
978-0-470-56520-9

Windows 7

Windows 7
For Dummies
978-0-470-49743-2

Windows 7
For Dummies,
Book + DVD Bundle
978-0-470-52398-8

Windows 7 All-in-One
For Dummies
978-0-470-48763-1

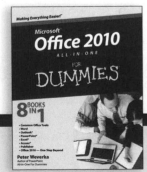

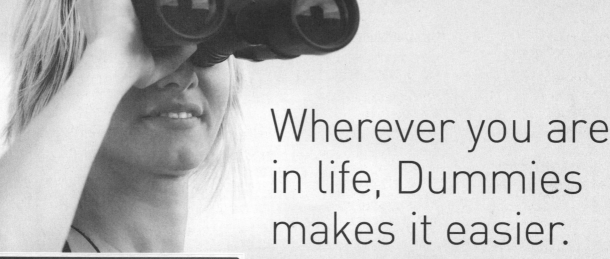

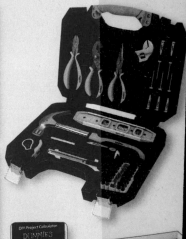